Anti-Americanism and the American World Order

Anti-Americanism and the American World Order

• • •

Giacomo Chiozza

The Johns Hopkins University Press
Baltimore

© 2009 The Johns Hopkins University Press
All rights reserved. Published 2009
Printed in the United States of America on acid-free paper
9 8 7 6 5 4 3 2 1

The Johns Hopkins University Press
2715 North Charles Street
Baltimore, Maryland 21218-4363
www.press.jhu.edu

Library of Congress Cataloging-in-Publication Data
Chiozza, Giacomo.
  Anti-Americanism and the American world order / Giacomo Chiozza.
    p. cm.
  Includes bibliographical references and index.
  ISBN-13: 978-0-8018-9206-6 (hardcover : alk. paper)
  ISBN-10: 0-8018-9206-6 (hardcover : alk. paper)
  ISBN-13: 978-0-8018-9208-0 (pbk. : alk. paper)
  ISBN-10: 0-8018-9208-2 (pbk. : alk. paper)
  1. Anti-Americanism. 2. United States—Foreign public opinion.
  I. Title.
  E895.C45 2009
  303.48'273—dc22   2008048591

A catalog record for this book is available from the British Library.

Special discounts are available for bulk purchases of this book. For more information, please contact Special Sales at 410-516-6936 or specialsales@press.jhu.edu.

The Johns Hopkins University Press uses environmentally friendly book materials, including recycled text paper that is composed of at least 30 percent post-consumer waste, whenever possible. All of our book papers are acid-free, and our jackets and covers are printed on paper with recycled content.

Contents

Tables

Figures

Acknowledgments

I would like to thank Joseph Grieco for his support, guidance, advice, criticism, comments, and suggestions on matters large and small throughout the years.

This book evolved from my dissertation at Duke University. For their guidance, support, and insights I would like to thank the members of my dissertation committee, which Joseph Grieco chaired: John Aldrich, Christopher Gelpi, and Hein Goemans.

I thank Pradeep Chhibber and Patrick James who read the entire manuscript and made many important suggestions. Several people generously offered comments and advice: Ericka Albaugh, Nora Bensahel, Lisa Blaydes, John Bowen, Jonathan Caverley, Maria Fanis, Ole Holsti, Jacques Hymans, Seth Jolly, Miles Kahler, David Karol, Peter Katzenstein, Bob Keohane, Charles Lipson, Doug McAdam, Luigi Manzetti, Henry Nau, Abe Newman, Samuel Popkin, Imke Risopp-Nickelson, Stephen Peter Rosen, Curt Signorino, Duncan Snidal, Paul Sniderman, Arthur Stein, and Rob Trager. I also thank Henry Y. K. Tom, Executive Editor at the Johns Hopkins University Press, for his supervision of my manuscript throughout the publication process.

Special thanks go to Ashwini Chhatre and Carol Atkinson. To Ashwini for the wonderful time at #9, the apartment we shared for three years, where this project originated. To Carol for all the suggestions, comments, challenges, and criticisms she has given me to improve my work, but above all for being by my side and for all the joy, love, and adventures she has brought into my life.

Portions of this book have appeared in Giacomo Chiozza, 2007, "Disaggregating Anti-Americanism: An Analysis of Individual Attitudes towards the United States," in *Anti-Americanisms in World Politics*, ed. Peter J. Katzenstein and Robert O. Keohane (Ithaca, NY: Cornell University Press), pp. 93–126. Portions will appear in Giacomo Chiozza, 2009, "A Crisis Like No Other: Anti-Americanism at the Time of the Iraq War," *European Journal of International Relations* 15(2): forthcoming.

Mistakes, omissions, and other assorted infelicities are my own responsibility.

PART I / Themes and Theory

CHAPTER ONE

Overview

Introduction

W hat is the image of the United States of America abroad? What opinion
do foreign publics have of the United States, its citizens and its institutions, its ideals and its culture, its policies and its symbols? What attitudes do
they have towards all things American? In the early years of the twenty-first
century, popular opposition to the United States seems to be on the rise in many
parts of the world: it reached horrendous proportions on the tragic day of September 11, 2001; it surfaces in opinion polls and flares up in mass demonstrations
against the war in Iraq; it manifests itself in the approval that foreign leaders
receive when they stand up against the United States. Nelson A. Rockefeller's
observation in 1973, when he instituted the Commission on Critical Choices for
Americans, is true again now: "The United States is not popular abroad these
days" (Free, 1976, xxv). It seems fair to ask again, as the newsmagazine *Newsweek*
did in 1958 when anti-American protests raged in Algeria, Burma, Lebanon, and
Venezuela, "Does the rest of the world hate the United States?" (quoted in McPherson, 2002, 16–17).

In this book, I investigate the character, the sources, and the persistence of
foreign attitudes towards the United States. Systematic studies of how the United
States is perceived by foreign publics are scarce, while impressionistic accounts
abound. Academics, policymakers, and journalists have so far offered overviews
rich in intuition at best or mired in prejudice at worst. My primary goal is to shed
empirical light on the phenomenon of anti-Americanism: that is, to identify the
features and the content of the perceptions of the United States among foreign
publics, to identify the features and characteristics of the societies that admire
America or reject America, and to assess the persistence of negative views of the
United States. I hope to fill in a wide gap in our understanding of the U.S. standing at the mass societal level internationally.

The Central Argument

This book shows how the popular opinion of the United States takes a loose and multifaceted form in which negative and positive elements coexist with no apparent tensions. My analyses demonstrate that popular anti-Americanism is mostly benign and shallow. It is far from being a prejudice or an ingrained view of ideological opposition, as we often hear among scholars and practitioners of international politics.[1] Periods of strong opposition often do occur. In different times and contexts, the balance between positive and negative elements changes. A particular action, policy, or aspect of the United States can capture public opinion and tilt the cognitive balance into the negative zone. A deep-seated ideological opposition to the United States certainly exists, and tragically so. But it is usually the aberration of a minority of people in few quarters of the world.

The reason for this optimistic view, which counters the current conventional wisdom about U.S. popularity abroad, is that there is more than one aspect of the United States that frames popular opinion. As publics balance likes and dislikes about the United States, they end up tempering the anger, resentment, and displeasure they occasionally feel towards the United States with ideas about U.S. freedoms, prosperity, and popular culture. Like a cubist painting where the image is broken into small multifaceted areas that represent the plural viewpoints of our vision, my theoretical account of anti-Americanism portrays the multiple sides of the United States that simultaneously shape popular attitudes. In Part 1, I present the theoretical underpinnings of this argument, which I call the *dimensions of America theory,* and place it within the bounds of a theory of public opinion formation.[2] In Part 2, I present extensive empirical tests of my argument. I show how the dimensions of America theory accounts for the popular views of the United States in a large sample of more than forty countries, and in a more in-depth analysis of eight predominantly Islamic countries and six European countries.

The dimensions of America theory points to a specific asset of the United States—its combination of values, political institutions, and popular culture— that helps assuage foreign anger and resentment. But does this asset then translate into a substantial political advantage for the United States? On the one hand, the existence of an underlying set of values and institutional norms that elicit the approval of foreign publics dampens the contestation of the normative basis of the American world order. On the other hand, the attractiveness of American values, political institutions, and popular culture is often credited with the ability to shape the policy preferences of foreign publics. Joseph Nye (1990, 2004), in particular, has argued that the United States has a unique reservoir of *soft power* that enhances U.S. ability to exercise global leadership. The argument in this book partially concurs with the soft power thesis. I show that foreign publics find plenty to admire in the United States.

If we then focus on the macro level of prevailing ideas, the *soft power thesis* identifies an important feature of the normative basis of the American world order. At the micro level, where popular attitudes are formed, however, soft power is hardly a fungible political resource. Approval of U.S. cultural norms and values does not necessarily ameliorate popular views about U.S. diplomatic and international behavior. Under the logic of the dimensions of America theory, each dimension of the United States remains compartmentalized, a single area that only marginally shapes how publics view the policy arena. The approval of U.S. culture, values, and institutions, then, is not sufficient on its own to facilitate U.S. efforts of public diplomacy.

The argument I put forward in this book possesses a common element with the *varieties of anti-Americanism typology* elaborated by Katzenstein and Keohane (2007b). Both my approach and theirs point to the multifaceted nature of anti-Americanism. Both reject a characterization of anti-Americanism as a uniform phenomenon of opposition to the United States. Despite their commonalities, these two approaches differ in their key intellectual aims and in their theoretical underpinnings.

The primary aim of the variety of anti-Americanism typology is "to understand variation in what is considered 'anti-Americanism'" (Katzenstein and Keohane, 2007b, 37). The identification of *types* of anti-Americanism then becomes its primary empirical strategy, as is exemplified by Sophie Meunier's (2007) analysis of French anti-Americanism and Bow, Katzenstein, and Santa-Cruz's (2007) analysis of the Canadian and Mexican cases. The dimensions of America theory instead provides a theoretical account—grounded in a theory of public opinion—of the individual-level processes that lead to the articulation of a negative opinion of the United States in a specific political and cultural locale.

Implications: Sources and Persistence

The dimensions of America theory and the empirical analyses in Part 2 characterize popular opinion of the United States as the collection of multiple considerations that temper the formation of an outright rejection of the United States.

The main contribution of my theoretical argument is to explain the nature of popular anti-Americanism. But this argument, thanks to its underpinnings in a theory of public opinion,[3] can also be extended to explore two additional aspects of anti-American sentiments: their sources and their persistence.

In Part 3, I explore the individual profile of the publics that express negative views of the United States. I show how anti-American sentiments are anchored in specific personal and political contexts. Negative views of the United States, for the most part, are not a whimsical reaction of hatred and prejudice that defies explanation. But, while it is possible to identify sources of anti-American opinion in demographic factors and specific attitudes, such as the rejection of a modern lifestyle or the projection of one's personal dissatisfactions onto the United States, none of these factors gains preeminence at the aggregate level. When we analyze attitudes towards the United States at the individual level of mass opinion, we find that there is no single overarching demographic or attitudinal factor from which anti-American attitudes stem. The set of motivations that might lead someone to express a negative opinion of the United States is always challenged by the many other motivations that instead elicit positive reactions.

The dimensions of America theory offers an account of the appraisal process that individuals in mass publics undergo when they assess the United States in light of their predispositions, formative experiences, and information. This account shows that anti-American attitudes have heterogenous sources. As a consequence, the multifaceted nature of anti-American sentiments is reflected not just in their multifarious content but also in the way they emerge in the belief systems of ordinary people.

In Part 4, I use the dimensions of America theory to address the persistence of anti-American sentiments. In times of crisis, such as the ones that have been triggered by the war in Iraq and the larger U.S. campaign against terrorism, it is not surprising to observe that the popular image of the United States is under strain. Within the terms of my theoretical argument, during times of crisis the perceptions of the United States would indeed worsen, as factors with negative connotations gain preeminence in people's minds. The dimensions of America theory, however, creates the opportunity to assess the persistence of the current wave of anti-Americanism, because the theory allows for a direct investigation of whether the current spike in opposition to the United States is a response to contingent political conditions, such as the personal character of the current U.S. president, or whether it is a manifestation of a deeper syndrome of opposition that is unlikely to subside even after the current crisis has passed. My analysis shows that the mélange of factors underpinning the U.S. image abroad has not yet congealed into a pattern of enduring opposition.

Relevance: U.S. Primacy and American Exceptionalism

The dimensions of America theory presents an explanation of how foreign publics view the United States, accounts for the sources of anti-American sentiments, and provides a systematic and empirically testable approach to making claims about the persistence of anti-American sentiments. Still, we need to ask, What is the relevance of this theory for international relations?

In a time when attitudes towards the United States are the subject of congressional hearings and State Department conferences and candidates for president express concern about the U.S. standing abroad, this question might appear unnecessary.[4] However, powerful voices have articulated skepticism about the political relevance of what the world thinks of the United States and, as a consequence, about the relevance of the theoretical arguments that explain popular views of the United States. Secretary of State Dean Acheson (1965) made the skeptic's case in the most scathing terms. In Acheson's view, the recurrent interest in foreign public opinion is no more than a reflection of a "Narcissus psychosis" that betrays a sense of insecurity on the part of the American public; for prudent politicians, who know better, "world opinion . . . is pure fancy—no more substantial a ghost than the banging of a shutter, or the wind in the chimney."

In the discipline of international relations, which has embraced explanations cast at the level of the system, the state, and the leaders, there does not seem to be space left for mass public opinion. The study of attitudes towards the United States matters for scholars and practitioners of international relations, however, because it addresses two major aspects of the American world order: popular acceptance of U.S. primacy and the implications of American exceptionalism for world affairs.

Twenty years after the end of the Cold War, the United States has reached an apogee of power that it is now customary to compare to that of Imperial Rome (see, for example, Lapham, 2002; Nye, 2002; Johnson, 2004). Charles Krauthammer (1990–1991) identified the emergence of the military, diplomatic, political, and economic preeminence of the United States and christened it a *unipolar moment* in which the United States had the historic opportunity to establish rules of world order that would command the allegiance of weaker states in the system.

In any international order, power is a fundamental currency that defines the patterns of relationships among states (Gilpin, 1981). But, as Daniel Deudney and

John Ikenberry (1999) have shown, international order involves more than just the distribution of power: it entails a structure of legitimate authority and therefore also is premised on ideational features—be they normative or institutional—that transcend material power realities. By looking at foreign attitudes towards the United States, my investigation shows how perceptions of the United States, of its ideals and its identity, shape the belief systems of foreign publics and how images of U.S. identity and ideals are related to the actions the United States takes. In the process, it offers an empirical analysis of the extent to which the ideational aspects of the American world order are accepted or resisted among foreign publics.

In this book I also explore a second fundamental theme, that of American exceptionalism. The idea that the United States is a "city upon a hill," exceptional in its achievements and the key point of reference for the rest of the world, has been part of U.S. cultural heritage ever since Puritan leader John Winthrop evoked the image in the immortal *Arbella Covenant* in 1630 (Lipset, 1997; Shafer, 1999; Ignatieff, 2005).[5] The United States has prided itself on being different from, and better than, any other country; America defines itself as powerful but benign, "the last best hope of earth."[6]

The United States has indeed an impressive track record to offer to make such claims more than self-congratulatory assertions, but still never impressive enough to assuage the tragic sense of power emanating from the realist scientific paradigm. Kenneth Waltz (1991, 670), the most prominent realist thinker of the last fifty years, sternly disputes any notions of exceptionalism and asserts, "I believe that America is better than most nations[;] I fear that it is not as much better as many Americans believe. In international politics, unbalanced power constitutes a danger even when it is American power that is out of balance." By looking at foreign publics' perceptions of the United States, I seek to understand whether America is "exceptional" in the eyes of the mass general foreign public or whether it is just a country like any other, only more powerful.

I conducted the empirical investigations using a wide array of data that tap into foreign nations' perceptions of the United States in Africa, Central and South Asia, Eastern Europe, East Asia, Latin America, the Middle East, and the industrial democracies of Western Europe and Canada. I gave prominent attention to two regions of the world: the countries of Europe and the countries in the Arab and Islamic world. This choice reflects the relevance that attitudes towards the United States have attained in those parts of the world and the extent to which popular opposition to the United States is alleged to be a defining feature of the political discourse in those societies.

The focus on Islam and Europe, therefore, places this book among a growing number of analyses and editorial commentaries that purportedly analyze the growing global chasm between the United States and the European and Islamic publics, allegedly identify causal explanations, and self-assuredly offer policy recipes. A hallmark of that growing literature is the pretense to distinguish between "rational policy criticism," which is legitimate and welcome, and "outright ideological opposition," which is a manifestation of bigotry or of a neurotic obsession (Hollander, 1995; Sardar and Davies, 2002; Berman, 2004; Joffe, 2004). However, while sharing topic and areas of investigation with these works, my analytical approach could not be more different. My argument eschews any imponderable distinction between legitimate criticism and pathological opposition and, instead, engages its readers in a more fruitful endeavor: to discover who says what of the United States and under what political conditions.

In the rest of this chapter, I present an overview of various facets of attitudes towards the United States. I then proceed to describe the patterns of anti-American sentiment during the Cold War, with an emphasis on how the United States was perceived among the general foreign public in the aftermath of the Vietnam War and during the Reagan administration. Finally, I present a preliminary set of empirical findings on attitudes towards the United States in the post–Cold War, post–September 11th world. The combination of these findings with the Cold War results indicate that the United States inspires benevolence and admiration even amidst tense controversies over policies and interests. This raises the central question of this investigation, which will be analyzed theoretically and empirically in the rest of the book: What political processes underlie this dynamic?

Attitudes towards the United States

If one were to type the word *anti-Americanism* into a web search engine, articles would be found in the thousands: from October 2001 to December 2007, 3,327 in the *Expanded Academic ASAP*, 3,221 in the *EBSCO Host*, 1,402 in *Proquest*, 5,320 on *Google Scholar*.[7] Book-length treatments of how the world is on a collision course with the American social and political systems have started to appear offering analyses from various ideological perspectives and in many styles, from the tentatively factual to the openly polemical, as the references at the end of this volume attest. The stiff opposition that the United States faced during the diplomatic crisis that preceded the war in Iraq has given further credence to the perception that the specter of anti-Americanism is haunting the globe.[8] Thomas Friedman (2003), a *New York Times* commentator, has summarized this state of affairs in terms that are much like those used by *Newsweek* in 1958: "After 9/11 people wondered, 'Why do they hate us?' speaking of the Muslim world. After the Iraq war debate, the question has grown into, 'Why does everybody else hate us?'"

A flurry of international opinion polls has appeared in recent years to convey a chilling message: the United States is disliked in many parts of the world. Andrew Kohut (2003), director of the Pew Research Center for the People and the Press—an organization that has conducted multiyear surveys of global attitudes in more than forty countries—warns that the survey results paint a dire picture of America's standing in the perceptions of ordinary people: "In 2002," he writes, "the U.S. global image had slipped. But when we went back this spring after the war in Iraq—conducting another 16,000 interviews in 20 countries and the Palestinian Authority—it was clear that favorable opinions of the U.S. had plummeted" (Kohut 2003). In a more recent iteration of the Pew survey (April 2006), the percentage of respondents expressing a favorable opinion of the United States was 56% in Britain, 39% in France, and 37% in Germany, a substantial drop from the results of the summer of 2002 when the favorable responses were 75% in Britain, 63% in France, and 61% in Germany (Pew Global Attitudes Project, 2006). Even more worrisome are the results indicating a solid reservoir of mistrust for the United States. When asked whether, as a consequence of the war in Iraq, respondents had more confidence or less confidence that the United States is trustworthy, in March of 2004 large majorities responded "less confidence" in all the countries included in the survey, with the exception of the United States itself (Pew Global Attitudes Project, 2004).

Beyond survey results, though, there is the growing sense that the opposition that we observe is more than just a momentary dissatisfaction with the United States or the administration in power. Anti-Americanism is viewed as the new ideology that shapes political discourse after the end of all ideologies. "What matters most," writes Ivan Krastev (2004, 6) of the Center for Liberal Strategies in Sofia, "is not that America suddenly has become hugely unpopular, but that blaming America has become politically correct behavior even among America's closest allies." In a commentary that appeared in the *Washington Post* in May of 2004 on the enlargement of the European Union to the countries of Eastern Europe, Robin Shepherd (2004) unwittingly underscored this point. Describing an anti-U.S. and anti-globalization protest rally in Warsaw, she wrote, "Totaling only

4000 or so, the protesters were easily outnumbered by police, journalists and the entourages of presidents, prime ministers and central bankers. Scarcely a rock was thrown, and Polish Radio wryly reported that the participants closed up shop promptly at 5:30 p.m., whereupon many retired to a party at a nearby club." In all seriousness, Shepherd points out that in Poland a rally with "only" four thousand protesters is a manifestation of warmth towards the United States.

Despite all these alarums, the spread of anti-American sentiment comes as a paradox and a surprise to Americans. Anti-Americanism is reportedly mounting, yet the United States is equally praised as the benign hegemon, the upholder of democracy and freedom, the symbol of progress and human flourishing. America, John Quincy Adams famously said, "is the well-wisher to the freedom and independence of all. She is the champion only of her own." People all over the world dream the American Dream: in the beautiful words of Immanuel Wallerstein (2003, 2), a social critic of America and its capitalistic system, it is "the dream of human possibility, of a society in which all persons may be encouraged to do their best, to achieve their most, and to have the reward of a comfortable life. . . . It is the dream that we are a beacon to a world that suffers from not being able to realize such a dream."

Indeed, in sharp contrast to the perception of growing anti-Americanism stands the appeal of the American ideals of liberty, equality, and opportunity, and the pervasiveness of American culture. Throughout the twentieth century, as Eric Hobsbawm (1994, 198) succinctly stated, "in the field of popular culture the world was American or it was provincial."[9] The United States is a symbol and a role model to be emulated. It is a country from which higher standards of behavior are expected. Samuel Huntington (1982, 37) preceptively summarized the aspirations that are associated with America, the land of the free and the home of the brave: "Critics say that America is a lie because it falls so short of its ideals. They are wrong. America is not a lie; it is a disappointment. But it can be a disappointment only because it is also a hope."

Underlying the notion of America, however, there is more than just the physical manifestation of a country, with its territory, its resources, and its people. There is also the myth of a successful revolution, of modernity achieved. Joseph Nye (1990, 2004) elaborated the political implications of these unique features of the United States in describing the concept of soft power. Soft power is a form of power in the classic sense of Robert Dahl (1957): the ability to get others— other countries, other nations, other societies, other people—to do what America wants, but it is power by co-optation instead of power by coercion. Soft power is premised on cultural values and political ideology, it operates through persuasion and example, and it is perpetuated within a network of institutions that defines rules and modes of legitimate behavior. It is a sublime form of power that the American society possesses in profusion above and beyond the military, economic, and technological power resources of its government. Movies, media, universities, software, technology, internet, skyscrapers, English, and jeans all contribute to the cultural clout of what Josef Joffe (2002, 173), in a felicitous phrase, calls "America the Beguiling." But regardless of its softness, it is still power; it shapes the realm of choice and action of other political actors, frames their references, and indirectly elicits compliance. In the words of Bachrach and Baratz (1963, 632), the two political scientists whose work on power and decisions underpins Nye's conception of soft power, it consists in "the practice of limiting the scope of actual decision-making to 'safe' issues by manipulating the dominant community values, myths, and political institutions and procedures."

The United States always appears to be two things at the same time: it is generous and exploitative, a republic and an empire, modern and retrograde, dynamic and stultifying, materialistic and spiritual. The ambivalence of sentiments that underlies world opinion of the United States underscores a love/hate relationship that might defy rational explanation. We might have the impression that we are traveling in the territory of the irrational when we discover that in the late 1920s and early 1930s French authors were publishing books with such disconcerting titles as *Qui Sera le Maître: Europe ou Amérique?, Le Cancer Américain, L'Impérialisme Économique Américaine,* and *L'Amérique à la Conquête de l'Europe* (Strauss, 1978, 123–138; Lacorne and Rupnik, 1990, 13). When the United States was enduring the economic collapse of the Depression years and American and French diplomats were drafting the articles of the treaty that outlawed all wars, French intellectuals felt threatened by the ascendance of the United States and its influence in Europe. This, of course, is just a quirky anecdote in the history of the relationship of two countries that never fought a war against each other but nonetheless seem not to have good chemistry with each other. It is indicative, though, of the fact that countries, their publics, and their elites, fall prey to waves of fear and resentment that do not have a clear connection with the actions of the country that is the object of their aversion. No country seems to be immune to this syndrome: from the Red Scare of 1919 and 1920 to the Japan-bashing of the early 1990s, foreign threats have been perceived on the American political scene that in retrospect were not commensurate with the fears that leaders and members of the public expressed.

Where does anti-American sentiment originate? What forms does it take? How does it change over time? How is it mediated by the political relations existing between the United States and a given country? These are empirical questions that I address in the chapters that follow.

A Historical Overview

The empirical lens of this study is primarily directed on foreign perceptions of the United States now, when the Cold War's international order has become history and a new order has emerged, an order that admirers or critics refer to variously as the era of American unipolarity, American hegemony, Pax Americana, or American empire (Bacevich, 2002; Brooks and Wohlforth, 2002; Mann, 2003; Odom and Dujarric, 2004). In less than half a century, Henry Luce's visionary hope of an American Century has come to fruition. In the dark year of 1941, Henry Luce spoke of a mission for America to build "an internationalism of the people, by the people and for the people," in which the promise of a "more abundant life" was wedded to the "passionate devotion to great American ideals . . . —a love of freedom, a feeling for the equality of opportunity, a tradition of self-reliance and independence and also of co-operation." For Henry Luce, these would be the features of the new "international moral order" that the United States of America would and should create.[10]

The United States is now, more than ever before, the "colossus" bestriding the world that Harold Laski described in 1947; but America, more than ever before, also symbolizes a polity and a model of a political economy. Perceptions of the United States in foreign lands, then, become an empirical venue for an investigation into the normative and ideational dimensions of the contemporary American world order. While the meaning and relevance of such an investigation are tightly tied to the features of the American world order since the end of bipolarity, nonetheless, its meaning and relevance should be placed into the context of how perceptions of the United States have fluctuated over time since America took on its internationalist mission in World War II.

Therefore, when we read that anti-Americanism is "in the air the world breathes," as Charles Krauthammer (2003) wrote, we are left to wonder whether attitudes towards the United States have acquired new polemical dimensions that they did not have when the Cold War was raging. The overcharged tones in which some people speak of a widespread anti-American sentiment convey the idea that popular opposition to the United States has attained new heights. However, historically, concerns over world opinion of America have recurrently emerged, attracted the attention of scholars and pundits, and then quietly subsided. For example, in the winter of 1974, the Institute for International Social Research conducted an opinion survey of the image of the United States in eight countries in Western Europe, the Americas, and Asia on behalf of the bipartisan Commission on Critical Choices for Americans convened by Nelson A. Rockefeller, then governor of New York. At the end of a tumultuous year that culminated with President Nixon's resignation amidst a wide moral and political scandal, the general and the elite publics in Canada, Mexico, Brazil, Britain, France, West Germany, Italy, and Japan were asked to evaluate several aspects of America's position in the international arena (Free, 1976). This investigation reflected Rockefeller's concern about the ability of U.S. institutions to cope with the domestic and international challenges the United States faced.

The image of the United States that emerges from the Commission on Critical Choices survey, shown in Table 1.1, is decidedly mixed and not at all catastrophic. In all three regions, both among elites and among ordinary people, the overall opinion of the United States is "only fair" or better for the great majority of the respondents, a finding that prompted the author of the survey, Lloyd Free (1976, 25) to comment, "While these results could, of course, have been worse, we cannot say that they are good." The attitudes towards America's international role were more sanguine; a year after the withdrawal of the American troops from Vietnam, solid majorities saw high degrees of commonality between U.S. interests and those of their country. Analogously, with the exception of the Japanese general public, most respondents had at least a "fair amount" of confidence in the U.S. ability to provide wide leadership in dealing with world problems. Not that respondents in the contentious 1970s were not living up to their reputation for antagonism: sizeable portions of the publics and the elites—from 9% to 25%—were still defining the United States as "politically imperialistic, and arrogant." But the bulk of negative aspects that the general publics associated with the United States pertained primarily to domestic problems or issues, from racial discrimination to social and economic inequalities (Free, 1976, 29).

Thus, the image of the United States that emerges in the immediate aftermath of the Vietnam War and of Watergate is hardly impressive, but far from dismal. The sober assessment expressed by foreign publics is not too dissimilar from the assessment that Americans themselves were offering of their nation. Surveyed in the spring of 1974, nearly two-thirds of American respondents concurred that the

Table 1.1.   Opinion of the United States, 1974

	Elites			Publics		
	Western Europe	The Americas	Japan	Western Europe	The Americas	Japan
Overall opinion of the U.S.						
Excellent	0.04	0.04	0.05	0.06	0.06	0.02
Good	0.33	0.27	0.23	0.34	0.29	0.16
Only fair	0.45	0.46	0.51	0.39	0.42	0.44
Poor	0.16	0.20	0.13	0.12	0.17	0.20
Mutuality of interests with U.S.						
Very much in agreement	0.15	0.25	0.05	0.13	0.22	0.04
Fairly well in agreement	0.61	0.46	0.58	0.57	0.42	0.47
Rather different	0.18	0.17	0.28	0.17	0.20	0.29
Very different	0.04	0.09	0.02	0.06	0.12	0.04
Confidence in U.S. leadership						
Great deal	0.11	0.20	0.10	0.14	0.18	0.03
Fair amount	0.44	0.36	0.48	0.46	0.36	0.41
Not very much	0.31	0.29	0.30	0.24	0.27	0.34
None at all	0.12	0.12	0.03	0.08	0.12	0.05

Note: Data are from Free, 1976, 24, 30, 51.

national situation had worsened over the previous five years, and about half of them agreed that the United States had lost ground in its ability to maintain respect in other countries (Watts and Free, 1974).

A similar dynamic unfolded in the early eighties, when a wave of anti-American protests swept across Europe. The reaction of the European publics to the security policies of the Reagan administration—primarily the deployment of medium-range nuclear missiles in Belgium, Britain, Germany, Italy, and the Netherlands and the break with the policy of détente—was charged with animosity, apprehension, and occasional contempt. For European commentators, their countries' relationship with the United States had reached a point of no return, and estrangement was its defining feature (Mueller and Risse-Kappen, 1987). "The relationship between Western Europe and North America, alias the Atlantic Alliance," wrote the British magazine *The Economist* in June 1981, "is in the early stages of what could be a terminal illness." Meanwhile, on the other

Table 1.2. Opinion of the United States, 1982–1987

Country	1982 Good		Neither	1982 Bad		1984 Good		Neither	1984 Bad	
	Very	Fairly		Rather	Very	Very	Fairly		Rather	Very
Belgium	–	–	–	–	–	0.04	0.41	0.22	0.30	0.04
France	0.06	0.62	–	0.26	0.06	0.05	0.44	0.24	0.24	0.04
Great Britain	0.11	0.52	–	0.28	0.09	0.07	0.46	0.14	0.26	0.07
Greece	0.06	0.21	–	0.40	0.34	0.06	0.27	0.10	0.41	0.17
Ireland	–	–	–	–	–	0.20	0.60	0.09	0.11	0.01
Italy	0.16	0.55	–	0.22	0.07	0.08	0.46	0.23	0.18	0.04
Netherlands	–	–	–	–	–	0.05	0.52	0.05	0.35	0.04
W. Germany	0.12	0.59	–	0.21	0.08	0.06	0.60	0.13	0.19	0.02

Country	1985 Good		Neither	1985 Bad		1987 Good		Neither	1987 Bad	
	Very	Fairly		Rather	Very	Very	Fairly		Rather	Very
Belgium	0.06	0.31	0.39	0.18	0.06	0.08	0.37	0.38	0.13	0.03
Denmark	0.06	0.45	0.20	0.24	0.05	0.08	0.40	0.24	0.24	0.04
France	0.07	0.47	0.26	0.18	0.03	0.06	0.45	0.25	0.21	0.04
Great Britain	0.09	0.55	0.11	0.19	0.06	0.11	0.53	0.11	0.20	0.06
Greece	0.09	0.20	0.23	0.26	0.22	0.12	0.26	0.30	0.21	0.11
Ireland	0.27	0.49	0.12	0.09	0.02	0.27	0.50	0.15	0.07	0.02
Italy	0.10	0.54	0.21	0.11	0.05	0.11	0.50	0.24	0.12	0.03
Luxembourg	–	–	–	–	–	0.22	0.52	0.13	0.11	0.02
Netherlands	0.05	0.51	0.13	0.25	0.06	0.06	0.53	0.14	0.24	0.04
N. Ireland	–	–	–	–	–	0.18	0.55	0.12	0.10	0.05
Portugal	0.13	0.49	0.27	0.07	0.04	0.15	0.44	0.36	0.05	0.00
Spain	0.05	0.28	0.29	0.27	0.12	0.08	0.29	0.33	0.22	0.07
W. Germany	0.06	0.42	0.36	0.13	0.03	0.08	0.42	0.38	0.10	0.02

Note: Data are from the following Eurobarometer surveys: 17 (1982), 22 (1984), 24 (1985), and 28 (1987).

side of the ocean, American commentators were portraying an analogous state of crisis. Andrei Markovits (1985, 3) wrote, "Reports of a dramatic increase in West European anti-Americanism have filled the American media in the past few years, giving casual readers the impression that the alternative and peace movements in these countries are motivated by an almost pathological hatred of the United States."

Again, however, when attitudes towards the United States are gauged by surveying public opinion, a more sanguine picture emerges. As Table 1.2 shows, the United States was in general seen in positive terms in Western Europe. In most countries, at least 50% of the public had a very good or fairly good opinion of the United States throughout the 1980s. Exceptions existed: the general publics in Greece, Spain, and to a lesser extent Belgium were less inclined to express warm feelings towards the United States. Moreover, while the data from 1982 and those from the later periods are not entirely comparable, given the different options respondents were given, it seems that the positive assessment of the United States remained fairly stable.

As Steven Smith and Douglas Wertman (1992, 128) conclude after an extensive overview of European public opinion, "American policy-makers and mass media greatly exaggerated the extent of anti-Americanism in Western Europe in the 1980s. . . . After eight years of Ronald Reagan as President, overall opinion of the United States in Western Europe as a whole, while probably no more positive, does not appear to be any more negative as we begin the 1990s than it was when we entered the 1980s." For a sentiment that has been defined as "one of the great psychological phenomena of our time" (Revel, 1974, 113), anti-Americanism proves more elusive than its critics maintain. A question, then, arises: Is this pattern any different in the post–Cold War, post–September 11 world?

The Current Era

In the summer and fall of 2002, when the Pew Research Center for the People and the Press asked more than 30,000 people in 42 countries what opinion they held of the United States, the responses were predominantly positive.[11] As shown in Table 1.3, in general the United States enjoyed a fairly favorable opinion in most countries. Contrary to the bleak renditions of these results in news reports, it appears that the United States was viewed in positive terms in most countries: at least 50% of the respondents held a positive opinion of the United States in 34 out of 42 countries (81%). In Ghana, Guatemala, Honduras, Nigeria, the Philippines,

Table 1.3. Opinion of the United States, 2002

Country	Favorable Very	Favorable Somewhat	Unfavorable Somewhat	Unfavorable Very	Country	Favorable Very	Favorable Somewhat	Unfavorable Somewhat	Unfavorable Very
Angola	23.59	30.90	15.77	5.00	Kenya	44.22	35.87	9.27	5.32
Argentina	8.72	25.43	25.68	23.46	Lebanon	8.50	26.80	21.00	37.60
Bangladesh	12.63	39.33	21.92	20.90	Mali	31.28	42.18	14.92	5.88
Bolivia	10.36	46.29	24.81	11.13	Mexico	15.16	49.40	14.56	10.34
Brazil	6.20	44.70	26.30	6.50	Nigeria	41.40	35.80	6.40	4.70
Bulgaria	27.04	43.97	12.65	4.67	Pakistan	2.36	10.53	13.63	58.42
Canada	24.20	48.80	17.40	7.20	Peru	26.02	45.29	13.50	4.50
Czech Republic	10.80	59.80	22.00	4.80	Philippines	39.43	51.71	4.71	1.86
Egypt	3.06	2.76	10.27	58.84	Poland	13.80	64.00	10.20	1.20
France	8.48	54.44	26.43	8.09	Russia	7.39	51.90	27.45	6.49
Germany	9.50	49.30	33.20	4.20	Senegal	22.68	41.97	24.51	9.30
Ghana	41.88	41.31	5.56	3.13	Slovakia	6.20	53.40	32.60	6.20
Great Britain	26.55	48.50	12.57	3.79	South Africa	32.71	32.14	10.29	19.14
Guatemala	30.60	51.20	9.80	3.00	South Korea	4.31	48.68	37.27	6.95
Honduras	42.69	37.55	2.96	2.17	Tanzania	17.36	35.97	15.69	9.58
India	22.57	40.66	10.92	13.66	Turkey	6.37	24.48	12.24	41.00
Indonesia	6.29	54.47	27.83	8.85	Uganda	41.17	33.23	7.14	6.45
Italy	12.99	56.69	17.72	4.72	Ukraine	30.80	51.20	12.80	4.00
Ivory Coast	41.10	43.50	10.45	4.94	Uzbekistan	34.29	51.00	9.00	1.43
Japan	12.68	58.55	23.36	3.28	Venezuela	48.57	33.14	10.57	3.29
Jordan	5.50	18.90	18.40	56.90	Vietnam	15.03	52.85	24.61	4.53

Notes: Data are from the Pew Global Attitudes Project, *What the World Thinks in 2002.* Percentage of "don't know" responses not included.

Poland, Uzbekistan, and Venezuela, fewer than 15% of the respondents reported an unfavorable opinion of the United States. Nonetheless, notable exceptions exist to the pattern of pro-American sentiment; in Bangladesh, Egypt, Jordan, Lebanon, Pakistan, and Turkey sizeable majorities of respondents had a somewhat unfavorable or a very unfavorable opinion of the United States.

Table 1.4 summarizes the large amount of information presented in Table 1.3 by showing the mean responses, along with the standard deviations, by region. The geographic area where the United States enjoyed the most favorable image is Africa; about 71% of the African respondents had a positive opinion of the United States and nearly half of that 71% of respondents had a very favorable opinion. The difference in opinion between the Eastern European countries and the Western democracies of Canada and Western Europe, on the other hand, is marginal. While Poland, Ukraine, Bulgaria, and the Czech Republic were very keen on the United States, with more than 70% of the respondents holding a somewhat favorable or very favorable opinion of the United States, the mass attitude in Russia and the Slovak Republic was analogous to that found in France or Germany. The United States also elicited large approval in Latin America, where nearly two-thirds of the public had at least a somewhat favorable opinion of the United States.

Table 1.4. Opinion of the United States, by Region, 2002

Region	Favorable		Unfavorable		N
	Very	Somewhat	Somewhat	Very	
Africa	33.74	37.29	12.00	7.34	10
	(9.69)	(4.60)	(5.79)	(4.61)	
Central & South Asia	15.63	39.20	16.66	20.65	5
	(12.93)	(17.30)	(7.96)	(22.27)	
East Asia	17.86	52.95	22.49	4.16	4
	(15.10)	(4.13)	(13.41)	(2.16)	
Eastern Europe	16.00	54.04	19.62	4.56	6
	(10.42)	(7.03)	(9.16)	(1.90)	
Latin America	23.54	41.62	16.02	8.05	8
	(16.10)	(8.85)	(8.65)	(7.07)	
Middle East	5.86	18.23	15.48	48.59	4
	(2.25)	(10.84)	(5.05)	(10.84)	
Industrial democracies	16.34	51.55	21.46	5.60	5
	(8.45)	(3.76)	(8.25)	(1.92)	

Notes: Data are taken from the Pew Global Attitudes Project, *What the World Thinks in 2002.* Standard deviations shown in parentheses.

A more tepid image is found in Central and South Asia, where about 55% of the respondents had a favorable view of the United States but as many as 20.6% held a very negative opinion of the United States. As the large standard deviation associated with this percentage attests, however, large variability exists among the five countries included in the Central and South Asian group. While about 58% of the Pakistani respondents strongly disliked the United States, small percentages did so in Uzbekistan and Indonesia, where only 1.4% and 8.9%, respectively, held a very negative opinion of the United States. Finally, it clearly emerges that the Middle East is the region where the perception of the United States was the least favorable. Nearly 49% of the respondents held a very unfavorable view of the United States, and about 15% manifested a somewhat unfavorable opinion.

A slightly rosier picture emerges from the analysis of the attitudes towards Americans as a people. Those who thought highly of the United States tended to think highly of its people as well, and conversely those respondents who did not hold a high opinion of America as a country did not hold a high opinion of its people. The high levels of congruence in the way respondents assessed the United States vis-à-vis the American people again underscores the widespread popularity of the United States among the general public in 2002. Any discrepancy to this pattern had a pro–American people connotation. For instance, in the Middle Eastern countries, about 31.3% of the respondents who expressed an opinion had more positive views towards the people than towards the country, which sets the overall percentage of people with an unfavorable view of the American people to 58.3%.

Moving beyond the geographic diffusion of anti-American sentiment, in Figure 1.1 I plot an index of anti-Americanism against a broad range of societal, political, and cultural variables.[12] Plotting these correlates indicates that attitudes towards America have uneven patterns of variability. For example, the range of variation of anti-American sentiment is higher in poor countries than it is in richer countries; the anti-Americanism index spans its whole range at low levels of GDP per capita, from the minimal presence of negative opinion of the United States in the Philippines and in Honduras to its peaks in Egypt and Pakistan. Analogous patterns emerge for all the other variables, possibly with the exception of U.S. economic aid and pro–U.S. elite discourse. Moreover, the finding on the positive relation between U.S. military assistance and presence of anti-American sentiment seems to be driven more by the combination of high military assistance and high anti-Americanism in Egypt and Jordan than by any more systematic relationship.

In sum, the findings from the analysis of the 2002 Global Attitudes Survey show, once again, not only the elusiveness of anti-American sentiment but also its adaptability. If we exclude countries a majority of whose inhabitants are Muslims, and countries selected for Peace Corps programs, anti-Americanism and its twin, pro-Americanism, flourish in a variety of political, societal, and cultural contexts.

Beyond 2002

How then have foreign publics viewed the United States in the trying times of the Iraq war and the torture scandals at Abu Ghraib and Guantanamo? To address this question, I analyze how attitudes towards the United States and the American people have fluctuated from mid-2002 into 2007 in Europe and in the Muslim world. Each of these data-gathering points captured reactions to certain political circumstances—the effects of the September 11 terrorist attacks in the 2002 wave; the invasion of Iraq in the 2003 wave; the transformation of Iraq amidst the insurgency, the first steps of an electoral process, and the torture scandals in the 2004 and 2005 waves—as well as conditions that are more specific to each of the countries, such as the consequences of the tsunami tragedy and the U.S. relief efforts in Indonesia.

In Figure 1.2, I track the pattern of attitudes towards the United States and the American people in Indonesia, Jordan, Lebanon, Morocco, Pakistan, and Turkey using data from four waves of the Pew Global Attitudes Survey. We see that attitudes towards the United States either declined or maintained their overall (low) levels after substantial drops to minimal levels of favorability in 2003 and 2004. Of the six countries listed in Figure 1.2, Lebanon and Morocco show rates of favorable responses above the 50% threshold with respect to the American people and just below 50% with respect to the nation, while the pro-American voices are still a minority in the other four countries.[13]

In Figure 1.3, I extend the analysis to Europe and Canada. In this context, we find that the appreciation of the United States has been declining since the summer of 2002, though the major drop in U.S. popularity that took place in March of 2003, at the peak of the Iraq crisis, turned out to be just a momentary aberration. Indeed, the change in the survey results between March and May of 2003 might be a fortuitous example of how the public readjusted its overall opinion of the United States as soon as the heated drama of war preparations and anti-war protests subsided. The perceptions of the American people, while they betray signs of slow deterioration, remained anchored to solid high rates of appreciation throughout the entire period.

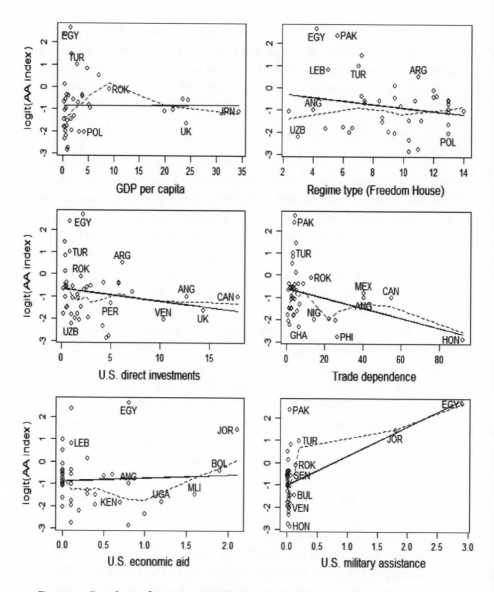

Figure 1.1. Correlates of Anti-Americanism, 2002

Note: Scatterplots of economic, cultural, political, and military variables against the aggregate anti-Americanism index, with a regression (solid) and a lowess (dotted) line superimposed. Labels identify selected countries. Data analysis is based on the 2002 wave of the Pew Global Attitudes Survey.

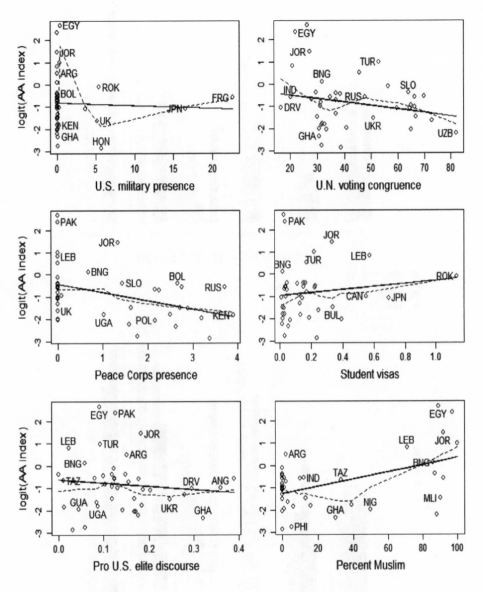

Figure 1.1. *(continued)*

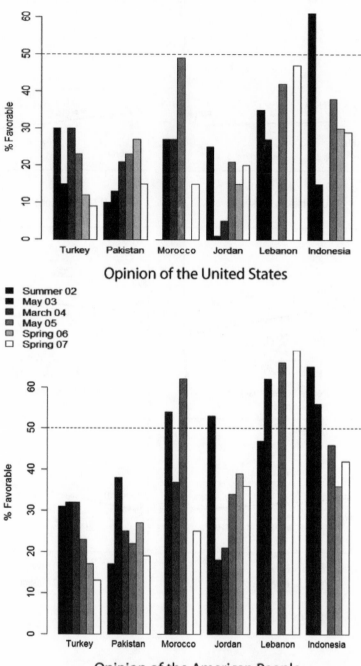

Opinion of the United States

■ Summer 02
■ May 03
▨ March 04
▨ May 05
▨ Spring 06
□ Spring 07

Opinion of the American People

Figure 1.2. Opinion of the United States and of Americans in Islamic Societies, 2002–2007

Note: Data from the Pew Global Attitudes Survey (various years).

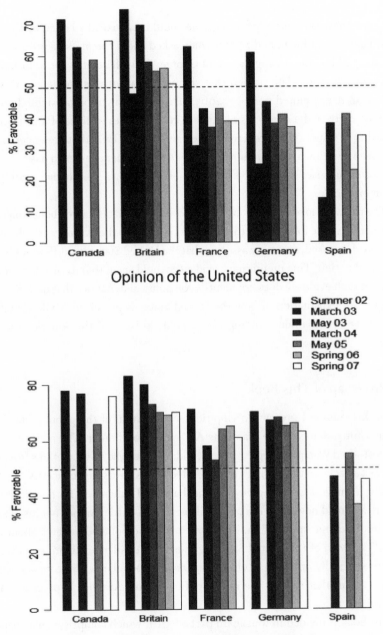

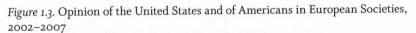

Figure 1.3. Opinion of the United States and of Americans in European Societies, 2002–2007

Note: Data from the Pew Global Attitudes Survey (various years).

Given these preliminary findings, we could paradoxically conclude that the First Lady, Laura Bush, had a point when asked about the massive protests taking place in London during President George W. Bush's state visit to Britain in November of 2003. She replied that she had seen only festive people waving American flags (quoted in Hoge, 2003). That reply might be far-sighted, given its glossing over the emotions of current controversies in light of a solid communality of values. It still remains a question how the United States engenders a mix of admiration and contempt, and how America manages to go past acrimonious controversies over choices and policies, retaining a good image among the common people.

The theme of love and hate, of what is loved and what is hated about America, then comes to the fore. Such a theme speaks directly to the claims of all who have described, invoked, or simply asserted that the United States is a different kind of powerful nation. This preliminary evidence would seem to indicate that indeed it is, but such evidence does not identify the political dynamics that underlie this finding. An explanation of how the United States is perceived would therefore contribute to our understanding of the political basis of the American world order.

Roadmap of This Book

In this volume I present an empirical investigation of the popular standing of the United States in the era of the American world order. The main focus is the post–Cold War, post–September 11 world, in which the reverberations from the terrorist attacks on the territory of the United States have given concerns over the country's image a new degree of immediacy and salience. The popularity of America abroad nowadays is a politically contested battleground, not just a subject for academic speculation. This book takes the political debates about the world's opinion of the United States seriously but challenges them, empirically and theoretically, in order to offer a portrayal of popular sentiments about the United States that reflects the rich variation in how America is perceived and appreciated abroad.

The book is divided in four main parts. Part 1, which comprises this chapter and Chapter 2, introduces the main themes of the book, its theoretical foundations, and its key terms. Part 2, which comprises Chapters 3 and 4, offers an analysis of the structural features of popular anti-Americanism. Part 3, which comprises Chapters 5 and 6, focuses on the sources of anti-Americanism. Part 4, which comprises Chapters 7 and 8, takes on the theme of the persistence of the current wave of anti-Americanism. Methodologically, the investigation relies upon the statistical analysis of survey data as its primary empirical strategy. An on-line appendix to this book presents the technical apparatus that underlies this investigation: the data, the measurement of the variables, and the statistical models.[14]

Chapter 2 presents the theoretical framework that informs the empirical analyses in the subsequent chapters and discusses how the analysis of popular perceptions of the United States contributes to understanding the basis of the American world order. The chapter begins with a discussion of how anti-Americanism can be defined and measured. It then contrasts two alternative views of anti-Americanism.

The first view posits that anti-Americanism is a cultural predisposition analogous to racism or anti-Semitism, that is, an ideological construct that systematically and deliberately misconstrues, rejects, and belittles the American people and the American polity. As such, this anti-Americanism is seen as pervasive and pernicious, an omnipresent cultural trait that both frames the intellectual worldview of ordinary people and dictates their basic political attitudes. This is anti-Americanism as a syndrome, a central theme in the analysis of Hollander (1995), Revel (2003), and Rubin and Rubin (2004).

The second view, on the other hand, challenges the depiction of anti-Americanism as a closed cognitive structure and instead characterizes it as the result of an aggregation of considerations, predispositions, and information. This view, which I call the dimensions of America theory, builds upon the theoretical work that such scholars of public opinion as Converse (1964) and Zaller (1992) have developed to account for the cognitive and attitudinal maps of the American electorate and then argues that the position of the United States in the cognitive mindframe of foreign publics is fluid and contingent. The popular perception of the United States reflects a balance of positive and negative elements, in which the appeal of the "American Dream" is not discounted by construction but is seen as an authentic factor that mediates how people relate to America, its power, and its actions. America is recognized as a cultural and political entity that is inherently multidimensional and multifaceted. From such a recognition, it follows that the United States is at times hated, at times loved, and very often hated *and* loved simultaneously, but rarely rejected altogether.

Chapter 3 presents the first set of systematic evidence about how ordinary people view the United States, investigating the worldwide perceptions of the

United States in a sample of forty-two countries in six regions of the world using the 2002 Global Attitudes Survey from the Pew Research Center for the
People and the Press. This broad overview identifies a series of systematic patterns that point to the multiple dimensions of the popular standing of the United
States. This chapter shows how the multifaceted nature of America tempers people's basic feeling towards the nation. This finding is consistent with the expectations of the dimensions of America theory. But, the empirical analyses also show
that such a pattern is not operative among Middle Eastern publics, where the
largest concentration of negative views of America is located.

Chapter 4 continues the empirical investigations with a more focused analysis
of the attitudes towards the United States among European and Islamic publics.
Chapter 4 relies on the batteries of survey questions from the 2002 Zogby International Ten Nation Impressions of America Poll and the Worldviews 2002—
European Public Opinion and Foreign Policy survey. The latter survey was conducted on behalf of the Chicago Council on Foreign Relations (CCFR) and the
German Marshall Fund of the United States (GMF). I distinguish two broader
frames through which ordinary people relate to America: the attitudes towards
American culture and society and the attitudes towards American policies. The
empirical analysis in Chapter 4 illustrates how respondents' propensities to oppose
America on its polity and policy dimensions are distributed within each country
and across countries.

The chapter then explores the relationship between the polity and the policy
attitudinal frames. From that relationship, we can distinguish between different
conjectures about the nature of anti-American sentiment at the popular level. In
particular, we can infer how systematic and ideologically consistent anti-
Americanism happens to be, that is, whether the attitudes towards culture and
society and the attitudes towards American foreign policy constitute a consistent belief system in which the image of America is either positive *or* negative
but not simultaneously positive *and* negative, depending upon which features
of America are more significant in the respondents' minds. We can also assess
the extent to which the appeal of U.S. culture and political values tempers concerns over the course of American foreign policy and resentment at the overwhelming power of the United States.

Chapter 4, therefore, takes another empirical stab at characterizing the nature
of the popular belief system about the United States. While Chapter 3 investigates
how the multifarious dimensions of America play into the formation of an overall
image of the United States, Chapter 4 investigates how the two fundamental

frames of policy and polity—of what America does and of what America is—hang together in people's cognitive maps. If foreign publics systematically distinguish between U.S. policies and U.S. culture and society in their evaluation of the United States, we must wonder whether this distinction has political consequences. In particular, the ideational appeal of U.S culture and ideals—that is, U.S. "soft power"—is often depicted as a major influence on the formation of attitudes towards U.S. diplomacy (Nye, 2004). By looking at whether the perception of U.S. culture and society shapes the perception of U.S. actions in the international arena, the empirical analysis in Chapter 4 goes to the core of the soft power thesis.

The main finding of Chapter 4 is that anti-American sentiments are mostly organized in loosely structured belief systems in which attitudes towards the American polity and attitudes towards American policies are only moderately connected. In line with the findings in Chapter 3, this chapter shows that one of the key components of U.S. soft power, namely the approval of American political ideals, does not have enough psychological force to engender approval of America's political choices in the international arena. Nonetheless, I also found that criticism of America's policies does not obscure the aspirations that America symbolizes, even among Islamic publics in the Middle East and South Asia.

Having established how the relationships between America as a symbol and America as a international political player shape popular attitudes towards the United States, the second empirical task is to analyze the types of individuals who have a positive opinion of America in its societal and policy domains and where they reside. In Chapters 5 and 6, I analyze a series of conjectures about the sources of anti-American opinion. The analysis emphasizes both the impact of standard demographic factors such as age, gender, and education and the impact of the broader ideational and ideological outlook of the mass publics.

Chapters 5 and 6 shift the analysis from the nature of anti-American opinion to the relationship between various individual-level characteristics and country-specific features and the patterns of popular opinion about the United States. The analytical focus is on the question of *who* and *where*—what types of individuals in what political contexts were more likely to articulate negative opinions of the United States. In these two chapters, the aggregate patterns investigated in Part 2 are deconstructed in order to specify the dynamics that underlie the formation of opinion about the United States.

The analysis of the sources of anti-American sentiments proceeds at two levels, which complement each other to provide an empirical map of the identity profile of the anti-American publics. First, we have a level of descriptive inference that pertains to variables such as gender and age. The descriptive inferences establish whether there is any systematic variation in the attitudinal patterns across demographic groups and how these patterns differ across world regions. These analyses are cast in terms of descriptive inferences because at this stage of development in the study of anti-American attitudes no clear *ex ante* expectations can be formulated. We are not yet ready to elaborate conjectures on a gender gap, for example, given that we are not aware of whether such a gap exists. The investigation proceeds on a second level, testing a series of conjectures that specify causal pathways linking attitudinal orientations with anti-American views. These conjectures go beyond *who* was more likely to hold the United States in low esteem and specify the reasons *why* such views were held.

Chapter 5 takes the survey data from the Pew Foundation's Global Attitudes Project and investigates four main hypotheses about the relationship between specific worldviews and anti-American attitudes. In particular, Chapter 5 investigates whether there was any systematic association between views towards the United States and respondents' levels of information, traditional family values, orientations towards capitalism and the market economy, and dissatisfaction with the state of affairs in the respondents' countries and in the world. Chapter 6 relies upon the data from the Zogby International survey and the CCFR/GMF survey, analyzed in Chapter 4, to corroborate, across surveys and samples, how information, educational levels, and the perceptions of U.S. military and economic power define the identity profile of the anti-American respondents.

Finally, Chapters 7 and 8 extend the empirical investigation beyond 2002 with an analysis of more recent surveys from the Pew Research Center. So much took place on the world scene since 2002 that it is important to investigate how the image of America fared among ordinary people. Scholars continue to bemoan the bleak status of America's image worldwide and attribute it to overwhelming American power, an unescapable structural factor that gives the United States unfettered influence (Pape, 2005; Walt, 2005; Mahbubani, 2005). Conservative intellectuals of all stripes, for their part, have already concluded that world opinion of the United States is steeped in bias and prejudice, a lost cause that should only be exposed and opposed (Revel, 2003; Rubin and Rubin, 2004).

Any evidence of how foreign publics manifest nuanced assessments of the United States, where criticism is accompanied by approval and admiration, however, would challenge these views regarding opinion towards America and place the ideational foundations of the American world order back at the center of the political and academic debates. This is the task undertaken in Chapters 7 and 8: to investigate whether current levels of anti-Americanism in Europe and the Islamic world are unlikely to subside even after the termination of the crisis unleashed by the Iraq war and by the U.S. response to the 9/11 terrorist attacks. In particular, in Chapter 7, I develop a series of hypotheses that probe whether the factors that shape popular perceptions of the United States reflect specific contingent circumstances or are indicative of a broader and deeper syndrome that is likely to persist over time. These hypotheses are then tested in Chapter 8.

The main finding of this analysis is that, even in times of crisis, the belief systems of ordinary people reflect diverse evaluations of the various aspects of the United States. In particular, attitudes towards the United States seem primarily to be shaped by the "human element," a president who personifies an era and the American people themselves. More specific misgivings about the use of U.S. power in the world enter into the cognitive calculus only as secondary factors. In other words, there is more nuance in the perceptions of the United States than is usually acknowledged. Nonetheless, for substantial portions of foreign publics between 2002 and 2008, a dim view of the American people overshadowed all other considerations in the formation of a negative view of the United States. This finding suggests that a change of U.S. executive will not be sufficient per se to alter popular attitudes towards the United States. For that to occur, views of the American people will have to improve as well.

In Chapter 9 I summarize the main findings of this study and evaluate how the popular standing of the United States in the collective imagination of ordinary people worldwide informs the nature of the American world order.

Two Theories on Anti-Americanism

Introduction

I f shelves in university bookstores count as reliable indicators of the fundamental political questions faced by a society, the message they convey in the
early years of the twenty-first century is clear: the position of the United States in
the world has emerged as the central issue for international relations scholars.
Title after title promises to define, explain, promote, or oppose a new phase in the
history of international relations in which the United States is the hegemon, the
new imperial power, the guarantor of stability, or simply the indispensable nation
(Bacevich, 2002; Ferguson, 2003; Johnson, 2004; Mann, 2003; Odom and Dujarric, 2004). Gone are the days when Richard Rosecrance (1976, 11) could write,
"Once so dominant in the international arena, America has become an ordinary
country in foreign relations." Also distant are the intellectual reflections that in
the immediate aftermath of the Cold War envisaged a new political era, in which
international law, collective security, and the United Nations would define the
fabric of the international community, as was the case in the doctrine of the *new
international order* most fervently advocated by President George H. W. Bush.[15]

Few commentators, if any, dispute the primacy of the United States in all the
dimensions that define the power status of a country: military, economic, political, and ideological. Even the doomsayers predicting a rapid collapse of America's dominant position in the international state system concur that the United
States towers over the world with its military might, its economic wealth, its
political influence, and its ideological appeal (see for example Kupchan, 2002;
Todd, 2003). The nature of the *American world order*, though, is the subject of
much controversy.

Opinions and conjectures clash over the stability of this order, the way it operates, and the extent to which it commands the allegiance of the people in "subordinate" countries. The essays in John Ikenberry's (2002) volume on the balance
of power in theory and practice in the era of the *Pax Americana* illustrate how eru-
dite scholars struggle to make sense of the American world order. What ensures

the stability of the international system in one point of view is the factor that, in another perspective, will bring the American era to an end; and what diffuses the sense of insecurity entailed in unbalanced power also makes America an existential threat, challenging the institutional identities and the cultural mores of weaker countries. America, as its sublime poet Walt Whitman said of himself, is large and contains multiple dimensions that might contradict each other.[16]

Popular anti-Americanism is similar; it is a protean entity that takes different forms and has different contents at different historical times in different countries. The anti-American attitude of a Marxist professor in a Western European institution of higher education is not directly comparable with the anti-American attitude of an unemployed worker in a developing country, nor is it comparable to the anti-American attitude of an Islamic extremist who commits terrorist acts against American people. Not only are the reasons behind a negative assessment of the United States likely to vary in these three cases, but they are also likely to vary in terms of levels and intensity of opposition.

When opposition to American values, symbols, and practices becomes politically salient within countries that are friends or allies of the United States and share its normative values, democratic institutions, economic practices, and individualistic lifestyle, anti-Americanism, then, can be seen as an expression of what Sigmund Freud would call the "narcissism of small differences." It may consist of the construction of minor differences between people that are otherwise alike into the basis for feelings of strangeness and hostility.[17] A separate situation exists when opposition to the United States emerges from cultural, religious, economic, or political divides. These are the allegedly "major differences" that set America's identity apart from that of other nations.

Most of the debate about the perception of the United States in foreign lands takes place under the subtext of one pointed question: "Why do they hate us?" Despite the centrality of that question in the current political debates, however, no simple answers can be found. Instead, any attempt at an answer should address all three elements of that question: Who are "they"? What beliefs or behaviors are subsumed into the emotion of hatred? What exactly about "us,"—America and the Americans—riles detractors, opponents, and enemies?

This chapter takes on those three questions and lays out the theoretical framework that underlies the empirical analyses persued in the subsequent chapters. I first review several attempts to define the meaning of anti-Americanism and its empirical referents. I identify the limitations in these attempts and elaborate an operational definition that directly places anti-Americanism within the purview of the data that are employed in this book, survey data that capture multiple dimensions of the popular perceptions of the United States among foreign publics. I then elaborate on two antithetical views of the nature of anti-American sentiment: anti-Americanism as a cultural syndrome in which opposition to America encompasses all that America does and stands for, and anti-Americanism as a feature of the belief system that is predominant in a society. Those two views portray divergent conceptions of the beliefs and attitudes that are usually subsumed under the same category of anti-Americanism.

Measuring Anti-Americanism

Measurement of a concept presupposes definition of the concept. Despite the fact that historians lament that "anti-Americanism has received little attention as a historical issue" (McPherson, 2003, 3), several attempts have been made to specify its defining attributes in different historical and geographical contexts. But while all definitions posit that anti-Americanism is some sort of opposition to America, agreement does not extend much further. This is because, as Richard Crockatt (2003, 43) has written, "like all essentially political terms, [anti-Americanism] proves difficult to define once you start peeling back the layers of meaning."

A key controversial issue in defining what constitutes anti-Americanism relates to the role that rationality, or irrationality, should have in the definition. The intent of writers who include those traits among the defining attributes of anti-Americanism is to separate "argument based" critiques of the United States from prejudicial or racist preconceptions. For example, in a broad overview of criticism of the United States at home and abroad, Paul Hollander (1995, 7) argues that "the concept of anti-Americanism implies more than a critical disposition: it refers to critiques which are less than fully rational and not necessarily well founded. It usually alludes to a predisposition, a free-floating hostility or aversion, that feeds on many sources besides the discernible shortcomings of the United States." He later reiterates the point, emphasizing that "anti-Americanism may be defined as an unfocused and largely irrational, often visceral aversion towards the United States, its government, domestic institutions, foreign policies, prevailing values, culture and people" (Hollander, 1995, 334–335).

Under Hollander's definition, "anti-Americanism" covers a wide spectrum. Graham Greene's novel *The Quiet American*, a scathing and prescient indictment of Western and U.S. involvement in Indochina, which was originally published in 1955, as well as the social doctrine of the Roman Catholic Church are taken by Hollander as examples of a "visceral aversion" to the United States. Given the disparate variety of critiques of the United States that would fall under Hollander's all-encompassing definition, it is hard to tell what critiques would not count as irrational.

In a similar vein, Josef Joffe (2004) tries to elaborate a set of theoretical criteria to distinguish between criticism of the United States and anti-Americanism. Critiques of the United States that are based on stereotyping, denigration, obsession, demonization, and the determination or desire to eliminate the adversary would count, in Joffe's opinion, as anti-American. But even granting that we were able to agree on when a critical comment slides into the realm of an obsessive stereotypical denigration, such definitional strategies would turn the concept of anti-Americanism into a social stigma on whoever is accused of holding such opinions rather than an analytical category whose origins, diffusion, and political consequences we can trace over space and time. The reciprocal accusations of anti-Americanism and anti-Europeanism that have cavalierly been lobbed back and forth over the Atlantic Ocean in recent times bear witness to this state of affairs (Garton Ash, 2003; Pond, 2004).

An alternative definitional strategy has been pursued by Ian Buruma and Avishai Margalit (2004). In their analysis, the cultural critique of America is subsumed within a broader category of criticism of the West which they call *Occidentalism*. Into that category they place all the descriptions that paint a dehumanizing picture of the West, such as "a machinelike society without a human soul." Anti-Americanism in this framework of analysis manifests a line of criticism that takes issue with the entire project of modernity to create a society based on the Enlightenment principles of freedom, equality, and national community.

Buruma and Margalit's approach has the advantage of showing how the discourse against modernity and the Enlightenment bears a family resemblance in a wide variety of historical contexts. But, in so doing, it transforms the political attitudes towards the United States into a chapter of the history of ideas and misses the extent to which negative attitudes towards the United States can be part of the belief systems of ordinary people who are by no means committed ideologues or dangerous fanatics. Moreover, by making anti-Americanism a subtype of a broader cultural syndrome, and thus paradoxically separating it from America, they exclude by default the possibility that America as a symbol of the West might be perceived in terms that are different from those in which any other modern, liberal democratic, country is perceived. In other words, Buruma and Margalit exclude by default the notion of an American exceptionalism.[18]

An additional challenge in the empirical analysis of anti-Americanism is the fact that "we are apt to resent criticism of our own society, voiced by an outsider, that we would deem legitimate, indeed possibly valid, from the mouth of an insider" (Cunliffe, 1986, 26). An example of this problem clearly emerges in the results of the 2005 wave of the Pew Global Attitudes Survey (Pew Global Attitudes Project, 2005, 5). In 2005, 70% of the U.S. public interviewed by the Pew Foundation stated that Americans are greedy, the highest percentage of respondents among the Pew sample of countries; and 39% of the U.S. public also stated that Americans are immoral, the second highest percentage in the sample. It is safe to claim that many Americans would react differently to the criticism if the respondents asserting that U.S. citizens are immoral and greedy were from foreign publics rather than Americans themselves. What does this imply for the concept of anti-Americanism?

On the one hand, this differentiation of outside and inside criticism raises a measurement problem. From the dynamics of in-group / out-group identification (Tajfel, 1982), we can expect that in-group favoritism potentially misconstrues conflicts of interests as ideological opposition and, thus, inflates measurements of anti-Americanism. But, at a more fundamental level, Cunliffe raises the issue of who can be accepted as a social critic of America and points out that the identity of the critic, rather than the content of the criticism, may determine what is recognized as legitimate discourse about America.

All these theoretical difficulties in finding the appropriate boundaries for anti-Americanism as an analytical category seem to call for a different approach. Instead of trying to specify the nature or content of anti-American sentiment and, in so doing, pass judgment on what constitute proper forms of criticism of the United States, this investigation defines the study of anti-Americanism as the analysis of popular sentiment towards the United States. "Popular" indicates that the feeling being reported is not just a matter for cultural elites but is an element of ordinary people's belief systems, from which they elaborate ideas about foreign affairs and international politics. "Sentiment" implies that anti-Americanism is not necessarily an encompassing ideology, a closed cognitive structure that elicits strong emotional reactions, but is a mood that ordinary people entertain about the United States. Such a mood is ascertained using public opinion polls, the instrument the social sciences have perfected to offer "the closest approximation to an unbiased representation of the public" (Verba, 1996, 1). And, as is the case with other attitudes gauged through opinion surveys (Zaller, 1992; Bartels, 2003), anti-Americanism is a mental construct and the result of the aggregation of considerations, cues, bits of information, emotions, and as such is subject to all the vagaries and the inconsistencies—Zaller's (1992, 29) "catalogue of horrors"— of public opinion.

Therefore, anti-Americanism can be defined as an ideational phenomenon, an attitude, and a political belief that can be measured through the answers individuals give to survey items. Those individuals who hold a low opinion of American citizens, American democracy, American society, American values, or American symbols are anti-American. In this framework, attitudes towards American policies constitute a separate dimension in foreign publics' system of beliefs about America, and this dimension's relationship to public orientations towards America in general can become a matter for theoretical and empirical elaboration. Negative attitudes about U.S. policies, however, are not per se sufficient to identify anti-Americanism. This operational definition sidesteps the difficulties regarding the appropriate meaning and comprehensiveness of the concept of anti-Americanism encountered in more elaborate definitional attempts, and it directly places the phenomenon of anti-Americanism within the context of the data that will be analyzed here.

It should be recognized that anti-Americanism as a mass popular phenomenon can also manifest itself in forms other than the attitudes revealed in opinion polls. Anti-Americanism can take the form of contentious political behavior, such as demonstrations, protests, riots, and other violent acts against American people, property, or symbols. Indeed, the few systematic empirical studies of anti-Americanism to date have focused on this dimension rather than the attitudinal dimension I analyze in this book (Midlarsky and Tanter, 1967; Tai, Peterson, and Gurr, 1973; Naghmi, 1982). But, while inherently relevant from a political and theoretical viewpoint, a focus on behaviorally contentious anti-Americanism masks the fundamental tension between admiration and opposition that seems to underlie the way foreign publics relate to the United States. A telling example, which could serve for many, comes from the student protests in Beijing after the NATO bombing of the Chinese embassy in Belgrade in 1999. When Chinese students chanted "Down with American imperialism" while drinking Coca-Cola, or when they lamented the state television's decision to stop broadcasting National Basketball Association (NBA) games protesting that "NBA games belong to the world" and saying that politics should not interfere with sports, they were manifesting this inherent tension to an utmost degree (Yan, 2002, 19–20). Focusing only on contentious behavior would, therefore, make it more difficult to identify the aspects of the United States that generate opposition from those that are admired.

Two major advantages underlie the choice of using survey data to assess the diffusion and intensity of anti-American sentiment: first, the possibility to elaborate an operational definition that does not have to establish whether critical opinions of America are "rational" or "misguided" and, second, the possibility to investigate various dimensions of the popular attitudes towards America and the relationship among these dimensions. Nonetheless, this choice comes at a methodological cost. To what extent are we to believe the responses of people who live in nondemocratic countries, where the public may enjoy, at most, partial political and civil rights? And to what extent are we confident that particular shades of opinion are not systematically underrepresented in the samples because some respondents feel that their responses might be socially or politically undesirable, a phenomenon that Adam Berinsky (2004) has documented in the case of American public opinion and that might emerge in other countries, democratic or not?

The methodological issue underlying these questions is that of *preference falsification*. In line with Timur Kuran's (1995) theoretical formulation, individuals have *private* and *public* preferences on any political issue: private preferences are those that are known to themselves only, while public preferences are those they decide to reveal to others. Such a decision is based on a strategic calculus in which individuals assess the benefits and costs of conformity—saying what their rulers or neighbors want to hear or pedantically repeating the received wisdom in their society—and the psychological costs of lying. Kuran shows how those calculations affect the pattern of participation in social movements and their success. He also shows how the mechanism of preference falsification leads to the unpredictable character of radical political change in nondemocratic regimes.

Thus, from the dynamics of preference falsification, we might conjecture that a hypothetical survey of anti-Americanism in the Shah's Iran would produce a substantial underestimate, while a survey of anti-Americanism in Khomeini's Iran or since Khomeini would result in an overestimate. Analogously, anti-Americanism should be less virulent in Kuwait, a close ally of the United States and a direct beneficiary of United States' Middle East policy, than in Indonesia or Lebanon, countries with less close political connections with the United States. One empirical strategy for dealing with the issue of preference falsification is to elaborate a set of expectations regarding the direction of probable bias depending upon the friendliness of state relations with the United States and the degree of repression of free speech and thought in the target country.

The survey data I analyze differentiate the attitudes towards America on a cluster of dimensions, including its democracy, technology, products, policies, and movies. Thus, a pattern of attitudes is examined, not just absolute levels of pro- or anti-Americanism. This approach should lessen the possibility that the effects of preference falsification will invalidate the findings reported in this book. This argument is analogous to the one offered by Geddes and Zaller (1989) in a classic study analyzing public opinion in nondemocratic countries. Geddes and Zaller wrote, "Finally, and most importantly, our analysis focuses on *patterns* of support for regime policies rather than absolute *levels* of support. We are unable to see how the complex pattern of regime support to be described below could be an artifact of the untruthful answers of fearful respondents." However, when considering the truthfulness of responses in nondemocratic societies, the repressive ability of authoritarian, but not totalitarian, states should not be overemphasized.[19]

The Popular Basis of Anti-American Sentiment

"Who's afraid of Mr. Big?" asked Josef Joffe (2001) while reflecting on the absence of strategic balancing against the power of the United States. The tone was humorous, as befit the summer of 2001, but the argument was serious. Lesser powers, Joffe claimed, might resent the overwhelming clout of America and might dream of institutional rules to harness its power and might even enjoy the bad-mouthing of the less refined styles of the pragmatic Americans. But when it comes to containing the United States, as the balance-of-power logic would predict, no one volunteers, because the United States, as the primary provider of the international public goods, is essential to their own interests. Thus, Joffe concluded, "as long as the United States continues to provide international public goods while resisting the lure of unilateralism, envy and resentment will not escalate into fear and loathing" (2001, 52).

But in the fall of 2001, when the United States came under attack, even the loud and popular opposition to the United States, its policies, and its ideals—the "psycho-cultural balancing" of the "chattering classes" which Joffe had dismissed as an inconsequential nuisance—started to be seen in a different light. Now that not just the armies of state organizations but also individuals loosely organized in terrorist networks could mount deadly attacks against the United States, the understanding of the popular basis of anti-American sentiment acquired a central place in the quest for American security. What Fareed Zakaria (2003, 15–16) aptly called the "democratization of violence" had struck home.

Simple connections cannot be drawn between the existence of an ideological climate in which America is vilified and its policies despised and the willingness to hurt the country and its people, as the literature on terrorist mobilization shows (see, in particular, Bueno de Mesquita, 2005). Terrorism expert Martha Crenshaw (2008, 6) has made this point very clear. Moreover, not all the forms of anti-Americanism are even remotely tainted with murderous intentions or criminal complacency. Investigating popular anti-Americanism, nonetheless, potentially offers a double contribution to the conditions for American security: it sheds light on the existence of fringes of *sympathizers* with whom the actions of the extremists could resonate, and more broadly it potentially shows the extent to which the rest of the world endorses the American leadership and respects the creed embodied in its political institutions.

The conservative commentators who have so deeply shaped the grand strategies of the George W. Bush administration would dismiss these concerns about the status of the United States among foreign publics as defeatist or morally dubious. In the words of Kaplan and Kristol (2003, 121), American foreign policy should be "unapologetic, idealistic, assertive, and funded well beyond current appropriations." The bring-'em-on bravado of William Safire (2003), who wrote "The more the elites here and in Europe holler, the solider the Bush support gets," turns the concerns about the image of America in the world on their heads, taking them as an indication of the probity of America's intentions.[20] But when Robert Kagan (2004, 67) writes that "for the first time since World War II, a majority of Europeans has come to doubt the legitimacy of U.S. power and of U.S. global leadership," we can conclude that "we have a problem."

Thus, ideas and perceptions become essential elements in the stability and viability of the American world order. Not just states and strategic interactions, but also masses and mass political attitudes delimit the ability to lead that the United States derives from the allegiance it commands from the subordinate subjects. E. H. Carr (1946, 132) approvingly quotes David Hume, who wrote, "The Soldan of Egypt or the Emperor of Rome might drive his harmless subjects like brute beasts against their sentiments and inclinations. But he must at least have led his *mamelukes* or pretorian bands like men by their opinions." America faces a similar predicament: in this age of mass politics and mass communications, power over opinion is more than ever a source of leadership and prestige.

Once we have established that masses and mass attitudes are the *locus* of the empirical analysis, what remains to be selected is the location of the empirical units to be investigated. As we have seen from the analysis of the attitudes towards the United States in forty-two countries in 2002, reported in Chapter 1, while more likely in countries of Muslim religion and less likely in countries with Peace Corps operations, negative opinion of the United States is not clearly associated with any specific factor in the large welter of political and societal circumstances. Anti-Americanism appears elusive and contextual, not easily reduced to a cause or a set of relationships.

To understand the phenomenon of popular opposition to the United States, therefore, we should go beyond the macro statistics of aggregate analyses and focus on individual patterns in selected groups of countries. This study offers both a broad analysis of anti-American sentiments in seven world regions and a more intensive investigation of two regions: Europe and the larger Islamic world. These two regions were chosen because they are perceived as the paradigmatic hotbeds of anti-American opposition in the new century and have deservedly attracted the attention of scholars and commentators. Europe, the allies of the Atlantic security community that should be forming stronger bonds with the United States, and a group of Islamic countries, civilizational opponents that may be expected to hold the United States and the West in contempt, clearly meet the criterion of being politically relevant.

But to go beyond what Amy Chua (2003, 229) calls "the tendency to generalize from an n of 2 or 3" in discussions of anti-Americanism, this study shifts the analytical focus from aggregate patterns to the interaction between political contexts and the dynamics of opinion formation at the individual level. This shift in analytical focus—from aggregate patterns of cross-sectional variation to individuals and the countries where they reside—avoids defining absolute standards of what would count as high levels of anti-Americanism. Each society appears more or less predisposed to be anti-American relative to the other societies in the same region, but by eschewing sweeping generalizations, my analysis preserves some level of homogeneity in the underlying dynamics through which anti-American sentiment emerges across regions.

Two Views on Anti-Americanism

In this book, I contrast two views about attitudes towards the United States among foreign publics. The first view is called *anti-Americanism as a syndrome.*

The second view is my own alternative account, which I elaborate in this book; I call this alternative view the *dimensions of America* theory. These two views portray anti-Americanism in very different manners. They have different theoretical and normative underpinnings, and they generate divergent implications about the relevance of U.S. standing in world politics.

Anti-Americanism as a Syndrome

Of the popular perceptions of anti-American sentiment that inform current political debates, the one commanding the most followers sees anti-Americanism as a unified, and undifferentiated, phenomenon striding across the world. In that view, anti-Americanism is an expression of a malevolent ill-disposition that defies any attempt at explanation. President George W. Bush declared, "Like most Americans, I just cannot believe [the vitriolic hatred of the United States] because I know how good we are" (quoted in Crockatt, 2003, 68). In a similar spirit, the newsmagazine *America* wrote in 1953, "We feel that anyone in his right mind ought to like us, or at least understand us. . . . After all, aren't we the most 'normal' people in the world?" (quoted in McPherson, 2003, 23–24). These expressions reveal an authentic feeling of bewilderment and outrage, but they also constitute the basic tenet of a popular conception that is deeply ingrained in the collective psyche of the American nation. The American people's "conviction that their interests and the world's interests are one," Robert Kagan (2003, 88) reminds us, "may be welcomed, ridiculed, or lamented. But it should not be doubted."

Those who stand to criticize or oppose the United States—so the logic goes—have ulterior motives that should be exposed and refuted. Jean-François Revel (2003) and Fouad Ajami (2003) offer two of the clearest statements of this reasoning. "The United States need not worry about hearts and minds in foreign lands," writes Ajami (2003, 61), "If Germans wish to use anti-Americanism to absolve themselves and their parents of the great crimes of World War II, they will do it regardless of what the United States says and does. If Muslims truly believe that their long winter of decline is the fault of the United States, no campaign of public diplomacy shall deliver them from that incoherence." Revel (2003, 159) would concur: "Europe in general and its Left in particular absolve themselves of their own moral failings and their grotesque intellectual errors by heaping them onto the monster scapegoat, the United States of America."

Hatred, envy, prejudice, and moral pettiness are, in this view, the driving forces behind anti-American sentiment. In the writings of such authors as Charles

Krauthammer (2003), Jean-François Revel (2003), and Dinesh D'Souza (2002), opposition to America is the disposition of people who embrace antidemocratic, antimarket, and antimodern ideologies; it is the psychological refuge of societies who eschew any responsibilities for their shortcomings or their failures; it is an all-encompassing cultural trait embodying values and beliefs inconsistent with "the American way of life."

Lest we be tempted to conclude that such sentiments are a recent phenomenon, merely a reaction to the assertive policies and the hectoring attitude of President George W. Bush and his administration, scholars have sifted through literary accounts, travel diaries, political speeches, and documents to show how the name of America has attracted scorn and derision, hatred and contempt since its colonial times. Thus, America was a degenerate land where no civilization could flourish for eighteenth-century critics, a failed society in the nineteenth century, a societal model to resist when its rise to power could no longer be denied from the Belle Époque to the Depression, and finally the scourge of fascists and communists in the ideological strife of the twentieth century. In an encompassing overview of anti-Americanism through history, Barry and Judith Rubin argue that this continuity can be explained in simple terms: it is "a response to the phenomenon of America itself, precisely because of that country's uniqueness and innovation, the success it has achieved, and the challenge it poses to all alternative ideologies or existing societies" (Rubin and Rubin, 2004, 243).

In the early years of the twenty-first century, such sentiments of opposition and rejection are allegedly rife, more than ever, in Islamic countries. "More than anything else," writes William McNeill (1993, 569), "reaffirmation of Islam, whatever its specific sectarian form, means the repudiation of European and American influence upon local society, politics, and morals." The theme of an irreconcilable separation between Islam and the West permeates the theory Samuel Huntington expounded in *The Clash of Civilizations* (1996). Again and again, Huntington depicts a history of bloody confrontations and fleeting truces that cannot be accounted for exclusively in terms of power and interests.

In clear words, Huntington (1996, 217) writes: "The underlying problem for the West is not Islamic fundamentalism. It is Islam, a different civilization whose people are convinced of the superiority of their culture and are obsessed with the inferiority of their power." In his theory, this normative divide affects the political institutions that Muslim societies can sustain and, by extension, molds the belief systems of ordinary people. Thus, from Huntington's clash of civilizations logic we derive the prediction that Muslim publics will be wary of the Western norms of individualism, pluralism, and relativism and be opposed to all America is and does, as America is the most pristine incarnation of the ideals of freedom, democracy, and opportunity. While several authors have cast doubts on the ability of Huntington's thesis to account for the patterns of peace and conflict in the post–Cold War international arena (Russett, Oneal, and Cox, 2000; Henderson and Tucker, 2001; Chiozza, 2002), the possibility remains that Huntington's civilizational dynamics are unfolding not at the state level but at the mass societal level.

By the anti-Americanism as a syndrome perspective, we should expect to find large majorities in Islamic countries and many people in Europe objecting to America, regardless of whether we inquire about their perceptions of American policies, society, or culture, and only negligible minorities approving of how the United States conducts its foreign policy and admiring what the United States has to offer as a society. We would also expect that the belief systems of the general public would be similar across countries, despite differences in political relations with the United States and levels of wealth and economic development. Should the data reveal this portrayal of America's image in the general public, anti-Americanism would indeed be the syndrome depicted by Krauthammer, Revel, D'Souza, and Huntington.

The Benevolent Nation and the Ambivalent Public

To say that the United States of America cannot be easily summarized into any single definition would seem to state the obvious (Singh, 2006). But, obvious though such a statement is to many, it captures an important point that is often missed in the current discussions about anti-Americanism, namely, that when people think of the United States, a large number of characteristics, events, and symbols come to mind. If we just contemplate the litany of statements that depict America as degenerate, immoral, hypocritical, and domineering, we see to what lengths the anti-American mind can reach.

The collection of three hundred years of anti-American discourse compiled by Rubin and Rubin (2004) is impressive in its thoroughness. It bears witness to how quickly the United States became a point of reference in political and cultural discourse, the "other" to disparage and to confront. But such a collection reflects two major limitations. First, it makes no distinctions among anti-American tropes from disparate historical periods, even though what constituted "America" varied radically in different periods. All the criticisms are conflated into the conceptual category of anti-Americanism, regardless of their specific targets. A historical continuity is thus established with no qualms about conceptual consistency.[21] A second limitation mars the Rubins' investigation. In their thorough review, they fail to emphasize that the name *America* also acquired a positive valence in the collective imagination of intellectuals and ordinary people from its inception on the world scene (Crockatt, 2003; Offe, 2005; Kennedy, 2007). The theme of America as the *New World* is the precursor to the theme of the *American Dream*, and it coexists with all the anti-American tropes so cogently dissected by the Rubins. America represented a new beginning and a social laboratory from which one could discern the laws of motion of a modern society constructed upon the pillars of freedom and equality, and with that, the future of the Old World (Offe, 2005).

Startling examples of this theme abound, but none is more startling than the one offered by Richard Crockatt (2003, 48), who reminds us that John Donne, the sublime English poet of the Elizabethan and Jacobean eras, eulogized his mistress in her full splendor with the epithet "Oh my America! My new-found-land." John Locke (1988 [1690], 301), in an oft-quoted line from the *Second Treatise of Government*, raised a similar point: "Thus in the beginning all the World was *America*" (emphasis in original). Claus Offe (2005), in particular, offers a perceptive portrayal of how the reflections over America shaped the analysis of Alexis de Tocqueville, Max Weber, and Theodor Adorno, three towering intellectuals who saw in the societal arrangements and cultural mores of the United States the possible bastions against the encroaching effects of bureaucratization and mass politics on liberty and equality.[22]

The Dimensions of America Theory

Given this rich intellectual history in which admiration and praise are intertwined with scorn and contempt, it should be no surprise that when ordinary people summarize their feelings about the United States, they rely upon a vast array of themes and features to formulate their opinions. Should they say "It depends" to a question asking them what they think of the United States, they would not be evading the question but offering a fair and appropriate characterization of their state of mind.

Scholars of American politics, where most of the theoretical advances in our understanding of public opinion are to be found, have long recognized that the general public rarely holds well-formed opinions reflecting a coherent assessment and evaluation of the issues at hand. More often, the general public has vague, contradictory, and unstable views—"non-attitudes" in Philip Converse's (1964, 1970) famous formulation.

Such "non-attitudes" have occupied a central place in the reflection of students of mass politics because they cast doubt on the capacity of ordinary people to coherently express their demands to the political system. Over time, however, skeptical views of mass publics have subsided as scholars have come to realize that those "non-attitudes" are not simply a manifestation of the public's inability to grasp complex issues, or a consequence of the public's falling prey to whimsical mood cycles, as Gabriel Almond (1960) emphasized. Those non-attitudes are instead real and systematic features of ordinary people's belief systems, and as such they are a reflection of a systematic process in which fundamental values, political attentiveness, and information flows interact to form public opinion (Zaller, 1992).

When we study the perceptions of the United States among ordinary people in foreign lands, it is reasonable to expect that similar dynamics might be at play. When people are asked what image or what opinion they hold of the United States, they generate judgments that conflate the multiple dimensions of America. Multiple considerations are behind the simple answer "I have a somewhat favorable opinion of the United States," or "unfavorable opinion" for that matter. These considerations are likely to be in the minds of the respondents at the time the survey is taken, either because they have been prompted by features of the questionnaire, such as question framing or wording, or because such opinions are part of the predominant pattern of elite discourse in their society. Far from representing the empirical manifestation of a cultural trait, survey items reveal the balance among predispositions, cognitive capacities, and levels of information across individuals in the mass public, a balance that is more contingent, more circumstantial, and more context dependent than is acknowledged in the current discourse on anti-Americanism.

In this perspective, John Zaller's (1992) and Alvarez and Brehm's (2002) theories of mass opinion loom large. Individuals are immersed in streams of political communication emanating from elites—be they political, religious, or cultural—and being conveyed through news and entertainment media and information channels. Insofar as they are politically attentive, individuals become aware of the elites' messages and filter them through their own basic predispositions, orientations, and aspirations. Survey responses emerge, then, as the outcome of a process in which individuals select from a multiplicity of considerations and summarize the ones they find immediately salient into a manifest statement, which is then recorded into an attitudinal scale.

Coherent classifications of the political referents in publics' belief systems need not be the outcome of the survey. On the contrary, contradictions and ambiguities are a staple of people's opinions and are reflected in surveys. In this model, a multifaceted and nuanced image of the United States emerges as respondents speaking of America are often of two minds: appreciative when some features are evoked and negative when they focus on other aspects. Contradictory perceptions coexist in people's minds because America is an inherently multidimensional "object."

Bruce Russett (1963, 213) warned, "One must be extremely careful to specify the content of the attitudes in question when using broad labels like 'anti-American.'" To abide by Russett's advice, in my analysis I carefully distinguish the specific referents that ordinary people assess in their evaluations of the United States. Such evaluations across multiple referents need not generate any syndrome of ambivalence, if we take ambivalence to mean the sense of anxiety and tension that apparently irreconcilable feelings generate.[23] There is nothing inherently contradictory in, for example, the simultaneous appreciation of American democratic ideals and concern over the excesses of its popular culture, nor is there any underlying conflict over competing core values when individuals express admiration for American technology while disapproving of American business practices.

More importantly, a fundamental condition of feelings of ambivalence is seldom present in the emotional and intellectual relations that members of general publics establish with the United States. If, as Neil Smelser (1998) clearly posits, ambivalence emerges in relations of dependence from which one cannot escape, such as those between parents and children or prisoners and guards, the connections that ordinary people establish with the United States are hardly so intense or so intimate. Despite its towering importance and its diffuse presence, the United States is far from being the primary concern in the ordinary lives of ordinary people.

But, if we strip the word ambivalence of its anxiety-inducing connotations and we limit its meaning to the existence of opposing, multifarious affective orientations towards an object, it can inform the hypothesis that this book puts forward, that the image of the United States is premised on a multitude of characteristics, the dimensions of America theory. The primary empirical task, then, is to show how world public opinion, and in more detail the public opinion in Islamic societies and in Europe, systematically discriminates among aspects of the United States and how these views coexist in respondents' minds.

The Soft Power Thesis

A central concern in the study of U.S. popularity abroad is whether there is a connection between the acceptance of the normative basis of U.S. world order and the acceptance of U.S. diplomacy. While opposition to U.S. policies does not count per se as anti-Americanism, it is important to assess how views about policies feed into views of U.S. polity and society. If indeed foreign publics look at U.S. policies and at U.S. culture and society through different lenses, we are left to wonder whether those two lenses influence each other or whether they remain distinct in people's minds, two different perspectives with no clear overlap.

This is far from being an academic question. Evidence of how positive opinions of American society and negative opinions of American policies coexist in the aggregate has been trenchantly dismissed as hypocritical or misguided. Fouad Ajami (2003, 54) exemplifies this line of reasoning when he ridicules the notion that much can be inferred from any finding purporting to differentiate among dimensions of the United States. "The pollsters," he writes, "have flaunted spreadsheets to legitimize a popular legend: It is not the Americans that people abroad hate, but the United States! . . . You can't profess kindness towards Americans while attributing the darkest of motives to their homeland." Roger Cohen (2004) sounded a similar chord when he wrote in the *New York Times*, with an emphasis worthy of Louis XIV, "Bush is America just as Chirac is France. The two nations' highest offices represent every shade of opinion that makes up their democracies."[24]

The distinctions and the nuances that characterize the attitudes towards the United States are as much decried as they are invoked as the panacea that would cure popular anti-Americanism. "It is the policies that people hate, not the people and the ideals" is a common refrain that is often heard in casual conversations as well as more learned analysis (Waterbury, 2003). More importantly, the ideational appeal of U.S. culture and ideals, its "soft power" (Nye, 1990, 2004), is often credited with the capacity to exert a positive influence on how people perceive U.S. diplomacy. Of the sources of soft power, one has been especially singled out as a major force that shapes the policy preferences of other people and nations: the character of U.S. culture. "If [a country's] culture and ideology are attractive, others will more willingly follow," wrote Joseph Nye (1990, 32). Commenting upon his own variation on the theme of soft power, which he calls "sweet power," Walter Russell Mead (2004, 39–40) concurs that "American sweet power, though limited and variable, clearly plays an important role in winning sympathy and support for American foreign policy around the world." The soft power thesis, therefore, makes an important claim about the nature of U.S. image, one that gives political meaning to the different frames that structure popular attitudes towards the United States.

Despite the interest in the connection between love of U.S. ideals and opposition to U.S. policies, however, the empirical investigations have systematically fallen short, bedeviled by many conceptual challenges. First, we should acknowledge that no empirical endeavors can go so far as to adjudicate the strong causal claim that the notion of soft power seems to imply. Nye (2004, 14) himself admits the possibility that the causal effect might flow in the opposite direction, from policies to political ideology and all the fixtures of the American dream; in his own words, "domestic or foreign policies that appear to be hypocritical, arrogant, indifferent to the opinion of others, or based on a narrow approach to national interests can undermine soft power."

More fundamentally, it is not possible to discern the direction of causality between these two sets of beliefs because, in the mental maps of ordinary people, attitudes towards policies and attitudes towards society do not exist in a hierarchical structure in which one set of attitudes constitutes a more general ideational posture encompassing the other set of attitudes. As Hurwitz and Peffley (1987) have explained in their classic model of foreign policy beliefs, both sets of beliefs would need to satisfy this condition if we wanted to establish a causal relationship between them. Opinions about policy and opinions about culture and society are, instead, elaborated at the same level of generality. Therefore, each might cause the other, and each could emerge from distinct dynamics of opinion formation.

If a causal relationship between these two dimensions of the attitudes towards America remains indissolubly elusive—a social science variant of the chicken-egg conundrum—their reciprocal relationship remains nonetheless of great relevance. The theoretical framework developed in this book provides a venue for testing the effectiveness of the soft power thesis at the mass popular level.

The starting point for this empirical test of the soft power argument is Converse's (1964, 207) definition of a belief system as "a configuration of ideas and attitudes in which the elements are bound together by some form of constraint or functional interdependence." A highly constrained belief system is one in which a person's opinions form a consistent aggregate, such that it would be possible to infer attitudes on one dimension from knowledge of a person's stances on another dimension. In this light, it is possible to ascertain whether attitudes towards U.S. culture and society and attitudes towards U.S. policies generate a consistent—or constrained, in Converse's (1964) terminology—belief system. Are the individuals who hold a negative view of U.S. policies those who hold a negative view of U.S. society and culture? Similarly, are the people who subscribe to the notion of an American dream more amenable to U.S. foreign policy? If that were the case, then, it would be possible to guess where a person would stand on one dimension from knowledge of where he or she stands on the other. And, from that knowledge, we would be able to infer that the mechanisms of soft power contribute to the formation of popular opinion about the United States, regardless of which attitudinal dimension "causes" the other in the mind of individual respondents in the surveys.

Conclusions

In the current discourse on the image of the United States in foreign lands, two master narratives compete on the intellectual field. One claims that anti-Americanism represents a consistent ideology of hatred and contempt targeting the United States, its government, its principles, and its people indiscriminately. The competing narrative claims that the attitudes towards the United States are contextual and mediated by the appeal that the United States exerts in the collective psychologies of ordinary people the world over. These two master narratives are premised on different normative perspectives and stem from different scientific traditions about international affairs. As is always the case with divergent interpretations of social phenomena, each narrative commands a degree of empirical plausibility and its own assortment of intellectual supporters.

If we seek to extend our understanding of the attitudes towards the United States beyond such prima facie empirical plausibility, such narratives should be subjected to intensive empirical investigation. In the next chapter, I start such an intense investigation with an analysis of how attitudes towards the United States were structured in the belief systems of the mass publics in a worldwide sample of forty-two nations.

PART II / Features

CHAPTER THREE

Patterns of Anti-Americanism

Introduction

To unravel the puzzle of the mixture of aspiration and opposition that is associated with the United States, that is, to understand *who* says *what* of the United States, I begin with an analysis of the status of America's image in 2002 in seven regions of the world: Africa, Central and South Asia, East Asia, Eastern Europe, Latin America, the Middle East, and the advanced industrial democracies of Western Europe and Canada. The analyses rely upon the extensive survey data of the Global Attitudes Project of the Pew Research Center for the People and the Press, a large survey that is often cited in commentaries and discussions of anti-Americanism but rarely systematically analyzed.[25]

We have already seen in Tables 1.3 and 1.4 in Chapter 1 that the U.S. image was largely untarnished and uncompromised in the summer and fall of 2002, when the survey was administered to 38,000 people in 42 countries.[26] Respondent after respondent in country after country manifested a favorable reaction whenever asked to offer an overall evaluation of their feelings towards the United States. Given the pervasiveness of the discourse on anti-Americanism, this finding is no doubt reassuring, as it shows that anti-Americanism was not a predominant orientation among foreign publics as recently as 2002, although, as Tables 1.3 and 1.4 show, substantial variation existed across and within regions. Dislike of the United States was widespread and intense among Islamic respondents in the Middle East, and it was the predominant attitude in such disparate places as Angola, Argentina, Bangladesh, and Pakistan, where solid majorities systematically indicated a negative appraisal of the United States. Dire apprehensions of a specter of anti-Americanism spreading over the world were mostly exaggerated. The regional variation, however, dispels any sense of complacency that the rosy figures from the Global Attitudes Survey superficially convey.

This chapter illustrates what lies behind this variation by evaluating the extent to which popular attitudes towards the United States have metastasized into a syndrome of rejection and opposition or, conversely, are mediated by the multiple aspects of the United States. First, I analyze how ordinary people assessed different features of the United States in 2002 and whether they formed coherent opinions of those features. Second, I analyze whether the apparent good standing of the United States in people's opinions reflected mere politeness rather than a genuine feeling of approval of the United States.

The analysis focuses on forty-two countries in seven regions: 1) in Africa, Angola, Ghana, Ivory Coast, Kenya, Mali, Nigeria, Senegal, South Africa, Tanzania, and Uganda; 2) in Central and South Asia, Bangladesh, India, Indonesia, Pakistan, and Uzbekistan; 3) in East Asia, Japan, the Philippines, South Korea, and Vietnam; 4) in Eastern Europe, Bulgaria, the Czech Republic, Poland, Russia, Slovakia, and Ukraine; 5) in Latin America, Argentina, Bolivia, Brazil, Guatemala, Honduras, Mexico, Peru, and Venezuela; 6) in the Middle East, Egypt, Jordan, Lebanon, and Turkey; and 7) a group of advanced industrial democracies, Britain, Canada, France, Germany, and Italy.

Dimensions of Anti-Americanism

As observed earlier, the anti-American discourse dissected by Rubin and Rubin (2004) or Revel (2003) coexists with the discourse about the American dream and American soft power theorized by Joseph Nye (2004). It is, therefore, important to go beyond summary statements of like and dislike, such as those we have discussed so far, and identify which characteristics feature prominently in people's mental frame of the United States. What about the United States attracts or repels foreign publics? Do the attitudes towards America form coherent patterns across these dimensions?

More focused inquiries, like those tabulated in Table 3.1, reveal that, beneath the surface of a widespread support of the United States and its people lay a more nuanced opinion of America. Positive attitudes towards the United States coexisted with negative appraisals of fundamental features of the American polity and society. Asked to state their opinion about American ideas about democracy, a sizeable number of people, 36.65%, responded that they disliked these ideas. The regional variation in the attitudes towards American democracy is also revealing: this percentage was lowest among the ten African countries, where only about 21.11% of the respondents disapproved of the American style of democracy, and highest in the Middle East, where more than half of the respondents expressed dislike. We can also see that in three very different regions—Central and South Asia, Latin America, and the group of industrialized Western democracies—

Table 3.1. Dimensions of Anti-Americanism

Region	U.S. democracy (%)		U.S. customs (%)		Popular culture (%)		U.S. science (%)	
	Neg.	NA	Neg.	NA	Neg.	NA	Neg.	NA
Africa	21.11	11.32	48.15	7.50	28.65	6.92	8.82	5.97
Central & South Asia	41.48	22.12	70.00	11.92	59.65	11.53	11.11	15.60
East Asia	29.47	7.50	49.08	9.30	35.26	6.22	12.37	3.87
Eastern Europe	35.55	17.52	57.57	13.28	37.12	7.20	31.46	9.16
Latin America	42.07	14.48	61.84	8.27	33.12	6.34	18.71	4.21
Middle East	54.41	8.79	77.75	8.11	50.90	6.37	28.27	6.84
Industrial democracies	43.50	10.31	61.17	8.39	25.73	5.27	25.03	4.44
Total	36.65	14.25	60.62	9.41	39.36	7.48	17.45	7.67

Region	U.S. business (%)		War on terror (%)		Econ. foreign policy (%)		U.S. unipolar power (%)	
	Neg.	NA	Neg.	NA	Neg.	NA	Neg.	NA
Africa	22.39	14.41	29.16	8.45	40.67	12.47	33.57	9.38
Central & South Asia	33.76	22.79	35.93	16.61	46.54	23.00	35.39	17.53
East Asia	30.21	11.20	37.50	5.77	57.52	8.81	28.17	6.88
Eastern Europe	29.55	22.33	16.18	7.68	53.67	11.89	30.86	20.76
Latin America	40.71	14.10	31.09	6.64	58.55	10.20	29.14	9.95
Middle East	46.37	11.35	69.39	8.98	61.85	13.89	33.42	12.42
Industrial democracies	55.31	12.04	24.20	6.37	65.25	7.76	27.95	11.24
Total	35.09	15.97	34.54	9.30	52.52	13.51	31.87	12.58

Notes: Percentages in first column of each pair are of respondents expressing an anti-American opinion concerning the American aspect listed. "NA" stands for "Don't know," or refused to answer. "Economic foreign policy" refers to attitudes towards the effects of U.S. policies on the gap between rich and poor countries; "U.S. unipolar power" refers to belief that power balancing makes the world safer. Data are from the 2002 wave of the Pew Global Attitudes Survey.

about 40% of the respondents expressed negative attitudes towards American ideas of democracy.

If these findings do not portray great appreciation of a central feature of U.S. soft power, a marginal variation on a similar theme, namely the attitudes towards the *spreading* of American ideas and customs, elicited even more negative reactions. Solid majorities declared that the spreading of American customs and ideas was a negative development for their countries. Even in Africa, where the United States seems to have received enthusiastic support on most other dimensions, the diffusion of American ideas and customs was seen with skepticism and apprehension by 48.15% of the respondents. Exceptions to this pattern are found in Japan and the Philippines where those concerned about the spreading of American ideas and customs were 36.9% and 34.6%, respectively, and Nigeria and the Ivory Coast where the percentages were 30.9% and 31.8%, respectively. It is worth noting that when American respondents were asked their opinions about the spreading of U.S. customs and ideas, as many as 3 in 4 saw it as a positive development.

Less politically charged aspects of America, on the other hand, revealed more favorable views. Admiration for American scientific and technological achievements was universally widespread: only a 17.45% average of respondents in the whole sample expressed a negative evaluation of the United States on this count. Against this pattern of strong support, however, stand a few telling exceptions, namely, Russia, the Czech Republic, and Slovakia, where the percentages of those who did not admire the United States for its scientific and technological advances were, respectively, 46.4%, 42.8%, and 39.4%. Pockets of resistance were also present in France and Germany, and in Egypt and Jordan, where between 32% and 39% of the publics were disdainful of U.S. scientific and technological prowess.

American popular culture, in the form of movies, music, and television, on the other hand, was very much liked in Western Europe and Canada and in Africa, regions where only 25.73% and 28.65% of the respondents did not like the primary products of the American entertainment industry; but it was less appreciated in the Middle East and Central and South Asia, where such percentages reached 50.9% and 59.65%, respectively. Similarly, U.S. ways of doing business were usually appreciated, with the exception of the countries of the advanced industrial democracies, particularly France, where 72.6% declared that they disliked such ways.

Respondents were also asked to evaluate the behavior of the United States in the war on terror, the effects of U.S. policies on the gap between rich and poor countries, and the extent to which the respondent believed that a military counterweight to the United States would make the world more secure. The most remarkable of these three survey items is the one investigating attitudes towards the U.S.-led efforts to fight terrorism. In the summer of 2002, a majority of respondents in six out of seven world regions said that they favored those efforts. Unsurprisingly, the exception was the Middle Eastern region, where the percentage of those against the U.S. war on terror ranged from 56% in Lebanon to 85% in Jordan.

Closer inspection of these results, however, reveals that substantial variation exists within each region. Thus, the regionally solid support for the U.S.-led war on terror in Central and South Asia is skewed by the strong approval in India and Uzbekistan, compensating for the solid majorities opposing it in Indonesia and Bangladesh. The Pakistani public, for its part, remained mostly ambivalent with 46.5% opposing, 22.7% approving, and as many as 30.9% refusing to state an opinion, a result that underscores the ambiguous relationship that Pakistan had with the United States under the leadership of General Pervez Musharraf. In East Asia and Latin America, the overall positive opinion is contradicted in two countries, South Korea and Argentina, where 71.6% and 66.5%, respectively, declared their disapproval of the U.S. antiterrorist policies.

On the other hand, the French and German publics, who would so vociferously oppose the war in Iraq only a few months later, were consistently behind the United States at the time these surveys were administered, with 75% of the French and 68.2% of the Germans *favoring* the U.S. efforts to combat terrorism. These results indicate that, in the aftermath of the defeat of the Taliban regime in Afghanistan, a consensus existed among the publics of the major industrial democracies on how to approach the problem of terrorism.

Disagreement over policies existed, however, in the realm of social and economic policy. About 52.52% of the publics in the entire sample believed that American policies had detrimental effects on the gap between rich and poor countries. This belief was particularly pronounced in France and Germany, where it was embraced by 68.6% and 71.9% of the respondents, as well as in Canada and Great Britain, where it was espoused by 66.6% and 53.5% of the respondents. Americans themselves surely did not overwhelmingly endorse the policies of their country. Still, the percentage of the American public blaming U.S. policies for an increasing the gap between rich and poor countries was 39.9%, that is, about 30 percentage points lower than it was in France and Germany and 13 percentage points lower than it was in Great Britain.

On the subject of the United States as the unmatched military power in the international arena, less than a third of respondents would welcome the emergence of another power balancing the might of the United States. Only 31.87% of the respondents believed that the emergence of another country equal in military power to the United States would make the world a safer place. The canonical *realpolitik* strategy of balancing against the dominant nation had little appeal among most of the general publics, at least when the great power was the United States. Bangladesh, India, and Venezuela, along with the African countries of Nigeria and Senegal, were the only five countries where substantial portions of the general public—between 45% and 49%—thought that the world would be safer if there were another country as powerful as the United States. But even there, popular support for the emergence of a balancing counterweight was less than 50%. What is even more surprising, however, is that, with the exception of the Bangladeshi public, the same Indian, Venezuelan, Nigerian, and Senegalese respondents overwhelmingly expressed positive attitudes towards the United States in general.[27] Conversely, many publics that did not express positive feelings towards the United States were also not keen on witnessing the emergence of a counter-balancing power. From a theoretical viewpoint, these patterns indicate that the straightforward application of standard international relations theory arguments, such as the balance-of-power theory, to the attitudes towards the United States does not appear a fruitful endeavor.[28]

These results also cast doubt on the proposition that the growing power imbalance between the United States and any other country had profoundly altered the perceptions of the United States, even before the tense controversies over the Iraq war. The only superpower was "lonely" for Samuel Huntington (1999) and for many other scholars of various persuasions and ideological stripes (Walt, 1998–1999; Cox, 2005; Mahbubani, 2005). Lonely though it was in its towering power, the United States was not yet feared in the spring and summer of 2002.

In sum, these patterns of responses show how individuals make distinctions among features of the United States when they are asked to express their attitudes. Even what might appear as a slight variation on the same fundamental aspect of the American polity—American customs and ideas vis-à-vis American ideas on democracy—induces different evaluative reactions. These findings, therefore, indicate that the status of the United States in the belief systems of ordinary people is multifaceted.

One figure that says much about U.S. popular standing is that there were only 1,374 individuals in this sample of about 38,000 from seven world regions who simultaneously disliked U.S. democracy, U.S customs, U.S. popular culture, U.S. technology, U.S. approach to business, and U.S. actions in the war on terror. If we add the respondents who also attributed to U.S. policies negative effects on the disparities between rich and poor countries and those who thought that balancing U.S. power would make the world safer, the head count drops to 264. For all the other respondents there was something about the United States to like. With so many distinctions and so much nuance among so many individuals, it seems that stereotyping, demonizing, and the attribution of evil intentions to the United States—three defining features of anti-Americanism as a cultural syndrome, as Josef Joffe (2004) so eloquently argued—were hardly part of the mindset of the mass publics in the summer of 2002.

The Multifaceted Opinions about the United States

How do opinions about these distinct aspects of America jibe with the overall view that ordinary people have of the United States? Which factors feature prominently in the minds of those who are well disposed towards the United States? Which turn ordinary people against America?

If all elements of the United States were consistently aligned in the cognitive maps of general publics, we would expect that individuals who harbored good feelings towards the United States would equally appreciate its polity, society, and policies, while individuals who expressed negative attitudes towards the United States would likewise express negative attitudes towards its polity, society, and policies. These polar opposites, though, do not represent the typical structures of the popular beliefs about the United States. Specific dimensions have different degrees of salience, generate different emotional responses, or simply are discounted when individuals form their overall evaluations.

We have already seen that in many countries widespread criticism of one aspect of the United States can exist hand in hand with strong approval of other specific aspects, and of the United States as a whole as well. Such aggregate patterns indicate that there is not a single encompassing image of the United States among large portions of the general public in many societies and world regions. What we now investigate is the extent to which such incongruent patterns were present at the level of individual respondents in the 2002 survey, and the implications that those patterns have on the nature of the constellation of beliefs about the United States. To address these issues, I rely upon two complementary approaches: first, a series of descriptive figures—fourfold display plots[29]—that map responses across dimensions and at different levels of amity towards the United States, and second, a series of regression models that measure the average weight that each specific dimension had in the respondent's overall evaluations.

A Graphical Representation

Belief system refers to a configuration of ideas and attitudes that are connected and interrelated. A belief system is said to be "constrained" if it would be possible to guess correctly what opinions an individual holds on one issue from knowledge of the opinions he or she holds on other issues (Converse, 1964, 207). We would expect, for example, that people who are opposed to the spread of U.S. customs and values would also be opposed to American democratic ideals if those beliefs are tied together in a constrained belief system about the United States. The pressures that individuals feel to be consistent in their attitudes and beliefs come from a variety of sources that can be logical, psychological, or social in nature. But those pressures, as Philip Converse (1964) showed for American public opinion, are not necessarily strong enough to lead to the resolution of inconsistencies.

Is it possible to identify any systematic relationship between overall attitudes towards the United States and attitudes on specific issues areas? Can we guess the attitudes respondents have towards U.S. political values and societal norms, towards U.S. popular culture and scientific achievements, and towards U.S. security and economic policies, respectively, by distinguishing between those individuals who have a favorable opinion of the United States and those who do not?

The plots in Figures 3.1 and 3.2 analyze the relationship between popular approval of U.S. democratic ideas and popular attitudes towards the diffusion of the customs the United States embodies. As is the case in conventional 2×2 tables, the plots present four alternative configurations associated with two (dichotomous) categories. For example, in each plot in Figure 3.1, we have (a) in the upper left corner the respondents who were opposed to both U.S. democratic ideas and the diffusion of U.S. customs; (b) in the upper right corner the respondents who were opposed to U.S. democratic ideas but were supportive of the diffusion of U.S. customs; (c) in the lower right corner the respondents who were supportive of U.S. democratic ideas and were supportive of the diffusion of U.S. customs;

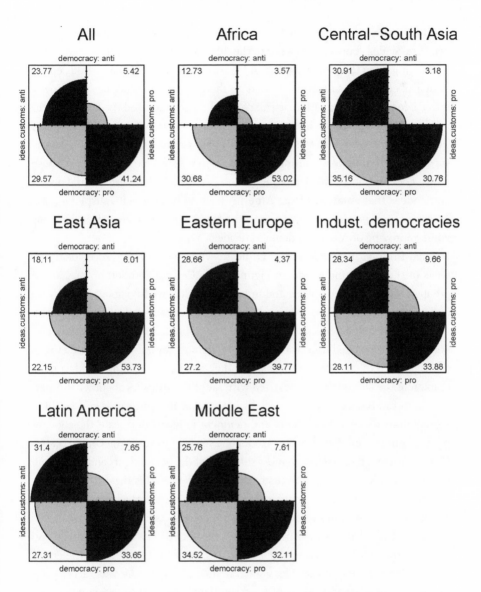

Figure 3.1. Support for U.S. Customs and Democratic Ideas in Respondents with Favorable Opinion of U.S.

Notes: The number in each of the cells represents the percentage of individuals who selected the indicated combination of responses. Data analysis is based on the 2002 Pew Global Attitudes Survey. (See also endnote 29.)

and (d) in the lower left corner the respondents who were supportive of U.S. democratic ideas but were opposed to the diffusion of U.S. customs.

Starting from the plot at top left in Figure 3.1, we observe that, in this entire sample of countries, support for U.S. ideas about democracy and the spreading of U.S. customs was the position of 41.24% of all those who liked the United States in general. Such a congruence between approval of two fundamental elements of the American polity and the general feeling about the United States is hardly surprising. What is worth noting, however, is that a sizeable proportion of those with a good opinion of the United States—23.77%—felt that customs and democratic ideas that emanated from America were to be seen with suspicion, and an even larger portion—29.57%—rejected the spreading of American customs while approving of American democratic ideas.

Such findings are even more significant when we look at the regional patterns in the remaining graphs in Figure 3.1. In Central and South Asia, in the group of Western democracies, and in Latin America, we find about as many individuals who said they liked U.S. ideas about democracy and favored the diffusion of American customs and ideas as we find individuals who were opposed to both or ones who liked American ideas about democracy but were opposed to the diffusion of U.S. customs and ideas. In other words, a recording of a favorable opinion of the United States coexisted with skeptical attitudes about what America stands for. Indeed, what is especially remarkable in Figure 3.1 is how conflicting opinions about U.S. customs and democratic ideals permeate the thought processes of the individuals who harbor good feelings towards the United States. Only Africa and East Asia, with more than half of the respondents endorsing *both* U.S. democratic ideas and U.S. customs, are different in this regard.

The respondents who did not have a favorable opinion of the United States, on the other hand, were more consistent in their beliefs. As Figure 3.2 shows, a dislike of the United States and a consistent dislike of two of its central political and societal aspects were found in about two-thirds of the respondents in the entire sample. Appreciation of U.S. ideas about democracy, however, was rather common even among the detractors of America. If we sum up the percentages in the bottom halves of the plots, we find that the percentage of those who declared that they liked U.S. ideas about democracy was by no means negligible. It ranged from a minimum of about 25.2% in Central and South Asia to 51.15% in Africa. While such a belief is not sufficiently strong to tilt the overall evaluation of the United States, it is still a remarkable feature in the cognitive maps of many individuals in many regions of the world.

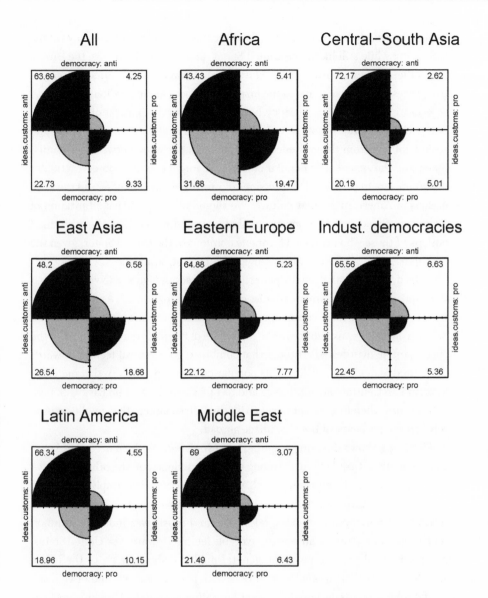

Figure 3.2. Support for U.S. Customs and Democratic Ideas in Respondents with Unfavorable Opinion of U.S.

Notes: The number in each of the cells represents the percentage of individuals who selected the indicated combination of responses. Data analysis is based on the 2002 Pew Global Attitudes Survey. (See also endnote 29.)

If we can easily find individuals who are critical of fundamental features of the U.S. polity while still liking the United States, and others who dislike the United States though they admire its democratic ideals, what else could affect the cognitive processes that give shape to the image of America among ordinary people? A conjecture is that the discrepancy between the overall approval of the United States and the criticisms of the fundamental features of the American polity and society follows from the existence of an implicit association between the United States and the appeal of its popular culture. We might expect to observe a tighter congruence between overall expressions of pro-American attitudes and the evaluations of American popular culture. We should also expect that admiration of American science and technology should feature prominently in the attitudinal outlook of those who expressed favorable opinions of the United States, given the widespread approval of U.S. technological and scientific advances.

Indeed, when we analyze the pattern of responses in Figure 3.3, we notice that the joint admiration of American science and technology and of American popular culture was the most common response in all the regions but in Central and South Asia. But we also notice in the top halves of the plots that about 30% of the entire sample manifested attitudes that combined good overall feelings towards the United States with a dislike of its popular culture, a percentage that increases to 52.79% in Central and South Asia and to 34.64% in the Middle East. U.S. popular culture, therefore, is not necessarily the "silver bullet" that might be used solve all the problems of the U.S. image abroad.

Figure 3.4 shows the same graphing for respondents with an overall unfavorable view of the United States. Among such respondents, on the other hand, we find that a substantial percentage—58.3% in all the countries sampled—disliked the popular culture aspects of the United States. Aversion to U.S. popular culture as it is portrayed in movies, television, and music was indeed a common sentiment among those who held unfavorable feelings towards the United States, but a nontrivial percentage of the general publics—about 34.3% of the entire sample—revealed an appreciation of both U.S. popular culture and of U.S. scientific achievements despite their overall negative view of the United States. For this latter group, in other words, two central features of American soft power were not very relevant in the formation of their attitudes towards the United States.

Finally, in Figures 3.5 and 3.6, we observe how people evaluated American security policies in the war on terror and the consequences of American action on the divide between rich and poor countries. Figure 3.5 shows the findings

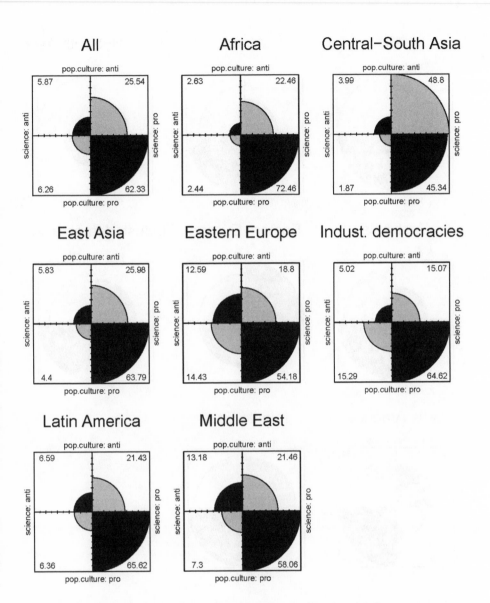

Figure 3.3. Support for U.S. Popular Culture and Science and Technology in Respondents with Favorable Opinion of U.S.

Notes: The number in each of the cells represents the percentage of individuals who selected the indicated combination of responses. Data analysis is based on the 2002 Pew Global Attitudes Survey. (See also endnote 29.)

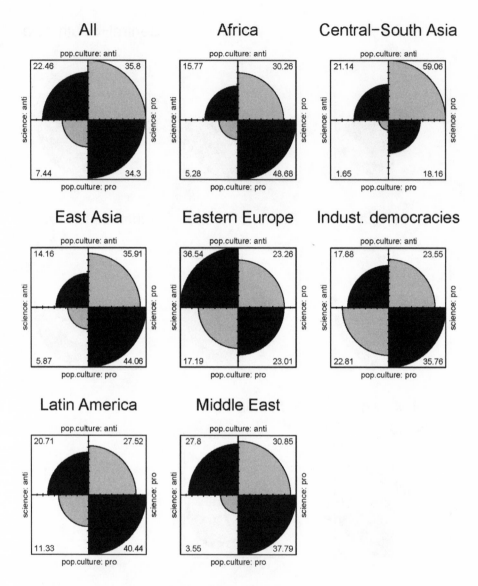

Figure 3.4. Support for U.S. Popular Culture and Science and Technology in Respondents with Unfavorable Opinion of U.S.

Notes: The number in each of the cells represents the percentage of individuals who selected the indicated combination of responses. Data analysis is based on the 2002 Pew Global Attitudes Survey. (See also endnote 29.)

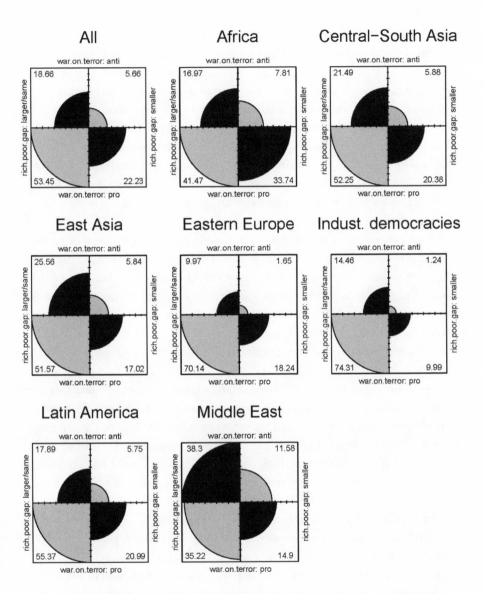

Figure 3.5. Support for the War on Terror and American Socioeconomic Policies in Respondents with Favorable Opinion of U.S.

Notes: The number in each of the cells represents the percentage of individuals who selected the indicated combination of responses. Data analysis is based on the 2002 Pew Global Attitudes Survey. (See also endnote 29.)

for the publics with favorable overall assessments of the United States, while Figure 3.6 shows the findings for the publics with unfavorable overall assessments of the United States. Of the two sets of policies, it was what America was doing in the international political economy that drew the ire of the mass publics. In Figure 3.5, we see that, while about 75% of the respondents approved of the U.S. led efforts in the war on terror, no less than 72% believed that American policies had a negative impact on global inequality. Indeed, few individuals had a positive outlook on the effects of U.S. economic and social policies worldwide. Only among African respondents do we find a sizeable group—41.6% of the sample—who saw a reduction in global inequality associated with American interventions.

Such concerns over U.S. social and economic policies largely permeated the views of those who held a generally low opinion of the United States. Indeed, as Figure 3.6 shows, about 6 in 7 individuals (about 85%) held a dim view of the impact of American policies on global inequality; a large portion—55%—was also critical both of U.S. economic policies and of the U.S. war on terror. It is worth noting that in Eastern Europe, and to a lesser extent among the respondents in the industrial societies of Canada and Western Europe, large numbers of respondents reached negative conclusions about the United States in general while approving of its efforts to combat terrorism. For those individuals, other factors, economic and social policies in particular, played a major role in influencing their overall cognitive and affective processes. The Middle Eastern publics, on the other hand, displayed a high degree of consistency in their negative assessment of U.S. policies, in both the security and the social and economic realms. This finding offers an indication of the importance of policies in the formation of the image of the United States in the Middle East.

In sum, if we had come across a person in the spring of 2002 who held the United States in low esteem, we should have expected that this person would be critical of American customs and American democratic ideals, wary of the American popular culture of movies, television, and music, and opposed to American policies and social and economic policies in particular. But, despite this negative opinion, we would also expect this person to be impressed with the scientific and technological achievements of the United States. Regional variation would qualify this image by emphasizing various features in the cognitive map of this individual who disliked the United States. There was a degree of consistency in the minds of those who harbored anti-American feelings.

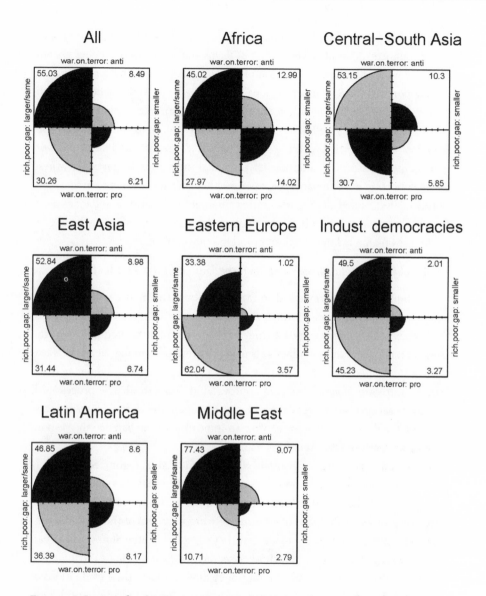

Figure 3.6. Support for the War on Terror and American Socioeconomic Policies in Respondents with Unfavorable Opinion of U.S.

Notes: The number in each of the cells represents the percentage of individuals who selected the indicated combination of responses. Data analysis is based on the 2002 Pew Global Attitudes Survey. (See also endnote 29.)

It is among those people who liked the United States, however, that we find a more nuanced or—in Converse's (1964) terms—less constrained belief system. A person who had a positive opinion of the United States in the spring of 2002 was supportive of U.S. democratic ideals, impressed with U.S. science and technology, happy to enjoy the product of the U.S. entertainment industry, and supportive of what the United States was doing in the war on terror. Such a person, however, was concerned with the spreading of U.S. customs and ideas and worried about the effects of U.S. policies on global inequality. In particular, these findings portray a discrepancy between popular evaluation of two issues very closely related, namely, U.S. democratic values and U.S. customs and ideas. Fundamental aspects of U.S. soft power, in other words, were not necessarily operating in unison among large portions of foreign mass publics.

Modeling the Relationship between the United States and Its Features

The figures we have reviewed so far have shown that many individuals can hold opposing orientations towards the United States. Likes and dislikes extensively coexist in people's minds as they evaluate the multifaceted nature of the United States. As much as individuals make distinctions among the various features of the United States as a country and as a symbol, they also aggregate these features into overall assessments of approval and disapproval. The processes of such aggregation reflect the salience of each feature of the United States for each individual and, as a consequence, offer an indication of the balance the respondent strikes between different dimensions.

We would expect that individuals who feel irritated, antagonized, or simply displeased about more and more aspects of the United States would reach the conclusion that they disliked the country as a whole. Conversely, we would expect that positive evaluations of cumulatively more aspects of the United States would lead most people to conclude that they liked the United States. But not all issues have the same impact on those assessments, as individuals attribute different weights to political, cultural, or policy dimensions in their evaluations of the United States. Thus, to assess the empirical relevance of the multidimensionality of the United States in the cognitive maps of mass publics, I estimate a series of regression models that predict what respondents think of the United States given their assessments of its dimensions. The models tell us how likely it is that individuals will hold an overall negative opinion of the United States based upon how they evaluate individual features of the United States.

The eight attitudinal items I investigate are coded as dummy variables on a 0/1 dichotomy, where 1 indicates that the respondent selected the option with an anti-American connotation. The baseline category, which occurs when all attitudinal items are coded as 0, identifies respondents who rated the United States positively on all the items. Each coefficient, therefore, assesses the average change in the probability of holding an overall unfavorable opinion of the United States as respondents shift their evaluations from positive to negative on each single dimension. The regression coefficients estimated in the statistical models serve as an empirical measure of the salience each dimension had in the respondents' overall assessments.

I estimate an ordered logit model, a type of regression model used to predict dependent variables that can be ranked on an ordinal scale, as is the case for the survey item asking whether respondents had a very favorable, somewhat favorable, somewhat unfavorable, or very unfavorable opinion of the United States (Long, 1997, 114–147). The model was estimated first on the overall sample of approximately 38,000 respondents and then, separately, region by region, in order to assess how the salience of each dimension varied in different political and cultural settings.[30]

I present the results of the regression models in two ways: first, with a graphical representation of the coefficients and their confidence intervals, and then, with a comparison of the substantive impact of feelings about each individual feature on the probabilities of holding a negative opinion of the United States under different attitudinal profiles. The comparison of the magnitude of the coefficients offers an overview of the different weights that the eight attitudinal items from the Global Attitudes Survey received in people's aggregate evaluations of the United States, while the analysis of the substantive effects on the probabilities gives an overview of the combination of factors that would tip the attitudinal balance towards a negative appraisal of the United States.

In Figure 3.7 I report the results of the regression model estimated on the entire sample of countries. There, we notice that all coefficients, except the one associated with the attitudes towards the emergence of a balancing military competitor, are positive and statistically significant. As we would expect, opposition to a specific dimension of the United States is systematically associated with higher probabilities of a negative assessment of the United States. The largest of these coefficients is the one associated with the attitudes towards the war on terror. This finding indicates that opposition to the actions taken in the war on terror was very salient

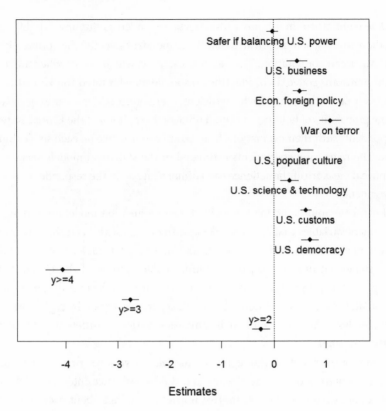

Figure 3.7. The Empirical Weights of Dimensions of America

Notes: The dark dots represent the regression coefficients, and the lines represent the 95% confidence intervals. Estimates are obtained from an ordinal logistic model, with Huber/White standard errors clustered by country. "Economic foreign policy" refers to attitudes towards the effects of U.S. policies on the gap between rich and poor countries. Data analysis is based on the 2002 Pew Global Attitudes Survey.

in the mass publics surveyed. While opposing the war on terror was, in general, a minority view shared by about one-third of the respondents, such a view carried a considerable pull in the mental calculus of those respondents, generating an overall opinion of the United States.

The second and third largest coefficients are the ones associated with the attitudes towards American ideas about democracy and the spreading of U.S. customs and ideas. Among the least salient indicators we find the one associated with the admiration of U.S. science and technology, which indicates that the overwhelming admiration of U.S. scientific and technological achievements exerted only a minor impact in the publics' belief systems. Finally, the coefficient measuring whether respondents believed that the emergence of a balancing competitor to the United States would make the world safer turned out to be negative and statistically undistinguishable from 0. The mass publics did not factor the overwhelming power superiority of the United States into their overall evaluations. It would appear that considerations of power balancing—the central tenet in realist political theory—did not engender a negative reaction to the United States.[31]

If so many factors tug at the cognitive calculus in people's minds, is there any combination of factors that would "tip the balance" and lead people to conclude that in the end they don't like the United States? In answer to this question, Table 3.2 reports a series of probability estimates computed by regressing, region by region, the overall attitudes on the eight attitudinal dimensions we have analyzed so far. In particular, the probability estimates show how likely it was that respondents would rate the United States negatively under various hypothetical scenarios. The first scenario concerns the individuals who chose a pro-American option on all eight indicators; the second identifies hypothetical individuals who disliked the United States on only one dimension, testing each one separately. In Table 3.3, I present a third group of hypothetical scenarios, in which individuals opposed the United States on a cluster of attitudinal dimensions at the same time.[32]

In Table 3.2 we see that, for the individuals who responded to all the separate issues in a pro-American fashion, the probability of holding an overall anti-American view was within single digits in all regions except the Middle East, where it was about 13.81%. That is to say, the image of the United States in the Middle East was tarnished enough that about one in eight respondents expressed an overall negative opinion of the United States, despite their positive assessment of what America did and stood for on eight different counts.

Of all the eight features of the United States, the one that was most closely associated with negative overall views of America was the U.S. war on terror. This was true in all seven regions. Statistically, this effect amounts to an increase in the probability to hold negative opinions of the United States between 5 and 20 percentage points, on average, when we compare the respondents who had no objections on any of the eight dimensions with those who opposed only U.S. actions in the war on terror. This propensity is particularly noticeable in the Middle East, where the likelihood that a respondent who opposed the American actions

Table 3.2. Effects of Issue Opinions on Overall Opinion of America, Simple Scenarios

	Africa	Central & South Asia	East Asia	Eastern Europe	Industrial democracies	Latin America	Middle East
No dimension opposed	7.12	7.32	5.54	3.85	2.95	7.22	13.81
	5.63 ~ 8.6	5.56 ~ 9.09	3.5 ~ 7.58	2.18 ~ 5.51	2.41 ~ 3.49	5.18 ~ 9.26	9.86 ~ 17.77
Anti-U.S. stance on:							
U.S. democracy	11.75	14.57	7.54	6.4	5.57	10.53	30.25
	8.66 ~ 14.84	10.66 ~ 18.47	4.6 ~ 10.47	4.06 ~ 8.75	3.9 ~ 7.24	6.94 ~ 14.12	17.6 ~ 42.89
U.S. customs	11	12.32	11.03	6.91	6.63	10.99	27
	8.74 ~ 13.27	8.4 ~ 16.23	6.62 ~ 15.43	4.72 ~ 9.1	4.99 ~ 8.28	7.85 ~ 14.14	20.28 ~ 33.71
U.S. science/tech.	10.61	12.94	5.32	5.89	4.49	10.59	14.61
	7.45 ~ 13.77	6.12 ~ 19.77	1.99 ~ 8.65	3.94 ~ 7.83	3.38 ~ 5.6	7.97 ~ 13.21	7.83 ~ 21.4
U.S. pop. culture	9.38	12.38	6.26	5.86	4.73	9.09	18.12
	6.81 ~ 11.95	6.96 ~ 17.81	2.83 ~ 9.7	3.42 ~ 8.31	3.72 ~ 5.75	6.43 ~ 11.75	10.19 ~ 26.05
War on terror	12.66	18.24	15.71	9.65	8.48	17.25	32.89
	9.95 ~ 15.38	12.27 ~ 24.21	11.15 ~ 20.27	5.8 ~ 13.5	5.79 ~ 11.16	13.02 ~ 21.48	26.98 ~ 38.79
Econ. foreign policy	9.79	10.39	9.72	7.23	4.97	10.9	21.37
	7.82 ~ 11.77	7.31 ~ 13.48	6.52 ~ 12.93	4.22 ~ 10.24	4.01 ~ 5.93	8.21 ~ 13.59	16.37 ~ 26.36
U.S. business	11.75	13.79	8.78	6.47	5.45	12.1	13.25
	8.8 ~ 14.7	8.82 ~ 18.76	5.41 ~ 12.15	3.73 ~ 9.22	3.78 ~ 7.11	9.39 ~ 14.81	8.58 ~ 17.92
U.S. unipolar power	7.03	5.98	4.79	4.69	4.14	5.84	13.73
	5.39 ~ 8.66	4.77 ~ 7.2	0.88 ~ 8.69	2.74 ~ 6.64	3.2 ~ 5.08	4.27 ~ 7.41	9.96 ~ 17.5

Notes: The main entries measure the probability of publics' holding a somewhat unfavorable or a very unfavorable opinion of the United States. The 95% confidence intervals, computed with the delta method (Wasserman, 2004, 131–134), are shown underneath the main entries. Estimated probabilities are obtained from an ordinal logistic model, with Huber/White standard errors. Data analysis is based on the 2002 wave of the Pew Global Attitudes Survey.

to combat terrorism would have negative attitudes towards the United States generally was as high as 32.89%. But, for the Middle Eastern publics, that was not the only dimension of the United States exerting by itself a large impact on people's evaluations. Substantial effects were also associated with disenchantment about U.S. democracy and concerns about the spreading of U.S. customs, in the presence of which the probabilities to express unfavorable views of the United States increased to 30.25% and 27%, respectively. While policy considerations were a factor of primary relevance in the formation of people's attitudes towards the United States, these two fundamental features of the U.S. polity were nearly as important in the Middle East, the region where opposition to the United States was most widespread. In other words, two dimensions associated with "what America stands for" and not just "with what America does" carried a predominant weight in the formation of an overall negative stance towards the United States.

This empirical result marks a major difference between the sources of negative attitudes towards the United States in the Middle East and in all the other regions. It is not just that for the Middle Eastern respondents both policy and polity of the United States, what it does and its political values, were the strongest determinants of their negative assessments. It is also true that in regions other than the Middle East we do not find a major issue framing the overall orientation towards the United States. Instead, outside the critical area of the Middle East, opposition to the United States is the result of a cumulation of factors. This result emerges whenever we come across respondents who were critical of several aspects of America.

In Table 3.3 we see the opposite end of the spectrum—respondents who selected the answer with anti-American connotation on all of the items. As we would expect, the probabilities of holding a negative overall opinion of the United States substantially increased, reaching levels well above 80% in the advanced industrial democracies, the Middle East, and Central and South Asia, but not in the countries of East Asia, where the probability of expressing an overall negative assessment of the United States spanned a very wide interval, from 32.3% to 88.96%, centered at 60.64%. For large portions of the East Asian publics, it seems, the United States had a positive connotation that went well beyond any of the specific characteristics of the U.S. polity and society that those publics found objectionable.

Respondents who were concerned about the spreading of American customs and opposed the American war on terror were likely to hold a negative opinion of

Table 3.3. Effects of Issue Opinions on Overall Opinion of America, Composite Scenarios

	Africa	Central & South Asia	East Asia	Eastern Europe	Industrial democracies	Latin America	Middle East
All dimensions opposed	67.39	87.33	60.64	77.43	83.24	68.42	87.86
	60.06 ~ 74.73	78.57 ~ 96.08	32.33 ~ 88.96	69.16 ~ 85.69	78.35 ~ 88.13	59.71 ~ 77.12	82.5 ~ 93.23
Anti-U.S. stance on:							
U.S. democracy & war on terror	20.13	32.49	20.58	15.45	15.25	23.97	57.01
	15.23 ~ 25.03	22.44 ~ 42.55	17.11 ~ 24.05	9.82 ~ 21.08	9.7 ~ 20.81	17.64 ~ 30.3	46.55 ~ 67.47
U.S. customs & war on terror	18.96	28.4	28.25	16.55	17.81	24.85	53.07
	14.75 ~ 23.16	18.59 ~ 38.21	17.43 ~ 39.07	12.07 ~ 21.03	12.36 ~ 23.26	18.01 ~ 31.69	42.83 ~ 63.3
U.S. democracy & customs & war on terror	28.91	46.11	35.37	25.33	29.63	33.34	75.37
	23.35 ~ 34.46	32.76 ~ 59.47	27.4 ~ 43.34	19.48 ~ 31.18	21.52 ~ 37.75	24.77 ~ 41.92	61.28 ~ 89.46

Notes: The main entries measure the probability of publics' holding a somewhat unfavorable or a very unfavorable opinion of the United States. The 95% confidence intervals, computed with the delta method (Wasserman, 2004, 131–134), are shown underneath the main entries. Estimated probabilities are obtained from an ordinal logistic model, with Huber/White standard errors. Data analysis is based on the 2002 wave of the Pew Global Attitudes Survey.

the United States with the following probabilities: 17–18% if they resided in a Western democracy, in Eastern Europe, or in Africa; around 25% if they resided in Latin America; and around 28% if they resided in Central and South Asia or in East Asia. Only in the Middle East, was that probability so high as to be larger than 50%.

If we add the criticism of American ideas about democracy to this hypothetical scenario, the probabilities of disliking the United States increase to about 75% in the Middle East and get high enough to have a confidence interval including a 50% chance in Central and South Asia. In no other regions do we find that the combination of the opposition to American democratic ideas, the spreading of U.S. customs and the war on terror affected popular perceptions to such an extent that respondents were more than 50% likely to say that they held a negative opinion of the United States.

Evidently, for the Middle Eastern respondents who had grown disenchanted with U.S. democracy and U.S. antiterrorist policy, none of the other factors that might still be appreciated about the United States had enough psychological leverage to keep the respondents from forming a negative opinion of the United States. Elsewhere, and in particular in Eastern Europe and in the advanced industrial democracies, as well as in Africa, Latin America, and East Asia, the United States still enjoyed a reservoir of good feeling generated by other facets of its society and culture.

By revealing the multifaceted nature of the attitudes towards the United States, these results validate the theoretical perspective I elaborated in Chapter 2. As we would expect in the dimensions of America theory, large portions of the general public are willing to entertain simultaneously positive and negative opinions of the United States on its multiple dimensions, while a systematically negative classification of any referents associated with the United States is more of an exception. Using a multifaceted evaluation of the United States helped temper the formation of an overall negative view of the United States that tended to emerge when respondents systematically felt at odds with feature after feature of America, a circumstance that was exceptionally rare in the spring and summer of 2002.

Reassuring though this finding may sound, a reluctance towards rejection of the United States was no longer operative even then among the Middle Eastern respondents, who disregarded the multifaceted nature of America and primarily based their negative assessment on their negative opinions of the American polity and its anti-terrorist policy. This finding, therefore, points to a qualitative difference between the popular standing of the United States in the Middle East and its standing in other regions.

Are People Just Trying to Be Polite?

The patterns of responses that we have uncovered so far paint a more encouraging picture of popular attitudes towards the United States than it is generally portrayed among public intellectuals and in the popular media (Revel, 2003; Krauthammer, 2003; Ajami, 2003). With the exception of the respondents in the Middle Eastern countries, ordinary people tended to like the United States overall. If the simple answer "I have a somewhat favorable opinion of the United States" is the result of a process of aggregation of multiple considerations, then we can conjecture that positive factors overwhelmed negative factors in people's minds. Any question that makes a reference to the United States in general cued the respondents to disregard any specific societal or political or cultural element. What is then evoked in their minds is an image of the United States that is larger and more encompassing than the sum of any single component.

Can we conclude, then, that the case of those who were proclaiming the rise of popular anti-Americanism has been disproved? If we take survey results as a fair representation of the status of public opinion, we might be inclined to answer affirmatively. Indeed, it is remarkable to see the extent to which pro-American views colored the attitudes of mass publics on issue after issue, when writers such as Revel (2003) and Rubin and Rubin (2004) declared otherwise.

An interpretation of these findings less flattering to America can also be formulated. Rather than regarding the survey responses recorded in the Global Attitudes Survey as representing deep-seated predispositions that preordain respondents' judgment, they could be discounted as a bowdlerized version of the popular feelings about the United States. Under this interpretation, the responses to the question "What is your opinion of the United States" would not reveal true appreciation of the United States but would overstate the levels of pro-American support, on the assumption that ordinary people might think it inappropriate to publicly display a wholesale rejection of a country, thus hiding the predispositions that truly condition their political behavior.

Scholars of public opinion would recognize in this conjectural interpretation another instance of the broader phenomenon of "preference falsification," to use Timur Kuran's (1995) label. In that logic, the behavioral manifestation of attitudes and preferences, whether it occurs in public rallies or survey questions should not be taken at face value but should be seen as the outcome of a strategic calculus by individuals who assess the consequences that might follow from telling the truth. Adam Berinsky (2004, 19), while eschewing the concept of preference falsification, raises an analogous point when he argues that "opinion surveys may fail to measure accurately the conscious will of individuals who are uncomfortable expressing opinions that are socially undesirable."

Given the robust prevalence of pro-American feelings in 2002, there might have been a tendency to report favorable assessments of the United States that could be called a "politeness norm," keeping to oneself one's dislike of the country. For conservative commentators, from Krauthammer to Ajami, these results would just reflect the mendacity of large portions of publics who would say positive things while being convinced of the opposite. Fouad Ajami (2003, 54) did not mince words when he urged dismissal of the more conciliatory conclusions on anti-Americanism emanating from the survey results: "There is no need to go so far away from home only to count the cats in Zanzibar."

Despite Ajami's skepticism, however, it is possible to gain some empirical leverage on the presence of preference falsification using survey data. The data collected in the 2002 Global Attitudes Survey make it possible to clarify some of the survey responses of respondents who did indeed eschew stating openly their negative opinions. To do so, we can conjecture that the view expressed in the reply to the question "What do you think of the United States" consists of two elements: the first element is true feelings about the United States, and the second element is adherence to the politeness norm. The goal would be to analyze answers after they have been purged of the effects of the desire to be polite.

If we assume that adherence to the politeness norm is a feature of each respondent, we can get additional leverage on the attitudes towards the United States by establishing a pair comparison between how a person assesses the United States and how that person assesses some other country. We might expect high degrees of congruence in how people rate certain countries, given that such ratings would respond to the same ideological outlook of each person and to an analogous set of social norms.

The discrepancies in people's evaluations of different countries open an additional window into individual attitudes towards the United States. We might distinguish four different types of subjects: a) the *contrarians*, who dislike the United States and other countries; b) the *politically correct*, who like the United States and other countries; c) the *anti-Americans*, who dislike the United States but like other countries; d) the *pro-Americans*, who like the United States but dislike other countries. The subjects in the first two categories—the contrarians and the politically correct—are the ones whose attitudes are more impervious to categorization, because their attitudes can be generated by alternative but observationally undistinguishable mechanisms. In those two groups we can indeed find, respectively, people who bear deep-seated, even visceral, grievances against the United States and other countries, and people who feel a sense of communality with the United States and other countries. But in the same groups we can also find people whose response style is to say always positive things of the United States and other countries or to say always negative things. We can also find people who find the expression of negative opinions inappropriate or shameful and who prefer hiding behind the mask of a "somewhat favorable" opinion. In other words, congruent responses are less informative.

The third and fourth categories, however, give us some leverage to assess the impact of the politeness norm. In those categories, we find respondents who might feel the pressure to conform to the norm of politeness but who decide to make a distinction nonetheless. The labels *pro-American* and *anti-American* should be seen as characterizing the higher level of deliberation that is inherent in the responses of those who make a distinction between the United States and other countries in their replies. Given that the desire to be polite is constant across the evaluations of the two countries, the discrepancies that we observe can be imputed to different predispositions towards the United States.

In the Pew Global Attitudes Project, along with the questions asking their opinion of the United States, respondents were asked to state their opinion of the country that the Pew Foundation researchers deemed the dominant country in the given region. Under this category, we can find a vast array of countries (listed in the on-line Appendix). For example, Japanese respondents were asked what they thought of China, Egyptians were asked what they thought of Turkey, Pakistanis of India, the French of Germany, the Argentineans of Brazil. Then we should ask whether the attitudes towards the United States are different from those towards the regionally dominant country.

As a general pattern, it is not very common to state an unfavorable opinion of the regionally dominant country: 52.1% of all respondents had a very favorable or a somewhat favorable opinion of it, a distribution that closely resembles the one we find for the United States. Not just the United States, therefore, but another powerful country is usually seen in a positive light, indicating an overall reluctance to state unfavorable opinions of a country. But to detect the impact of the politeness norm on survey responses, we analyze the joint distribution of the attitudes towards the United States and the respondents' opinion of the dominant country. Figure 3.8 shows the percentage of respondents in each of the four categories obtained by cross-tabulating respondents' opinion of the U.S. with their opinion of the dominant country in their region.[33]

Overall, we find that in this classification scheme the most common attitudinal stance was that of the politically correct, with two remarkable exceptions, the Middle East and Central and South Asia, where the modal category was that

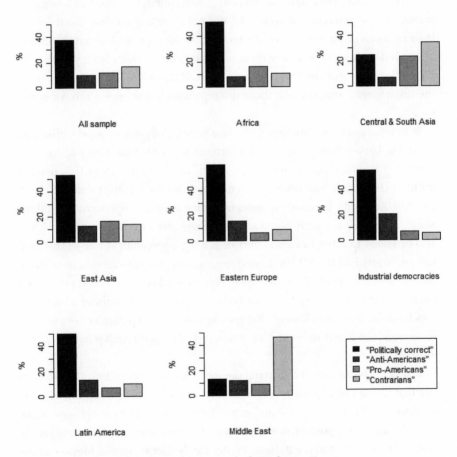

Figure 3.8. Opinion of the United States and of a Referent Country

Notes: The bars show the percentage of respondents in each of the four classifications obtained by cross-tabulating respondents' opinion of the United States and their opinion of the dominant country in their region. Data analysis is based on the 2002 Pew Global Attitudes Survey.

of the contrarians. The least common category in the whole sample was anti-Americans. In other words, the dislike of America in conjunction with appreciation of some other country—which we take as manifestation of anti-American predispositions—pertained to a minority of respondents.

As we could expect from these aggregate results, there was a high level of congruence of opinion: if we look at all the respondents who thought highly of the referent country, we find that 72.6% of them also thought highly of the United States and, analogously, we find that 72.8% of those who thought highly of the United States also thought highly of the other powerful country they were asked to evaluate. Conversely, the respondents who had a negative opinion of the referent country—and did not have any qualms about letting their opinions be known—were less inclined to think likewise about the United States. Indeed, a sizeable 40% of those who disliked the other country had fonder dispositions towards the United States. Thus, if there are any discrepancies in the respondents' assessments, those discrepancies had overall a pro-American slant.

While the aggregate findings describe a bedrock of genuine good feelings towards the United States, the regional patterns reveal that the image of America was not one of admiration all over the world. The bleaker state of U.S. popular status in the Middle East once again emerges from these patterns of data. With 64.1% of the Middle Eastern respondents holding a negative opinion of the United States, America was clearly not much loved there. But, this negative outlook was also extended to other foreign countries playing a geopolitical role in the area. Indeed, nearly half the Middle Eastern respondents could be labeled as *contrarians*. None of the Middle Eastern respondents were asked to express their opinion towards Israel. This finding thus reveals the pervasiveness of a sense of frustration, hopelessness, and encirclement that goes beyond the deep enmity between the Israelis and the Palestinians and has embraced relations of Arab publics with the external world.

It was in the advanced industrial democracies of Western Europe and Canada that, using this approach, a notable level of anti-American sentiment could be detected. About three in four respondents with a negative opinion of the United States had a positive opinion of their referent country—Germany for the British, the French, and the Italians; France for the Germans; and Mexico for the Canadians. It was rare to find respondents of the advanced industrial democracies willing to openly express negative opinions of the other countries: only about 12.7% offered a negative view of their referent country, either as *contrarians* or as

pro-Americans. Hence, the findings in Figure 3.8 show that the lack of appreciation for the United States was strong enough to displace the countervailing effect of the desire to state an "appropriate" opinion. Still, such a negative sentiment pertained to a minority of respondents—21% of them—not to hordes of
effete barbarians lacking any common purpose but disdain of America, as we so
often read in commentaries and editorials during the diplomatic crisis preceding
the war in Iraq.[34]

To a smaller degree, we find a similar pattern among the Eastern European
and the Latin American publics, where about 15.6% and 12.9% of the respondents, respectively, rated their referent country more favorably than they did the
United States. Such percentages are slightly higher than the percentages of respondents who rated the America above their referent country. Otherwise, we
are more likely to find respondents who were "pro-American" in this classification scheme than respondents who were "anti-American."

Conclusions

At the end of this investigation of the image of America in 2002, we find that
there was not an all-encompassing element that subsumed popular perceptions
of the United States in the post–Cold War, post–September 11 world. Multiple
perceptions were the main theme that underlay the way the United States fea-
tured in the belief systems of ordinary people. In general, relatively good feelings pervaded ordinary people's attitudes, and while not all about the United
States was always liked by all people, very few rejected the United States altogether. For some aspects of America that are disliked, there are many more that
are appreciated. The wholesale rejection of the United States was not a common
stance among this sample of 38,000 respondents the world over in the year
of 2002.

However, important variation in the appreciation of the United States exists
across regions. In the Middle East, among Muslim respondents, we find a greater
propensity to express views that are critical of the United States. It should be
stressed that there is not just a quantitative difference in the popular standing
of the United States among Middle Eastern respondents but a qualitative one as
well. Not only are Middle Eastern publics more inclined to manifest negative attitudes towards the United States, but they are also more likely to make negative
assessments about the United States as a whole even if, among American dimensions, they disapprove only of U.S. policies and U.S. democratic ideals. In all

other regions, opposition to the United States appears to be the state of mind of those who dislike the United States on issue after issue, not just a few topical dimensions. Outside the Middle East, appreciation of one or more American features tempers the opposition and the disagreement generated by other aspects of the United States. Multidimensionality—that incommensurable asset of the United States—seems to have lost its psychological appeal among Middle Eastern respondents.

CHAPTER FOUR

Testing the Soft Power Thesis

Introduction

As we have seen, attitudes towards the United States are far from homogeneous. Ordinary people elaborate a variety of opinions that reflect their individual assessment of the United States, its society, and its international political behavior. Taken at face value, that evidence challenges some of the most widely held arguments about the diffusion of popular anti-Americanism, and it indicates that the appeal of U.S. ideals persists even amidst sharp disagreement over the course of U.S. policies. The findings in Chapter 3 indicate that the popular sentiment about the United States in the Middle Eastern region is qualitatively different, as it appears less responsive to the appeal of the soft power of American polity and culture.

This chapter probes deeper into the findings discussed in Chapter 3 by analyzing the relationship between two frames: the attitude towards U.S. culture, society, and political system, on the one hand, and the attitude towards U.S. foreign policies, on the other. This distinction—which we may call the polity/policy distinction—is as often belittled as it is invoked in recent discussions of anti-Americanism (Ajami, 2003; Waterbury, 2003; Joffe, 2004), but it is rarely subjected to systematic empirical analyses that go beyond the politically charged overtones of conservative intellectuals and their liberal critics.[35] More importantly, the relationship between popular views of U.S. policy actions and popular views of U.S. culture and society serves as an empirical battleground for Nye's (2004) soft power thesis.

First I describe the patterns of variation in popular sentiment about U.S. polity and U.S. policies. I analyze how the patterns in anti-American opinion are distributed across countries and how they differ across the sociocultural and policy dimensions. I then analyze the relationship between the polity and policy frames in the belief systems of the foreign publics in the Islamic world and in Europe. Specifically, I explore whether the relationship between attitudes towards U.S.

culture and society and towards U.S. policies exhibits the degrees of consistency that we expect from the soft power thesis.[36]

Description of the Data

We will investigate the patterns of attitudes towards America in the mass public in eight predominantly Islamic countries—Egypt, Indonesia, Iran, Kuwait, Lebanon, Pakistan, Saudi Arabia, and the United Arab Emirates—and in six European countries—France, Germany, Great Britain, Italy, the Netherlands, and Poland. The survey data for the Islamic countries are taken from the Ten Nation Impressions of America Poll, which was conducted on behalf of Zogby International in the spring of 2002 and included 5,345 respondents: 700 from Egypt, Indonesia, Iran, and Saudi Arabia; 500 from Kuwait, Lebanon, and UAE; and 1,045 from Pakistan.[37] The survey data for the European countries are taken from Worldviews 2002—European Public Opinion and Foreign Policy, a survey conducted on behalf of the Chicago Council on Foreign Relations (CCFR) and the German Marshall Fund of the United States (GMF) in the summer of 2002 and which include 6,001 respondents, 1,000 in each the countries but France, where the number of interviewees was 1001.

The Islamic Countries

The respondents in the Zogby International survey expressed their feelings towards the United States in a battery of survey items capturing various aspects of the polity/policy distinction. With respect to the polity dimension, the respondents were asked to express their overall impression on six different aspects of America: (a) science and technology; (b) freedom and democracy; (c) the people; (d) movies and television; (e) manufactured products; (f) education.

With respect to policies, respondents were asked to assess their overall impression of six policies: (a) U.S. policy towards the Arab nations, (b) U.S. policy towards the Palestinians, (c) the American-led effort to stop ethnic cleansing in the Balkans, (d) the American-led effort to free Kuwait, (e) the American-led fight against terrorism; (f) U.S. policy towards Iraq.

Responses were coded on a four-point scale ranging from "Very favorable" (1) to "Very unfavorable" (4). Intermediate Scale points were "Somewhat favorable" (2) and "Somewhat unfavorable" (3). Table 4.1 and Table 4.2 summarize the distribution of responses, distinguishing the percentage of respondents who ex-

Table 4.1.   Attitudes among Islamic Publics towards U.S. Culture and Society, 2002

Country	Science & technology	Freedom & democracy	People	Movies & TV	Products	Education
Egypt						
% Favorable	77.86	52.71	34.71	53.29	50.14	67.57
% Don't know	11.57	9.14	18.57	7.14	4.57	15.14
Indonesia						
% Favorable	82.86	36.43	45.71	77.00	71.29	79.00
% Don't know	9.29	10.86	13.43	3.29	13.29	12.43
Iran						
% Favorable	92.57	6.71	33.71	75.29	84.29	19.86
% Don't know	0.29	1.71	18.57	0.57	0.14	13.57
Kuwait						
% Favorable	85.60	58.40	49.60	53.80	57.40	57.00
% Don't know	2.40	2.20	12.40	2.00	4.00	14.20
Lebanon						
% Favorable	82.40	58.40	63.00	63.60	72.40	81.00
% Don't know	2.00	2.00	4.00	1.00	2.20	3.20
Pakistan						
% Favorable	82.58	63.64	62.39	64.02	75.31	79.71
% Don't know	3.44	10.81	10.14	8.42	8.42	4.59
Saudi Arabia						
% Favorable	71.14	52.14	42.57	54.29	52.86	57.71
% Don't know	3.14	3.71	6.71	3.71	3.14	7.57
United Arab Emirates						
% Favorable	80.60	49.60	42.80	63.80	68.00	79.00
% Don't know	5.40	6.00	14.80	4.60	5.00	4.60
Total						
% Favorable	81.89	47.39	47.26	63.50	67.09	65.24
% Don't know	4.77	6.40	12.40	4.28	5.52	9.34

Notes: Data are taken from the Zogby International's Ten Nation Impressions of America survey. "% Favorable" = sum of "Somewhat favorable" and "Very favorable" responses.

pressed at least a somewhat favorable opinion of the United States and the percentage of non-responses.

As Table 4.1 shows, attitudes towards the American polity among Islamic publics in 2002 ranged from supportive to critical, depending upon which dimension of America was under investigation. Large majorities expressed a very favorable or somewhat favorable opinion of American science and technology (82%), of U.S.-made products, of U.S. education, and of U.S. movies and television (about two-thirds). Attitudes towards American freedom and democracy and towards the American people were less warm but hardly hostile. The sample split about in half with respect to American freedom and democracy, with around 47% expressing a very or somewhat favorable opinion and 47% thinking otherwise, while around 47% had a favorable opinion of Americans as a people. A sizeable 12% expressed no opinion.

Variation also existed across countries. Iranian respondents stand out for their reportedly intense disapproval of U.S. ideas about freedom and democracy and skepticism of U.S. education, yet strong admiration of U.S. science and technology, products, and movies and television. In general, then, U.S. technology and popular culture are accepted in the belief systems of large portions of the individuals surveyed. But even more "political" or "value-laden" features of the American polity do not appear to be systematically rejected.

When we shift our focus to attitudes on U.S. foreign policy, the picture changes. There, we indeed find decidedly negative attitudes. As Table 4.2 shows, solid majorities had a very unfavorable opinion of U.S. policies towards the Arab nations, the Palestinians, and Iraq, which makes an overall negative assessment of U.S. actions in the Middle East at the time nearly unanimous (around 90%). The interventions in the Balkan conflicts and in Kuwait, and the war on terrorism policy, on the other hand, received slightly more approving responses; they generated substantially large percentages of "don't know" responses, as well, which indicates how controversial those policies were. The intervention to stop ethnic cleansing in the Balkans, a pro-Muslim policy for which ulterior motives are not easily found, may not be part of the cognitive map of many respondents. An analogous interpretation of the "don't know" responses with respect to the war to liberate Kuwait in 1991 would be unlikely, given the widespread commotion that those events generated in the Islamic world. In the latter case, non-responses more likely indicates areas of unspoken, or unarticulated, support rather than authentic lack of opinion.

If we look at the figures in Table 4.2, the Iranian respondents again stand out as the least keen on what the United States was doing in its foreign policy: *not one* of the 700 individuals interviewed in Iran expressed a favorable opinion of the Iraq policy. Analogously, the opposition to U.S. anti-terrorism policy was overwhelmingly strong in the mass public. But the question remains whether, even among the Iranians, those apparent "non-attitudes" belied a more circumspect assessment of the United States' actions, given that about 50% of Iranian respondents were unwilling or unable to assess the interventions to liberate Kuwait and to protect Muslim populations in the Balkans.

Table 4.2.   Attitudes among Islamic Publics towards Specific U.S. Policies, 2002

Country	Arab Nations	Palestinians	Iraq	Freeing Kuwait	Fighting Terror	Balkan Conflicts
Egypt						
% Favorable	3.86	3.00	3.86	22.71	19.00	16.29
% Don't know	10.14	3.14	12.71	24.86	13.71	50.14
Indonesia						
% Favorable	6.29	5.43	7.29	43.43	47.43	24.71
% Don't know	16.43	17.00	12.43	19.71	7.43	24.14
Iran						
% Favorable	0.86	0.14	0.00	0.57	0.14	0.57
% Don't know	15.00	5.41	5.29	54.86	2.00	47.43
Kuwait						
% Favorable	5.40	1.80	17.20	82.80	29.60	38.60
% Don't know	6.40	4.60	27.60	2.80	8.20	38.40
Lebanon						
% Favorable	8.80	5.60	4.00	35.40	29.80	34.20
% Don't know	5.40	5.40	5.80	12.60	4.80	17.60
Pakistan						
% Favorable	18.09	10.05	13.11	49.38	54.83	34.16
% Don't know	7.37	11.29	9.09	13.49	7.56	27.85
Saudi Arabia						
% Favorable	7.86	5.29	8.57	23.14	30.43	14.00
% Don't know	3.86	5.00	8.29	17.71	12.29	27.29
United Arab Emirates						
% Favorable	14.80	9.60	11.00	37.60	37.00	27.60
% Don't know	9.40	7.20	14.00	23.00	14.60	33.40
Total						
% Favorable	8.72	5.37	8.16	36.00	32.44	23.35
% Don't know	9.37	7.78	11.28	21.57	8.70	33.32

Notes: Data are taken from the Zogby International Ten Nation Impressions of America survey. "% Favorable" = sum of "Somewhat favorable" and "Very favorable" responses.

The European Countries

Attitudes among European publics towards U.S. policies were recorded in the CCFR/GMF survey using seven questions. Respondents were asked to rate the George W. Bush administration's handling of the following problems or issue areas: (a) overall foreign policy, (b) international terrorism, (c) the Arab-Israeli conflict, (d) the situation in Iraq, (e) global warming, (f) the war in Afghanistan, (g) relations with Europe. Responses were coded on a four-point scale: "Excellent" (1), "Good"

Table 4.3. Attitudes among European Publics towards Specific U.S. Policies, 2002

Country	Overall foreign policy	International terrorism	Arab-Israeli conflict	Iraq	Global warming	Afghanistan	Relations with Europe
France							
% Favorable	21.78	35.36	12.59	11.99	6.19	22.68	29.87
% Don't know	4.40	2.60	4.40	6.39	9.19	5.00	2.70
Germany							
% Favorable	36.30	50.10	20.80	22.70	12.60	34.50	48.10
% Don't know	2.60	1.50	3.10	3.80	5.30	1.90	1.60
Great Britain							
% Favorable	29.20	47.70	18.70	17.70	6.30	39.40	37.70
% Don't know	4.10	1.50	4.10	5.00	7.20	2.10	2.10
Italy							
% Favorable	57.00	50.50	27.80	29.00	15.60	39.20	64.80
% Don't know	5.70	3.00	6.10	8.50	10.50	5.80	4.80
Netherlands							
% Favorable	27.70	44.70	16.40	22.70	7.50	36.50	37.00
% Don't know	3.00	2.10	4.10	5.10	8.00	4.50	1.80
Poland							
% Favorable	61.80	52.40	22.70	27.20	28.80	37.70	69.00
% Don't know	12.20	8.30	21.10	24.20	32.80	18.40	10.90
Total							
% Favorable	38.96	46.79	19.83	21.88	12.83	34.99	47.74
% Don't know	5.33	3.17	7.15	8.83	12.16	6.28	3.98

Notes: Data are taken from the CCFR/GMF Worldviews 2002 survey. "% Favorable" = sum of "Good" and "Excellent" responses.

(2), "Fair" (3), "Poor" (4). Table 4.3 summarizes the distribution of responses, distinguishing the percentage of respondents who expressed at least a good opinion of the U.S. policies and the percentage of non-responses.

Responses varied across issue areas and among countries. While none of the seven policies of the Bush administration received the endorsement of a majority of respondents, the critical assessment of the European publics was uniform and prominent on the issues of global warming and the Arab-Israeli conflict: in these two areas, only about 13% and 20% of all respondents expressed at least a good opinion. In contrast, on the way the Bush administration had been handling the global war on terror and relations with Europe, the European publics split in half.

The Polish and Italian respondents appear to have been more inclined to support U.S. policies than were the respondents of the other nationalities. French citizens were the least appreciative of the actions and decisions taken by President Bush and his cabinet. About two-thirds of the Italians and the Poles expressed at least a good opinion of the way relations with Europe had been handled, and a majority of the Polish and Italian publics offered a positive evaluation of the overall foreign policy of the Bush administration.

These seven survey questions provide a means of evaluating the European publics' perceptions of U.S. policies, but the CCFR/GMF Worldviews survey does not offer a comparable battery of indicators of opinions about U.S. culture and society. Instead, the CCFR/GMF survey asked respondents to rate their attitudes towards the United States on a "feeling thermometer". This type of scale allows respondents to evoke whichever dimensions of America come naturally to their minds without superimposing any frame of reference.

In order to ease comparisons across surveys, I rescaled the CCFR/GMF feeling thermometer so that a score of 0 indicates a very favorable feeling, a score of 100 indicates a very unfavorable feeling, and a score of 50 indicates a neither favorable nor unfavorable feeling. In other words, on the rescaled feeling thermometer high numbers indicate greater levels of dislike of the United States. This scale is employed in Table 4.4.

The United States generally elicited somewhat positive feelings in all six European countries sampled. The mean scores on the anti-American feeling thermometer ranged from a "temperature" of 32° in Italy and Great Britain to 40° in France. These figures are below 50°, the neutral point on the scale, but far from denoting enthusiasm. The overall positive feelings towards the United States, nonetheless, fluctuate considerably among respondents; the standard deviation

Table 4.4.   European Publics Measured on Anti-American Feeling Thermometer, 2002

Country	Mean	Std. dev.	% Selecting 50°	Don't know
France	40.08	24.18	23.38	1.20
Germany	36.95	21.15	24.50	1.30
Great Britain	32.23	22.18	15.00	0.70
Italy	31.77	27.22	24.20	1.00
Netherlands	40.56	20.59	19.70	0.30
Poland	35.32	21.81	28.10	1.60
Total	36.16	23.21	22.48	1.02

Notes: Data are taken from the CCFR/GMF Worldviews 2002 survey. 0–100 index, where 0 = very favorable feeling towards the United States and 100 = very unfavorable feeling.

ranged from 21 points in Germany and the Netherlands to 27 in Italy. Moreover, while very few "don't know" responses were cast, a sizeable portion of respondents—from 15% in Great Britain to about 28% in Poland—selected a score of 50, which could indicate either no opinion or ambivalence.

More importantly, a comparison of the moderately positive image of the United States that emerges from Table 4.4 and the less appreciative image that emerges from the policy survey items in Table 4.3 offers some tentative evidence that the feeling thermometer does capture aspects of the United States beyond U.S. conduct in world affairs. The anti-American feeling thermometer can therefore serve as a partial surrogate for more explicit survey items measuring various aspects of America's culture and society.

Finding the Patterns of Anti-Americanism

These data from different surveys of Islamic and European publics provide further empirical support for the contention that attitudes towards the United States do not cluster around hardened ideological positions but instead reflect the separate evaluations respondents make of the multiple aspects of America, as the dimensions of America theory maintains. A description of the data, however, cannot give adequate empirical answers to the conjectures about the U.S. image that were elaborated in Chapter 2, nor can it evaluate how the normative and ideational dimensions of the American world order shape the belief systems of ordinary people worldwide. The statistical modeling is devoted to explaining how the polity/policy frames inform the belief system of the mass publics. Thus, the modeling helps us to evaluate how the dimensions of America theory relates to the soft power thesis, as was discussed in Chapter 2.

As we saw in the descriptions above, the Zogby International data and the CCFR/GMF surveys offer an array of indicators that tap into a variety of features of the United States. To analyze the Zogby and CCFR/GMF data in all their richness, I use a statistical estimator that is specifically designed to summarize information from multiple indicators, the item response theory (IRT) model.[38] The IRT model allows for an encompassing measurement of anti-American sentiments, in which clusters of indicators are taken as empirical manifestations of respondents' attitudes across the polity/policy frames (Fox and Glas, 2001, 2003; Fox, 2003).[39] The IRT model retrieves an estimate of the latent propensity to articulate a negative view of the United States.[40]

I use a different estimator for the anti-American feeling thermometer, a single indicator of overall attitudes towards the United States. For this data, I estimate a random-effect model, a variant of the standard linear model, which includes two stochastic components, one at the individual level of the survey respondent and one at the level of the country in which all respondents are clustered. The model yields estimates of the mean and variance of the feeling thermometer measurements in each country and in the entire sample of countries, and measures how much variation occurs at the individual level within each country and how much variation can be attributed to differences between countries, all of which are parameters that have an immediate and direct interpretation (Raudenbush and Bryk, 2002). With this in mind, we can now turn to the empirical results, which are summarized in Figure 4.1.[41]

The Islamic Countries

In the top half of Figure 4.1, I present the mean levels of the two latent propensities to be anti-American as attested in eight Islamic societies, estimated by the IRT statistical model. Lower scores indicate that a country is less opposed to the United States. The overall mean level of latent propensity shown on the left indicates that the perceptions of U.S. culture and society are fairly positive.[42] In general, this result is corroborated by the distribution of latent propensities: about 56% of all respondents have a level of sociocultural anti-Americanism smaller than −1, and a sizeable 16% has a score lower than −3. On the other hand, only about 8% of the respondents reach a level of propensity greater than 1, and just about 1.5% is above a level of 3.

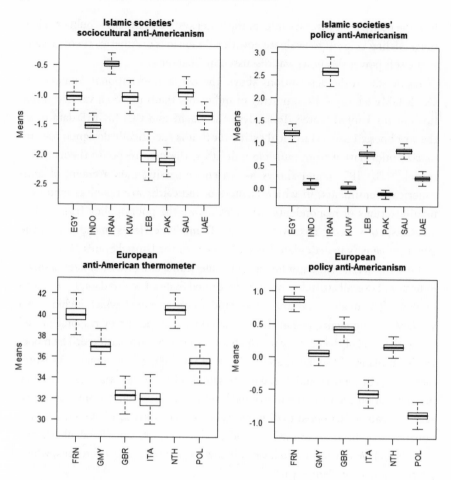

Figure 4.1. Levels of Anti-Americanism in Eight Islamic Societies and in Six European Societies

Notes: Box plot of the mean levels of anti-Americanism from the Bayesian IRT and random-effects models. Data analysis is based on the Zogby International Ten Nation Impressions of America Poll (2002) and the CCFR/GMF Worldviews 2002 survey.

Differences in the diffusions of anti-American sentiment exist among countries. The highest level of sociocultural anti-Americanism is reached in Iran[43] while the minimum levels are found in Lebanon and Pakistan. Most of the variation in latent propensity, though, occurs within countries; only about 13% of the variation in the latent propensity to oppose the United States occurs between countries.[44] These empirical patterns, challenge the view of an irreducible incompatibility between Islamic culture and society and the United States. Contrary to the arguments of Samuel Huntington (1996) and Barry Rubin (2002), but in line with the findings of Pippa Norris and Ronald Inglehart (2004) and Mark Tessler (2002), the low magnitude of the propensity to dislike U.S. culture and society in this survey data is indicative of the existence of large similarities in the values and aspirations of ordinary citizens in the West and in the Islamic world.

On the foreign policy dimension, however, the image of the United States appears much more poorly received. The anti-American propensity reaches a much larger score than was the case for the sociocultural dimension; this translates into fairly high probabilities to oppose U.S. policies.[45] The distribution of the latent propensity shows that about 38% of the respondents are given a score of 1 or higher, and about 5% reach a level of at least 3, whereas only about 8.5% of the public is attributed a score of −1 or lower. Again, Iranian respondents manifest the most negative attitude towards U.S. policies, and again the Pakistani respondents manifest the most favorable attitude towards the United States in this group of countries.[46]

In sum, from the top section of Figure 4.1 we can see a summary measure of the levels of opposition to U.S. society and culture, on the one hand, and U.S. policies on the other in eight Islamic societies. We can also see how different those overall scores are across societies. Thus, on the societal and cultural dimension, Iran reaches the highest levels on the latent scale, to be followed by Egypt, Kuwait, and Saudi Arabia. United Arab Emirates and Indonesia rank third on the scale, while Pakistan and Lebanon are the least anti-American in this group. On policy, Iran has by far the highest mean level of anti-Americanism, a level about twice as high as that of the second ranking country, Egypt. Lebanon and Saudi Arabia are ranked third on the scale, with Indonesia, Kuwait, Pakistan, and UAE the least anti-American.

The comparison of the country variances (which is reported in the on-line Appendix) shows how concentrated the distribution of anti-American sentiment is in these eight countries. On both the polity and policy dimensions, Lebanese respondents have the largest variability in their attitudes towards the United States. On the other hand, countries such as Iran and Indonesia have much lower variances, which might be taken as an indication of how the mass public in these countries has either reached a societal consensus on the United States or has coordinated on a common position under some specific political circumstances.

The European Countries

In the bottom half of Figure 4.1, I present the findings with regard to levels of anti-American sentiments on the polity and policy dimensions in Europe. The anti-American feeling thermometer, a comprehensive measure of anti-American sentiment, serves as a proxy for individual issue questions in measuring the popular perception of U.S. culture and society. The model estimates the same country means and country variances that are presented in descriptive statistics in Table 4.4. Again, we find that the image of the United States is more positive in Italy and Great Britain than in France or the Netherlands and that the variability of the responses on this survey item is larger in Italy than in the Netherlands. More importantly, however, the statistical model also estimates how much variability exists across countries and, thus, locates the sources of variation in the data.[47] From this quantity, it is possible to compute that about 16% of the overall variance is due to country differences. In other words, individual level factors seem to have a much larger role in accounting for the patterns of survey responses than country level factors.[48]

Overall, the mean level of policy anti-Americanism among European publics is centered around 0, a score that generates a response pattern of either moderate criticism or moderate approval of U.S. foreign policy. Negative assessments are more likely to be found in France and Great Britain than in Italy or Poland. The variability in anti-American sentiment (presented in the on-line Appendix) appears to be more marked in Italy, where the country variance is about 4 points on average. But if we consider the 95% confidence intervals around the country variances, we observe that they overlap for the most part. The exception is the Netherlands, where the distribution of respondents' latent propensity scores is tighter around its country mean. Finally, the variation within each country, at the level of the individual respondents, is more pronounced than the variation across countries. About 24% of the overall variation is due to country differences.

To summarize, in this sample of European countries, popular anti-American sentiment appears to be at most moderately affected by the political context within which respondents formulated their opinions about the United States. In the summer of 2002, when the most heated controversies over a war in Iraq were looming on the horizon but had not yet been unleashed, the European publics had moderately good feelings towards the United States. And while they were more critical of a few policies, those on the environment and the Middle East in particular, they hardly appear estranged Venusians sharing no common bonds with America, as Robert Kagan (2003) colorfully described them. Moreover, as we can observe from the plots in Figure 4.1, not only are the differences across countries rather limited, but they do not neatly fall along the lines of "old" and "new" Europe, the geopolitical distinction Defense Secretary Donald Rumsfeld did so much to popularize.

Such was the status of European perceptions of America in the summer of 2002, just before European and American elites would engage in a no-holds-barred dispute over a war in Iraq and over the proper conduct of international affairs, a dispute whose consequences resound in their relations, as we will explore in Part 4 of this book.

Policy, Polity, and Soft Power

So far in this investigation, the patterns in anti-American attitudes have been analyzed in isolation, one dimension at a time; but a key question about the underlying nature of anti-Americanism is whether the two frames of policy and polity are related. As we saw in Chapter 2, a connection between those two dimensions underlies Joseph Nye's (2004) concept of soft power: the more one is socialized into the U.S. political culture and ideology, the more prone one is to accept the policy goals pursued by the United States.

The analytical discussion in Chapter 2 also showed how problematic it is to know if a causal relationship exists between the approval of America's diplomacy and endorsement of its societal model, and to discern the direction of the causal relationship. What we can ascertain, however, is whether attitudes towards culture and society and attitudes towards policies fit into a consistent—or constrained—belief system. Are the individuals who hold a positive view of U.S. policies those who hold a positive view of U.S. society and culture? If that is the case, then it is possible to guess where a person stands on one dimension from knowledge of where he or she stands on the other, and from that knowledge to infer that the mechanisms of soft power contribute to the formation of popular opinion about America, regardless of which attitudinal dimension "causes" the other in the mind of survey respondents.

To this end, Figure 4.2 plots the latent propensities to oppose U.S. culture and society versus U.S. policies for the group of eight predominantly Islamic countries surveyed by Zogby International. Figure 4.4 does likewise for the group of European countries canvassed in the CCFR/GMF survey, juxtaposing the latent propensity to oppose policies and the anti-American feeling thermometer.[49] The

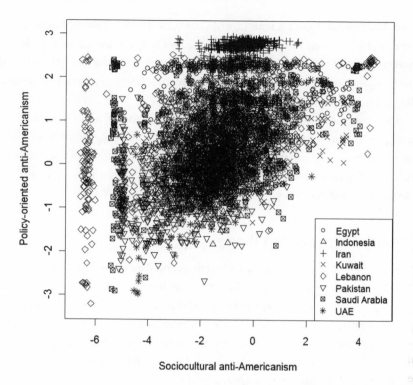

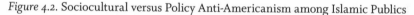

Figure 4.2. Sociocultural versus Policy Anti-Americanism among Islamic Publics

Notes: Dots in the figure represent the estimate of the latent propensity to oppose the United States estimated by the Bayesian IRT model for each respondent in the survey. Data analysis is based on the Zogby International Ten Nation Impressions of America Poll (2002).

quantities represented, as we have discussed in the previous section, offer a comprehensive measure of how inclined each respondent is to oppose either dimension of the United States.

It appears that, in the Islamic publics surveyed, the sociocultural and foreign policy dimensions of anti-Americanism were, unsurprisingly, related: high levels of anti-Americanism on one dimension coincide with high levels of anti-Americanism on the other dimension. This connection is reflected in a Pearson's correlation coefficient as high as 0.424. But there is more to this relationship than a mere correlation.

At low levels of sociocultural anti-Americanism, policy-oriented anti-Americanism spans the entire spectrum, from low levels to high levels. Thus, a good disposition towards U.S. society and culture is not necessarily incompatible with a strongly negative assessment of U.S. policies. On the other hand, at high levels of sociocultural anti-Americanism, the policy-related responses are much more concentrated, which indicates a syndrome of outright opposition to the United States for what it is and for what it does. Analogously, if we look at the relationship between the two types of anti-Americanism from the perspective of the policy variant, we can infer that opposition to U.S. policies is compatible with the entire range of attitudes towards U.S. culture and society. On the other hand, no respondents expressed a positive view of U.S. policies while being contemptuous of U.S. society.

In sum, it appears that, as Joseph Nye (2004, 14) has written, "government policies can reinforce or squander a country's soft power." Yet, finding U.S. cultural and political ideals appealing does not turn mass publics into keen supporters of American diplomacy; it makes them at most amenable to holding positive views of U.S. foreign policy. Figure 4.2's triangle-shaped scatterplot of the estimated propensities to sociocultural and policy anti-Americanism indicates that a large portion of respondents speak of the United States with two minds, appreciatively about aspects of America's polity and negatively when asked to focus on U.S. foreign policy. The pattern of attitudes in Figure 4.2 exemplifies the structure of a loosely constrained belief system in which approval of U.S. cultural norms and values coexists with negative views of U.S. diplomacy and international behavior.

Beyond the visual inspection of the scatterplot in Figure 4.2, patterns in the variability of the latent propensities can be ascertained using formal statistical tests. The hypothesis under investigation is the extent to which the variance in one attitudinal dimension is conditional on the values of the other. Focusing first on the latent propensity to oppose U.S. policies, the statistical test divides the sample of respondents in the Zogby survey into two sections, those who have a high score on the sociocultural anti-Americanism propensity and those who have a low score on that dimension, and then it computes the ratio of the variances in the two subsamples.[50] If a high score is defined as a value of propensity to oppose U.S. culture and society greater than the 80th percentile, and a low score is a value smaller than the 20th percentile, we obtain a variance ratio equal to 0.789, with a 95% confidence interval spanning 0.700 to 0.890. It is then possible to reject the hypothesis of equal variances, as we could conclude from visual inspection of the data.

Interestingly, though, the statistical test of the ratio of variances of sociocultural anti-Americanism yields a statistic equal to 1.001, with a 95% confidence interval from 0.893 to 1.136, if the thresholds to identify low and high scores on the policy anti-Americanism are set at the 20th and 80th percentiles. It would then appear that there is no difference in the dispersion of the propensity to oppose U.S. culture and society at low and high values of the policy attitudinal dimension. This result, however, is primarily driven by the distribution of the two latent propensities among the Iranian respondents (the bright green dots in the online color version of Figure 4.2). If Iran is excluded from the sample, the ratio of the variances is 0.541, with a 95% confidence interval from 0.476 to 0.616, which again indicates how much less dispersed societal and cultural anti-Americanism was among the respondents appreciative of U.S. policies.

Figure 4.3 shows the connection between polity and policy anti-Americanism in each country. The pattern of ambivalence that emerges from the aggregate analysis also characterizes the opinions of the respondents within the eight predominantly Islamic countries in the Zogby survey. This pattern is particularly prominent in the cases of Egypt, Lebanon, Pakistan, and Saudi Arabia; it is less so for Indonesia, Iran, Kuwait, and the United Arab Emirates, where opinions about policies and opinions about polity appear to be more consistently aligned.

Shifting our focus to the European publics, the anti-American feeling thermometer and the latent propensity to oppose U.S. policies show a fairly high positive correlation, with a Pearson's coefficient equal to 0.398, but the pattern that the two attitudes form in Figure 4.4 does not resemble a constrained belief system, in which a respondent's anti-American stance on one dimension is a good predictor of his or her stance on the other. Nor does the pattern look like the triangle-shaped configuration plotted for the Islamic publics, in which ambivalence becomes the identifying feature of the mindset through which the United States is perceived.

Instead, in Figure 4.4, we observe nearly as much variability in the attitudes towards policies among those who harbor low anti-American feelings as among those who feel strongly against the United States. Respondents who expressed their good feelings about America by selecting a "temperature" below 50° on the feeling thermometer entertained the entire range of opinions about America's policies, from very negative to very positive. It is only for the group of respondents who disliked the United States to the extent of selecting a thermometer score higher than 70° that we start to observe higher concentrations of negative opinions about U.S. foreign policies. If we exclude the few odd respondents in the lower right corner of Figure 4.4, high opinion of policies becomes less common among those with high degrees of anti-American feeling.

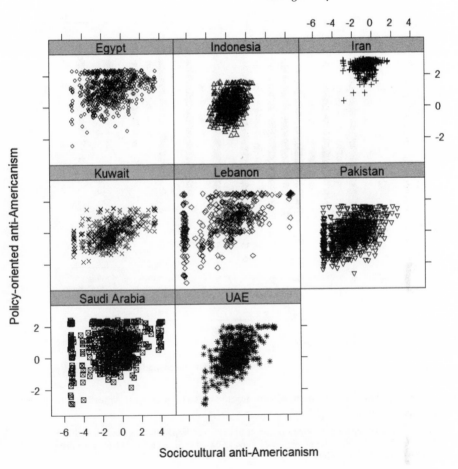

Figure 4.3. Sociocultural versus Policy Anti-Americanism among Islamic Publics, by Country

Notes: Dots in the figure represent the estimate of the latent propensity to oppose the United States estimated by the Bayesian IRT model for each respondent in the survey. Data analysis is based on the Zogby International Ten Nation Impressions of America Poll (2002).

The statistical test of the variability of opinions about U.S. policies gives further credence to the conclusion that the European belief system lacks a clear structure. With the 20th and 80th percentiles as the thresholds for low and high scores on the anti-American feeling thermometer, the variance ratio is 0.930 with a 95% confidence interval from 0.820 to 1.057, which does not reject the hypothesis of equal variances.

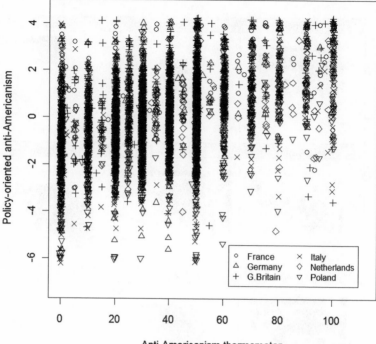

Figure 4.4. Anti-Americanism Thermometer versus Policy Anti-Americanism among European Publics

Notes: Dots in the figure represent the estimate of the latent propensity to oppose the United States estimated by the the Bayesian random effects and IRT models for each respondent in the survey. Data analysis is based on the CCFR/GMF Worldviews 2002 survey.

If we look at Figure 4.4 from the perspective of the latent propensity to oppose policies, we observe that the individuals who scored high on that dimension can feel as coldly about the United States as they can feel warmly, which indicates that dislike of policies is not a good predictor of overall feelings. Again, it is only at fairly low levels of policy opposition—a score of -2 on the latent propensity—that opinions start to concentrate at low anti-American thermometer scores. Indeed, the variance is about 414.3 when the values of policy opposition are in the bottom 20% and is about 664.3 when the values are in the top 20%. Such variances yield a ratio equal to 0.624, with a 95% confidence interval from 0.557 to 0.699, which rejects the hypothesis of equal variances.

In sum, the attitudinal map that is portrayed in Figure 4.4 indicates that the belief system about the United States is largely unconstrained for a substantial portion of European publics. Strong feelings against the United States in general are not a defining feature of the mental map of those who dislike U.S. policies. Nor is the endorsement of U.S. policies the typical response of those who feel positive about America. It would seem that it takes more than the appeal of U.S. political ideology to foster acceptance of U.S. diplomacy among citizens who already share strong commitments to the principles of democracy and modernity, as is the case in European countries.

These overall patterns play out in a very similar way in each of the six European countries under investigation. In Figure 4.5, the scatterplots for Germany and Italy reveal the mildly triangular shape implying that respondents who are attracted by America are more likely to experience ambivalent opinions about U.S. policies. Such a structure emerges among the British respondents as well, and would be more pronounced if it were not for the presence of several respondents whose anti-American feelings hit very high temperatures even though they were partial to American policies. In the Netherlands, France, and Poland, on the other hand, the two attitudinal dimensions seem to go hand-in-hand, moderately increasing while maintaining constant variances. Despite the differences in their mean levels, attitudes towards the United States in the Netherlands, France, and Poland seem to form a consistent map more than in the other three countries.

This analysis of the relationship between the polity and policy frames of anti-American opinion generates two major findings about soft power at the level of mass politics. On the one hand, soft power, the attractiveness that the United States derives from its cultural and societal characteristics, finds empirical confirmation in the overall views of ordinary people. In both Islamic and European societies, in 2002, the societal and cultural aspects of the United States elicited an overall sense of support. Granted, qualifications are often made, as we also saw in Chapter 3; and if we were expecting an unquestioning enthusiasm about U.S. popular culture and society, these findings would certainly contradict that expectation. But, the features of U.S. society and culture are far from being disparaged, as the conventional rhetoric about anti-Americanism often implies.

On the other hand, soft power as the ability to lead that the United States derives from its ability to attract is not reflected in the patterns of responses presented in this analysis. Ordinary people's views of U.S. policies are only marginally affected by their views of U.S. culture and society. There is no automatic transference of appreciation of the United States as a society based on freedom,

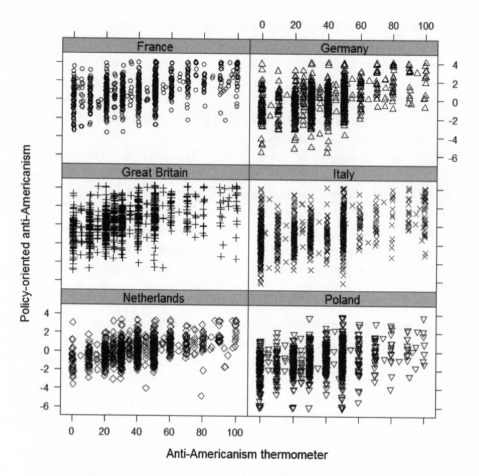

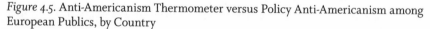

Figure 4.5. Anti-Americanism Thermometer versus Policy Anti-Americanism among European Publics, by Country

Notes: Dots in the figure represent the estimate of the latent propensity to oppose the United States estimated by the the Bayesian random effects and IRT models for each respondent in the survey. Data analysis is based on the CCFR/GMF Worldviews 2002 survey.

opportunity, and achievement into an appreciation of the policies the country pursues in the international arena. While both policy and polity underlie popular opinion about the United States, these two frames are not tightly tied.

As an empirical description of a belief system about the United States, this finding corroborates the expectation of an unconstrained belief system that I derived from the dimension of America theory in Chapter 2. From the broader perspective about the viability of the popular appeal of the United States as a tool of public diplomacy, however, this finding conveys a more chilling conclusion. The ability to attract that the United States possesses is not a substitute for wise leadership in the international arena.

Conclusions

For a sentiment that has been described as a malevolent ill-disposition, a uniform and undifferentiated syndrome that has taken hold of the world's ideational outlook, anti-Americanism appears too variable and too differentiated to be consistent with such popular views. Even in Islamic countries and in Europe—two of the areas that are conventionally seen as the hotbeds of popular anti-Americanism—the United States as a cultural and political symbol attracts more than it repels. When the United States is seen in terms of its freedom and democracy, its movies and products, its technological achievements and its educational attainments, majorities are inclined to express their admiration. It is when respondents are asked to assess U.S. foreign policy that opposition is more likely to emerge.

The empirical patterns in anti-American sentiment define a loosely constrained belief system in which attitudes towards the U.S. polity and U.S. policies are only moderately connected. Approval of the U.S. political ideals does not guarantee approval of U.S. political choices in the international arena. But the disapproval of U.S. policies does not have the psychological force to displace the aspirations that the United States symbolizes. Although not a trump card that wins over the sympathy and approval of ordinary people, the mechanism of soft power nonetheless can be an antidote to the most blatant forms of opposition to the United States. In other words, soft power generates an ideational environment in which the foreign policy goals the United States pursues might be seen in a more positive light.

Among many citizens the world over, the United States is a source of contending feelings, of love and hate, of admiration and disdain, of acceptance and frustration. Who are the people who articulate these ambivalent views of the United States? In the next two chapters, I will explore in depth to what extent various individual-level characteristics and country-specific features are significantly associated with these divergent strands in anti-American sentiment, how modernity, information, and material progress affect popular views of the

United States. The processes that shape popular attitudes towards the United States turn out to be primarily individual-level processes, mediated by political ideology and socialization. Country-level effects, such as economic, military, and cultural connections to the United States, are at best only marginally related to the distribution of anti-American sentiments worldwide.

PART III / Sources

CHAPTER FIVE

Profiles of Anti-American Opinion

Introduction

The empirical investigations conducted in Chapters 3 and 4 demonstrate the multidimensional nature of anti-American sentiment. When ordinary people are asked to express their feelings towards the United States, their responses reflect their evaluations of a variety of national characteristics of a democracy, territory, and cultural symbol that, as the British novelist Martin Amis once quipped, "is more like a world than a country" (1986, ix). The findings go beyond showing that people were better disposed towards U.S. institutions than they were towards U.S. policies. They also show that sizeable portions of ordinary people entertained conflicting views of the United States in which likes and dislikes closely coexisted. Those analyses, thus, indicate that ordinary people's belief systems about the United States are loosely structured, and hardly ever harden into an ideological framework. Moreover, they indicate that, in 2002, except in the Middle Eastern publics, the multiple dimensionality of the United States served as a key asset that tempered the formation of an overall rejection of the United States.

This chapter initiates a second phase of this investigation of popular attitudes towards the United States. Having analyzed what anti-Americanism is and is not, I now shift the focus of the analysis to *who* among ordinary people the world over expresses a negative overall opinion of the United States, and I elaborate an empirical profile of the individuals who are more likely to express anti-American opinions.

Using regression modeling, I evaluate several propositions about the demographic and attitudinal characteristics of the individuals who expressed anti-American views in the sample of countries surveyed in the Pew Research Center 2002 Global Attitudes Survey. Identity markers such as gender, age, levels of education, and religious affiliation are examined along with indicators that distinguish the ideological outlooks and broader belief systems of the respondents.

As in Chapter 3, these propositions are tested in seven geographical regions—Africa, Central and South Asia, East Asia, Eastern Europe, Latin America, the Middle East, and a group of Western democracies—allowing us to investigate whether there is any regional variation in which aspects of America shape how different people think about the United States. First I review the variables used, to distinguish the demographic characteristics of the respondents. I then present four causal conjectures about the presence of anti-American attitudes: (a) the information-and-contacts hypothesis, (b) the traditional worldview hypothesis, (c) the antimarket worldview hypothesis, and (d) the scapegoat hypothesis. Third, I discuss the modeling strategy and explain how regression modeling contributes to our understanding of the causal pathways through which negative opinions of the United States emerge.

This chapter offers additional evidence that the popular perceptions of the United States are a largely heterogenous phenomenon that differs in both qualitative and quantitative terms across regional domains. The individual profiles of the respondents who harbor negative feelings towards the United States reflect the fundamental experiences of their socialization and are mediated by the information they possess about the United States, their overall attitudes toward modern life and market economies, and their reactions to U.S. foreign policies. But while each of these mechanisms gives structure to the views of the United States among ordinary people, it is their combination that shapes the profile of the anti-American respondent in each of the regional samples.

Profiles of Respondents

What kinds of respondents were more likely to formulate negative attitudes towards the United States? We first consider a series of demographic indicators, the standard fare of public opinion analysis. The goal is to identify some basic characteristics of the respondents and to compare whether there were any differences across regions in the basic profile of the anti-American respondents. In particular, I consider the following demographic characteristics: (a) gender, (b) age, (c) education, and (d) religious affiliation.[51] Each demographic indicator likely captures alternative motivations that animate popular opposition to the United States. What irritates, upsets, or enrages younger women probably differs from what irritates, upsets, or enrages middle-aged men. The literati are likely to be turned off by the less refined tastes of the practical Americans, which instead may appeal to ordinary folks with less education and a passion for blockbuster movies. Agnostics and atheists would likely feel disconcerted when confronted with the messianic streak in the American political identity. Any patterns would also differ in emphasis and content across regions, given that the social and political contexts differ. While these predictions are safe to make, it is more difficult to pinpoint *ex ante* what underlying motivations structure the variation in U.S. popularity across demographic groups.

An example of such difficulty is that the differential impact of generational experiences may very well be reflected in the presence of clusters of similar opinions about the United States in each age group, caused by a collective encounter with the United States in a specific historical contingency. Memories of past wrongs actually or allegedly perpetrated by the United States would form a legacy of anti-American sentiments as much as memories of acts of friendship or generosity on the part of the United States would generate a reservoir of good feelings (Keohane and Katzenstein, 2007, 29–30). When massive protests took place in Western Germany in the mid-1980s to oppose the security policies of the Reagan administration, for example, scholars were able to trace the motivations of the younger activists to the key experience of their political socialization regarding America—the Vietnam War—whereas the Marshall Plan and the Berlin crises served as the main referents for the older generations (Mueller and Risse-Kappen, 1987). Clearly, past experiences mattered. But to specify *ex ante* what those generational experiences would be and how they might translate into opinion patterns goes beyond the theoretical frames about anti-Americanism that have so far been elaborated. Anything from the bombing of the Chinese embassy in Belgrade to the downing of an Iranian airliner by the U.S.S. *Vincennes,* from the killing of two Korean girls by a U.S. Army vehicle in Seoul to the scandal at the Abu Ghraib prison in Baghdad can potentially serve as the focal point for resentment against the United States for entire generations of people in a country. To corroborate this point, Doug McAdam (2007) has shown that both negative and positive legacies emerge through dynamic processes that are usually contingent and idiosyncratic.

In this light, the empirical analyses can offer at best descriptive inferences about the profile of the respondents who articulated negative views of the United States in the survey. But, as I explain below when I directly address the modeling strategy, these empirical analyses can take an inductive stab at explaining why we observe variation in the attitudes towards the United States among people with different demographic profiles. In particular, the modeling strategy tests the extent to which any of the four causal conjectures evaluated here can act as the causal pathway through which demographic factors exert their effects. The test is inductive, given that no prior hypotheses are formulated; the test is also demanding, given that clusters of motivations are likely to be subsumed within any aspect of a respondent's identity. With these caveats in mind, however, regression modeling can help highlight some aspects of the cognitive and affective dynamics that shape anti-American opinion.

Four Hypotheses

The regression models allow for the testing of conjectures about the connections between a cluster of belief systems and the presence of anti-American attitudes. I consider four causal hypotheses: the information-and-contacts hypothesis, the traditional worldview hypothesis, the antimarket worldview hypothesis, and the scapegoat hypothesis. These hypotheses can be engaged in a confrontation of the empirical record, to go beyond the description of *who* says *what* of the United States and evaluate some of the reasons *why* such opinions are held.[52]

The *information-and-contacts hypothesis* subsumes the claim that people who have closer contacts and better information about the United States are less likely to hold negative views of the country. This perspective undergirds the argument advanced by Joseph Nye (2004), who claims that social interactions with the United States foster socialization into the values and goals of the United States. For that reason, Nye advocates cultural exchange programs as a way to promote and sustain the image of the United States. In his perspective, information about the United States would shatter the walls of ignorance and prejudice and give U.S. soft power a chance to exert its influence.

A similar prediction about the effects of information and contacts emerges from models of strategic interaction. Using a model of opportunistic politicians with no qualms about spreading hatred for political purposes, Edward Glaeser (2005) shows that hostility towards a social group—be it an ethnic minority or the population of a country—declines with the increase of incentives to dismiss the false stories manufactured by the "entrepreneurs of hate." In Glaeser's theoretical formulation, increased economic interactions serve as the mechanism that makes believing in hate-creating stories counterproductive. The lack of social interactions is explicitly selected by Glaeser (2005, 79) as a key cause for the low status of the United States in the Middle East: "This combination of America's relevance (which creates the incentives for supply) and the absence of interactions (which ensures that there is little desire to know the truth) fosters the spread of hatred in this region."

I employ two measures to test whether the information-and-contacts hypothesis is reflected in the patterns of responses recorded in the Pew Foundation Global Attitudes Project survey. The first measure identifies the respondents who declared that they watched an international news channel such as the BBC or CNN. People who did so were arguably interested in expanding their sources of information beyond their domestic channels. In this respect, watching an international news channel might be seen as a proxy for Glaeser's "incentive to learn the truth" about an out-group. The potential drawback of this measure is that watching international news channels might very well be a consequence, rather than a cause, of attitudes towards the United States. For instance, a correlation between information seeking and positive attitudes towards the United States might be the result of respondents' attempts to avoid domestic news channels and acquire information from an American or Western perspective more attuned to their ideological outlook.[53]

Because of this drawback, I consider a second indicator that is less likely to be endogenous to attitudinal stances towards the United States, namely whether the respondents had friends or relatives living in the United States that they visited regularly or with whom they corresponded regularly in writing or by telephone. The risk of endogeneity associated with this second indicator is lower, given that the bonds of kinship and friendship drive the contact with the United States. Learning about the United States is then a byproduct of a personal relationship that goes beyond any prior interest in the United States. This second measure also has the advantage of offering an individual-level measure of the mechanism that underlies Nye's (2004) proposal to foster cultural exchanges with the United States.

The traditional worldview and the antimarket worldview hypotheses place the origins of popular opposition to the United States in the perception of a gap between individual normative and ideological predispositions and the implications that the societal and political model of the United States entails for those predispositions. These two hypotheses share a common logic insofar as they derive from the perception of a value gap. They differ, however, with respect to the content of the values they emphasize.

In the *traditional worldview hypothesis*, popular anti-Americanism stems from a reaction to the challenges that the individualistic and egalitarian ethos of the

United States presents to traditional systems of authority and to the subordinate position of women in some societies. This argument has been advanced in particular with respect to distinctions between Western and Islamic societies. In challenging Samuel Huntington's thesis in *The Clash of Civilizations*, for example, Pippa Norris and Ronald Inglehart (2004) show that the cultural cleavage existing between the Western and the Islamic societies pertains to social beliefs about gender equality and sexual liberalization and not to the appreciation of or disdain for democratic values and ideals. At the macro level, a similar argument has been elaborated by Steven Fish (2002), who places the roots of authoritarianism in Islamic societies in a repression of women's rights permitted by authoritarian institutions.

Four indicators are used to identify the respondents who embrace a traditional worldview: (a) The first distinguishes the respondents who declared that they "like the pace of modern life" from those who did not. (b) The second identifies the respondents who declared that a marriage where "the husband provides for the family and the wife takes care of the house and children" creates a more satisfying way of life than "a marriage where husband and wife both have jobs and both take care of the house and children." (c) The third indicator distinguishes respondents who believed that "birth control or family planning was a change for the better" from those who believed that "birth control or family planning was a change for the worse or did not make much difference." (d) The fourth indicator identifies the respondents who agreed that their way of life "needs to be protected from foreign influences."

The third conjecture—the *antimarket worldview hypothesis*—summarizes the position of that part of the surveyed publics who felt concerned about the societal consequences of unfettered market competition. The allegation is that the U.S. political economy is based on unregulated labor markets and puts a premium on efficiency and profit making at the expense of the social protection of the lower and middle classes. In this logic, an anti-American orientation emerges from a disagreement with the prevailing positions in the U.S. political system about the balance between efficiency and equity and about the importance of the welfare state as an institution that mediates between the market and social outcomes.[54]

But a second element pervades the opposition to the United States described by the anti-market hypothesis. This element pertains to the broader forces that drive success in life. It is often emphasized that the American way of life values individual achievement over ascriptive status in determining one's position in society. The *American creed* is premised on the belief that individuals are arbiters of their own success in life and that a competitive marketplace is the institutional setting where individuals can see their talents thrive.

This belief is often invoked to account for differences in political preferences over a large variety of social and economic issues. For example, in an original investigation comparing the sources of happiness in the United States and Europe, Alesina, Di Tella, and MacCulloch (2004) attribute societal differences in the effects of inequality on happiness among the rich and the poor to the different degrees of social mobility on the two sides of the Atlantic Ocean. What accounts for the aversion to inequality embodied in the European social model is not simply a matter of different "taste," but—Alesina, Di Tella, and MacCulloch (2004, 2036) conclude—it is a reflection of the fact that "opportunities for mobility are (or are perceived to be) higher in the US than in Europe."

By extension, the logic of this argument implies that negative attitudes towards the United States should be more likely among those individuals who are dissatisfied with the opportunities they have to improve their own and their families' position through effort and talent. They feel that their happiness and well-being would be more negatively affected by the income disparities generated in a competitive market economy, so they are less keen on the United States as the beacon of a better life.

Two indicators are used to distinguish the respondents who embraced the worldviews implicit in the antimarket hypothesis. The first identifies all the respondents who asserted that they *disagreed* with the statement "most people are better off in a free market economy, even though some people are rich and some are poor." The second indicator identifies the respondents who *agreed* with the statement "success in life is pretty much determined by sources outside one's control."

The final conjecture—the *scapegoat hypothesis*—claims that the origins of popular anti-Americanism are to be found in a psychological mechanism that induces individuals to transfer dissatisfaction with the state of affairs in their countries onto the United States. This conjecture is a staple feature in the rhetorical repertoire of the *anti*-anti-Americans, the cadre of pugnacious intellectuals who denounce any form of criticism of the United States, be it mild or preposterous.[55] It would be difficult to match the scorn that Jean-François Revel (2003, 170) bestows on all those who express negative views of the United States to deflect shortcomings of their own country: "Here we see how the Americans are useful to us: to console us for our own failures, serving the myth that they do worse than we do, and that what goes badly with us is their fault."

The converse of the scapegoat conjecture is that people who are satisfied with their own country are less compelled to blame the United States in all its manifestations and actions, because they do not feel the need to project their inadequacies onto the United States. To assess the extent to which this conjecture is reflected in the survey responses, I rely upon an indicator in the Pew survey that directly taps into the sense of dissatisfaction with the state of affairs in the respondent's own country.

By extension, I also analyze whether individuals' concerns about "how things are going in the world" were related to the patterns of responses they gave when asked about the United States. This additional indicator assesses whether respondents systematically held the United States responsible for the political dynamics shaping the international arena.

The Empirical Tests

To test these arguments, I estimated two sets of regression models, one focusing on the demographic factors, the other focusing on the casual hypotheses. As in Chapter 3, I analyzed the data from the Pew Research Center 2002 Global Attitudes Survey. In both sets of models, the dependent variable was the survey indicator measuring the respondents' overall opinion of the United States, which is coded on a four-level scale ranging from very favorable to very unfavorable. Positive coefficients indicate that a given factor is associated with a higher likelihood of expressing negative opinions of the United States, while negative coefficients indicate that respondents who share a given characteristic were less inclined to view the United States in negative terms.[56]

In the first set of models, I tested for a direct relationship between the demographic factors and respondents' attitudes. This modeling specification, depicted as Model 1 in Figure 5.1, is straightforward: the two boxes represent variables, whereby X stands for the demographic factors and Y stands for the dependent variable. The regression findings report the effect of each demographic characteristic, net of all the others.

The second set of models takes the form depicted in Model 2 in Figure 5.1, whereby X stands for the demographic factors, Z stands for the causal factors from the four hypotheses, and Y stands for the dependent variable, that is the attitudes towards the United States. The key relationship is the one between Z and Y, which is labeled C. In order to test whether there is any consistent connec-

Model 1: A Direct Relation

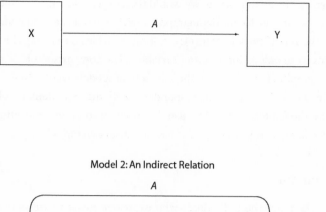

Model 2: An Indirect Relation

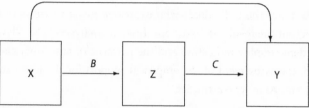

Figure 5.1. A Causal Diagram

tion between the causal variables Z and the dependent variable Y, we need to control for X, given that the demographic variables are plausibly correlated with Z factors and *prior* to them. If the coefficients associated with any of causal conjectures turn out to be statistically significant, we can conclude that there was consistent evidence linking specific worldviews and motivational stances to the popular perceptions of the United States. Model 2 allows us to adjudicate between the casual hypotheses about the sources of popular opposition to the United States.

Model 2 also generates a second set of findings, this time pertaining to the demographic factors. This is because the variables for the four causal conjectures are potentially an intervening factor between demographics and attitudes. Men and women, for example, might subscribe to the traditional worldview to different degrees. Moreover, men and women might make different assessments of the United States because of their different penchant for a traditional worldview. Under this scenario, controlling for a traditional worldview as the intervening factor would eliminate the association between the gender variable and the dependent variable. In general, we would then expect that in the Model 2 regressions the coefficients for the demographic variables would be "deflated," shrunken towards the zero threshold of no effect, if the variables measuring the four causal dynamics were indeed intervening variables. The comparison of the findings on the demographic factors across the two sets of models would establish some of the motivations that might lead respondents with different demographic profiles to oppose the United States. The usual injunction to avoid controlling for intervening variables can be exploited to assess causal dynamics.[57]

The Findings

Who, then, are the individuals who expressed negative views of the United States? I present the results in two steps: first, an analysis of the relationship between the demographic indicators and the patterns of anti-American attitudes, and second, the assessment of the empirical support for the four causal conjectures about anti-American attitudes.

The Demographics

Figure 5.2 presents the main results associated with the demographic variables region by region. By presenting the empirical findings separately in each region, I can highlight the interactions between the demographic characteristics of the respondents and the context within which they lived. The figure reports the coefficients and the 95% confidence intervals around the point estimates, offering a visual representation of the direction and the magnitude of the effects associated with each demographic predictor. Positive coefficients indicate that a given factor is associated with a greater propensity to assert negative opinions of the United States; negative coefficients indicate a decrease in the propensity to state negative opinions of the United States. Confidence intervals that straddle the zero vertical line indicate that the data do not contain enough information to reject the null hypothesis of no connection between an explanatory variable and the pattern of responses on the dependent variable.

Africa

Starting with the ten African countries surveyed in the Pew Research Center Global Attitudes Survey, we find that gender, age, education, and religious affiliation were significantly associated with the overall evaluations of the United

States. In particular, negative opinions of the United States were more likely to be found among males than females, though the difference in attitudes between genders was very small.

More interesting is the generational pattern: respondents of older generations, especially those between their mid-thirties and mid-sixties, were more likely to reveal negative opinions of the United States than respondents who were at most 35 years old at the time of the survey. No groupwide conclusions can be reached with respect to the respondents who were born before 1936; the coefficient corresponding to the age group above 65 years old was positive but insignificant. If we consider the small size of the oldest age group, such a finding reflects a degree of uncertainty in the estimates rather than more antagonistic attitudes towards the United States. The United States was regarded as "cool" among the young, the largest demographic cohort in the African sample.

The results associated with education indicate that anti-American feelings became less common in groups with higher levels of educational attainment. People with middle and high school education were less likely to manifest negative opinions of the United States than those with no education, the group that serves as the reference category in the models. The small and statistically insignificant coefficient for the cohort with college education indicates that there was no difference in their response pattern from that of the people with no education, but this finding can be associated with the small size of the college educated group rather than with the lack of a substantive difference in the attitudinal patterns.

All three religion indicators are associated with positive and significant coefficients. Muslim respondents expressed more negative attitudes than the Christian respondents, who serve as the referent category in the regression models. Atheists and people who followed other forms of religion were also more likely to be found on the anti-American side, as the positive coefficients reported in Figure 5.2 indicate. Those effects, though, were less pronounced than the effect of the variable identifying Muslim respondents. If we compare the coefficients and the confidence intervals associated with the three variables identifying religious affiliation, we notice that not only is the coefficient for the Muslim indicator of larger size, which denotes a stronger impact on the propensity to manifest anti-American attitudes, but its confidence interval is also narrower, which indicates less variability in the pattern of negative assessments.

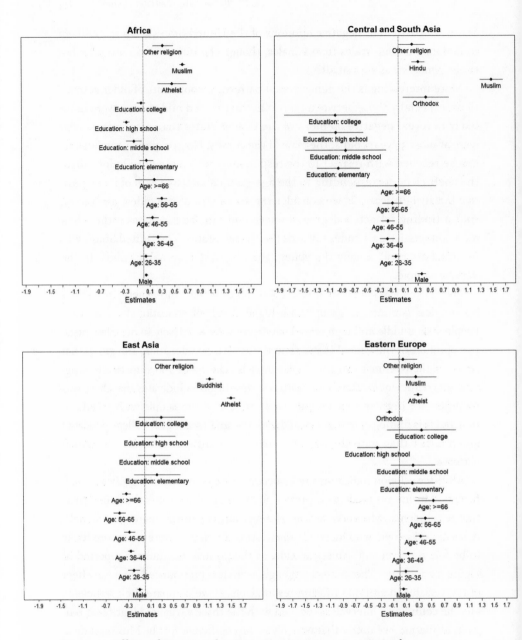

Figure 5.2. Effects of Demographic Factors on Anti-American Attitudes

Notes: The reference category is "Age: 18–25" for the age variables, "No education" for the education variables, "Christian" for the religious affiliation variables. Data analysis is based on the 2002 Pew Global Attitudes Survey.

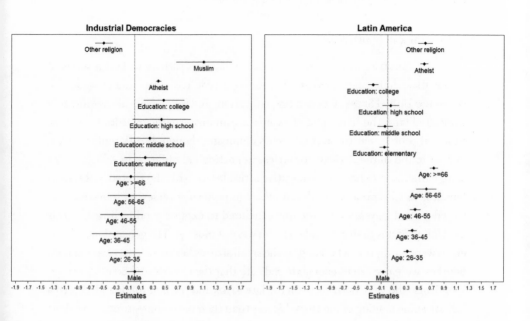

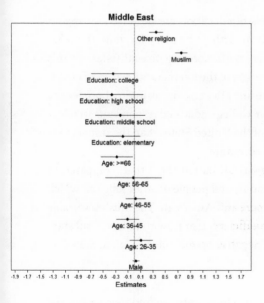

Figure 5.2. (continued)

Central and South Asia

In the countries of Central and South Asia, we continue to find a series of systematic relationships between key demographic indicators and attitudes towards the United States. Gender, age, education, and religion are all significantly associated with the likelihood of expressing an anti-American attitude. The attitudinal profile that those coefficients delineate, though, is different from the one we found in the African countries. In particular, while, as in Africa, males were more likely to have more negative attitudes towards the United States than females, in Central and South Asia the age pattern reverses. Respondents between 36 and 55 years old were more inclined to express good feelings towards the United States than respondents who were at most 35. The generational differences were hardly overwhelming, as the small size of the coefficients clearly shows, but they were consistent enough to indicate that the Central and South Asian respondents who were born between the late 1970s and the mid-1980s had formed a less sanguine opinion of the United States than their older compatriots. No cohort effect is found in the oldest age group.

All four coefficients measuring levels of education are negative and significant, which indicates that the respondents with no formal education, the reference category in the model, were the ones with more negative attitudes towards the United States. Given the similarity in size of the four educational coefficients, type of education does not seem to have any effect on the attitudinal propensity to dislike the United States in this region. College-educated respondents were not any more or less inclined to be critical of the United States than the respondents with only elementary or middle school education.

The four variables measuring religious affiliation show that, compared to Christian respondents, Muslims, Orthodox, and people of other religion, which includes Buddhists and atheists, were more anti-American. The Muslim variable is the one associated with the largest coefficient, that is, with the most substantial impact on the propensity to hold a negative opinion of the United States.

East Asia

Moving to the results about East Asian respondents, we find a small, but significant, gender effect. This time, men were less inclined to voice negative views of the United States than were women. Negative attitudes towards the United States were more likely to be found in the youngest generation of people, those who had come of age in the 1990s (the reference category in the model), and became less likely in older cohorts. With the slight exception of the coefficient for the group of 66-year-olds, the size of the coefficients increases (in absolute terms) as we move up the age ladder.

No educational effects emerged in the East Asian sample. All the four coefficients associated with the levels of educational attainment were positive, but with large confidence intervals straddling the zero line of no effect. The coefficients for religious indicators were positive and significant. Negative attitudes were less likely among Christians than in any other religious groups or atheists.[58]

Eastern Europe

The empirical profile of the anti-American respondent in Eastern Europe shows that negative opinions of the United States were concentrated among males, by a small margin. A more marked pattern emerges with respect to cohort effects: the probability of negative views towards the United States gets progressively larger as we compare older age groups. The lingering effects of socialization during the Communist era are reflected in the views that older people expressed towards the United States, the Eastern Bloc's adversary in the ideological struggle of the Cold War. Education levels, on the other hand, have a weak relationship to views of the United States: at most, only the respondents with high school education had more favorable attitudes than the illiterate respondents, whereas respondents with some education as well as the college educated did not differ in their answers.

In general, respondents of Orthodox religion were less likely to report negative opinions than were Protestant and Catholic respondents. The presence of a larger number of people of anti-American opinion among atheists and respondents with no religion can be seen as another lingering manifestation of socialization during the Soviet period, beyond the effect found in the age cohorts. The lower propensity to state negative opinions of the United States among Orthodox respondents primarily reflects the response patterns among Bulgarian and Ukrainian respondents. Russian Orthodox respondents were not any less likely to dislike the United States than were Russian atheists. From these findings at the mass popular level, therefore, it appears that in 2002 the fault line between Eastern and Western Christianity, yet another of the civilizational dividing lines in the "clash of civilizations" paradigm, did not affect respondents' attitudes towards the United States, the quintessential bearer of the Western civilization flag.

Industrial Democracies

In the industrial democracies (Britain, Canada, France, Germany, and Italy), we find that a negative attitudinal stance towards the United States was more likely among the college educated. All other coefficients have a larger magnitude at every step on the educational ladder without reaching statistical significance. If we consider that nearly 50% of the respondents had at least a high school diploma, these findings give some empirical support to the popular claims about the elitist nature of anti-Americanism in Western Europe and Canada.

The second relevant finding for the countries in this group is the one associated with the religious variables. We find that both atheists and Muslims were more likely to express negative attitudes towards the United States compared to the Christian respondents. The finding about Muslim respondents needs to be qualified; people of Muslim religion form only 1.5% of the sample. But once this caveat is taken into account, the data from the Global Attitudes Survey indicate that residence in the West did not temper the negative attitudes that Muslim respondents revealed in all regions. Respondents of other religion were markedly less inclined to oppose the United States. Finally, no generational effects and no gender effect distinguish the patterns of responses in this group; anti-American attitudes were as likely among the young and the old, as well as among both men and women.

Latin America

The findings for the group of Latin American countries show that anti-American feelings were more likely among people of older generations. As we can see in Figure 5.2, the coefficients associated with the age cohorts progressively increase in size, thus indicating that the likelihood of a dislike of the United States increased with age of the respondent. The close connections and the long legacy of U.S. interventions definitely soured the older Latin Americans' perceptions of the United States, but not those of people who came of age in the late 1990s, in the heyday of the Clinton presidency.

Education, on the other hand, did not differentiate popular perceptions of the United States. Across the levels of educational attainment, the college educated rated the United States only slightly better. A minor but significant effect is associated with gender: male respondents evaluated the United States more favorably that females. Finally, Christian respondents were less likely to have anti-American views than those with no religion and those who followed a religion other than Christianity.

Middle East

We conclude the overview of the regional patterns in the profiles of anti-Americanism with the group of Middle Eastern countries. In the spring and summer of 2002 when the Pew Global Attitudes Survey was administered, respondents with pro-American views were rare in the Middle Eastern region. As we saw in Table 1.4, unfavorable views of the United States were by far the most common response among Middle Eastern respondents. What then is the demographic profile of the minorities who expressed favorable views of the United States?

Clearly, the large coefficient on the indicator that identified Muslim respondents indicates that Christians, who predominantly resided in Lebanon, manifested warmer feelings towards the United States than the Muslim respondents. People of other religion and atheists were also more inclined to see the United States in a negative light than the Christians. But granted this marked distinction, few other differences stand out in the patterns of responses in the Middle East. For the clash of civilizations argument that so strongly delineates a value incompatibility between the Islamic world and the countries in the West, this result would suggest that the rejection of the United States among Muslim respondents trumped all other considerations that might be channeled through education or age effects.

In particular, we find that negative views of the United States were equally likely among women and men and among the uneducated as among the educated. Only the coefficient associated with the respondents with college education barely reaches statistical significance. Its negative sign would suggest that the people with college education were less likely to have negative views of the United States, but the effect was small.

The final element to consider is the effect of generational differences. If anything, the coefficients for the Middle Eastern countries show that the oldest people, above 66 years old, were the most inclined to say that they appreciated the United States. This finding indicates that a reservoir of good feelings towards the United States in these countries is about to evaporate, as respondents of older generation pass away and the negatively disposed younger people reach leadership positions in their countries.

Findings on the Four Causal Hypotheses

The four causal conjectures mentioned earlier point to different possible causal dynamics for the emergence of anti-American views. We now review the empirical record, by focusing first on the indicators pertaining to the four causal hypotheses, that is to say, by analyzing first the C link in Figure 5.1. In the next section, we will revisit the findings on the demographic factors by analyzing the direct and indirect links—the B and C links—implied by the regression models. The results are summarized in Tables 5.1 through 5.4, which show the coefficients and the 95% confidence intervals.

The Information-and-Contacts Hypothesis

Starting from the information-and-contacts hypothesis, which claims that higher levels of information about the United States lead to more pro-American opinions, we observe that the data reveal widespread support for such a conjecture across world regions. As we can see from Table 5.1, the indicator measuring whether the respondents watched news on international channels and the indicator identifying the respondents who had friends and relatives in the United States are both associated with negative, and statistically significant, coefficients. This suggests that respondents with more information about the United States were consistently more likely to hold more positive views. The only exception to the pattern linking information to pro-American views occurs in the Central and South Asian sample, where the respondents following international news channels were more inclined to state negative views of the United States. Exceptions for the contact factor are Eastern Europe and Central and South Asia, where respondents with contacts in the United States did not rate it differently from their less cosmopolitan countrymen.

The findings on the information-and-contacts hypothesis place the lack of connection between the aggregate levels of anti-Americanism and the number of students visas granted to a country—as was shown in Figure 1.1—in a different light. The relevant comparison is not across countries, where we saw no relationship between the number of student visas granted and popular anti-Americanism, but within each country, between the individuals who are directly affected by the flows of information that they receive from friends and relatives in the United States. It appears that the claims Nye (2004) and Glaeser (2005) made from different theoretical perspectives about the importance of information in fostering favorable opinions of countries and groups receive empirical support.

Even more directly, however, these findings may speak of the success stories that innumerable immigrants have been able to build in the United States, the proverbial land of the free and home of the brave. Even in the Middle East, a re-

Table 5.1.   Estimates for the Information-and-Contacts Hypothesis

	b	Lower bound	Upper bound
Africa			
Has contacts in the U.S.	−0.206	−0.236	−0.176
Follows int'l. news channels	−0.176	−0.233	−0.119
East Asia			
Has contacts in the U.S.	−0.246	−0.354	−0.138
Follows int'l. news channels	−0.279	−0.419	−0.140
Latin America			
Has contacts in the U.S.	−0.522	−0.578	−0.466
Follows int'l. news channels	−0.487	−0.544	−0.430
Western democracies			
Has contacts in the U.S.	−0.456	−0.594	−0.317
Follows int'l. news channels	−0.299	−0.348	−0.251
Central/South Asia			
Has contacts in the U.S.	−0.090	−0.188	0.008
Follows int'l. news channels	0.308	0.212	0.404
Eastern Europe			
Has contacts in the U.S.	0.008	−0.023	0.040
Follows int'l. news channels	−0.369	−0.467	−0.270
Middle East			
Has contacts in the U.S.	−0.561	−0.781	−0.340
Follows int'l. news channels	−0.296	−0.332	−0.260

Notes: Entries represent the coefficients, and their 95% lower and upper bounds, of ordered logit models. Confidence intervals are based upon Huber/White variance estimates, clustered by country.

gion where pro-American views were not very common, respondents who were able to obtain direct information from friends and relatives living in the United States had a more positive outlook towards the country. It would appear that when ordinary Middle Easterners correspond with their friends and relatives in the United States, they become aware of their relatives' achievements and of the opportunities that the United States offered them. As people move to the United States and are given a chance that they would not have in their native country, they become the most vivid examples of the opportunities that the United States affords. The "American uncle," a common fixture in popular folklore, does not just bequeath a rich inheritance to his dispossessed nephews overseas, but contributes to the diffusion of the good name of the United States and the American dream.[59]

The Traditional Worldview Hypothesis

The evidence associated with the traditional worldview hypothesis is less clear-cut but generally supportive. On the one hand, in Table 5.2 we observe that respondents who had a positive view of modernity were usually more inclined to reveal positive attitudes towards the United States; the connection between appreciation of the "pace of modern life" and pro-Americanism obtains across regions, which underscores the psychological attraction that the United States exerted as the quintessential embodiment of a modern society.

On the other hand, the evidence associated with the other three indicators relating to this hypothesis is less consistent. The beliefs of those who would like their culture to be protected from foreign influences were not systematically related to the popular perceptions of the United States. In central and South Asia, Eastern Europe, and Latin America the respondents who felt their way of life under threat from foreign influences viewed the United States less favorably than did those who did not perceive such a threat, in line with the traditional worldview hypothesis. It would appear, then, that in these three regions respondents with protectionist feelings about their way of life viewed the United States as a force that would disrupt their cultural mores and extrapolated this view to the country in general.

No such effect was found in the Middle East and in East Asia, where respondents were unlikely to base their perceptions of the United States on concerns about their own way of life; and the conjecture appears to be turned on its head in two regions: Africa and the Western democracies. There, negative and significant coefficients indicate that those who favored measures to protect their own way of life also had positive views of the United States. In Africa and in the Western democracies the effects of favoring cultural protection are the smallest among the four indicators investigated here. Nonetheless, in two regions at opposite ends of the world income distribution, we find that pro-American views were more common among those with cultural protectionist feelings.

We could speculate that the United States was not viewed as a cultural threat but the cultures of other countries might have been. For example, if Western European respondents felt a cultural threat coming from Islamic immigrants, then we would not expect that a desire to protect one's culture from outside influences to translate into anti-American views. This line of reasoning also dovetails with

Table 5.2. Estimates for the Traditional Worldview Hypothesis

	b	Lower bound	Upper bound
Africa			
Favors protecting way of life	−0.082	−0.135	−0.029
Likes pace of modern life	−0.405	−0.469	−0.342
Favors traditional marriage roles	0.193	0.136	0.250
Family planning for the better	−0.205	−0.244	−0.166
East Asia			
Favors protecting way of life	0.031	−0.015	0.078
Likes pace of modern life	−0.612	−0.685	−0.539
Favors traditional marriage roles	−0.048	−0.154	0.058
Family planning for the better	−0.541	−0.618	−0.465
Latin America			
Favors protecting way of life	0.030	0.002	0.059
Likes pace of modern life	−0.360	−0.444	−0.277
Favors traditional marriage roles	0.072	0.018	0.127
Family planning for the better	0.001	−0.059	0.062
Western democracies			
Favors protecting way of life	−0.089	−0.169	−0.008
Likes pace of modern life	−0.487	−0.674	−0.301
Favors traditional marriage roles	−0.157	−0.275	−0.040
Family planning for the better	−0.100	−0.152	−0.049
Central/South Asia			
Favors protecting way of life	0.170	0.145	0.196
Likes pace of modern life	−0.498	−0.673	−0.324
Favors traditional marriage roles	0.263	0.175	0.351
Family planning for the better	−0.472	−0.563	−0.381
Eastern Europe			
Favors protecting way of life	0.227	0.199	0.256
Likes pace of modern life	−0.516	−0.578	−0.454
Favors traditional marriage roles	−0.048	−0.107	0.012
Family planning for the better	−0.007	−0.087	0.074
Middle East			
Favors protecting way of life	−0.071	−0.235	0.093
Likes pace of modern life	−0.526	−0.767	−0.285
Favors traditional marriage roles	0.103	−0.155	0.362
Family planning for the better	−0.303	−0.415	−0.191

Notes: Entries represent the coefficients, and their 95% lower and upper bounds, of ordered logit models. Confidence intervals are based upon Huber/White variance estimates, clustered by country.

the effect of high levels of education reported in Figure 5.2 for the group of industrial democracies, if we accept that the highly educated were more likely to have cosmopolitan worldviews. This interpretation qualifies several anecdotes that depict concerns over nefarious consequences of American popular culture, as illustrated by Sophie Meunier (2007) in the French case, and locates them at the elite level, not at the level of the mass public.

In general, respondents wary of the empowerment of women in modern society manifested colder attitudes towards the United States than did respondents supportive of gender equality in the household and in the workplace. Support for traditional marriage roles was systematically associated with negative views of the United States in Africa, Central and South Asia, and Latin America; while the belief that family planning or birth control had been "a change for the better" was linked to more positive perceptions of the United States in Africa, Central and South Asia, East Asia, the Middle East, and in the Western democracies.

In all other cases, no relationship was found between the four indicators and anti-Americanism; with only one, puzzling, exception. The only instance in which belief that "women should stay home and raise children while husbands provide for the family" was systematically related to *pro*-American views was in Western Europe and Canada. From this finding I deduce that social conservatives in Western Europe and Canada saw the United States in a more positive view than did their more liberal compatriots, as if they were looking to the puritan side of the United States to be a bulwark against the far-reaching consequences of the dreaded sexual revolution. In other words, this suggests that Canadians and Western Europeans viewed the United States as a more conservative society. The mixed reactions that the United States generates in different societal and cultural contexts on issues of gender equality are yet another powerful example of how the multifaceted nature of the United States shatters simple generalizations and allows for the coexistence of contradictory perceptions in which the United States is retrograde for some and excessive for others.

The Antimarket Hypothesis

The third hypothesis posits a connection between antimarket views and anti-American attitudes. Of the two indicators selected to identify respondents holding such beliefs, only the one measuring acceptance of market outcomes even in the face of income disparities is consistently associated with the popular dispositions towards the United States. People who expressed a preference for equity over efficiency, by disagreeing that the market makes people better off in general despite the inequalities it engenders, tended to be more inclined to distance themselves from the United States. This result obtains in all regions but East Asia.

On the other hand, the second indicator for the antimarket worldview—the survey item measuring a fatalist outlook on life—is usually uncorrelated with anti-Americanism. In two of the seven regions, fatalist respondents had more negative attitudes towards the United States—Central and South Asia and the Western democracies. Again, the African sample yields surprising results: the negative and significant coefficient estimated in the African region indicates that pro-American views were associated with a fatalistic attitude to life. If we consider the wide-

Table 5.3.   Estimates for the Antimarket Worldview Hypothesis

	b	Lower bound	Upper bound
Africa			
Approves of market	−0.178	−0.207	−0.149
Fatalist	−0.064	−0.089	−0.040
East Asia			
Approves of market	−0.048	−0.175	0.079
Fatalist	0.029	−0.027	0.084
Latin America			
Approves of market	−0.191	−0.252	−0.130
Fatalist	0.039	−0.002	0.080
Western democracies			
Approves of market	−0.367	−0.414	−0.321
Fatalist	0.109	0.043	0.175
Central/South Asia			
Approves of market	−0.081	−0.120	−0.042
Fatalist	0.107	0.075	0.138
Eastern Europe			
Approves of market	−0.282	−0.329	−0.235
Fatalist	0.012	−0.040	0.063
Middle East			
Approves of market	−0.454	−0.666	−0.243
Fatalist	0.018	−0.017	0.053

Notes: Entries represent the coefficients, and their 95% lower and upper bounds, of ordered logit models. Confidence intervals are based upon Huber/White variance estimates, clustered by country.

spread approval of the United States that was recorded among African respondents, this finding could indicate that, in this region where poverty, war and disease have caused so much suffering, the United States was seen as an image of hope when all hope was lost. Like the two protagonists in Samuel Beckett's famous play who dream of an unfathomable knight who will terminate their plight, Africa is "waiting for Godot."

The Scapegoat Hypothesis

Last, we analyze the evidence for the scapegoat hypothesis in Table 5.4. In this conjecture, respondents unsatisfied with the state of affairs in their countries or globally are expected to be more likely to transfer that dissatisfaction onto the United States. This process uniformly holds across regions with respect to the dissatisfaction about the state of world affairs. Respondents who were "satisfied with the way things were going in the world" were more favorably disposed to the United States. Conversely, those who did not approve of the status of world affairs were more likely to dislike the United States. The relevance of America to world politics in the popular perception is clearly reflected in these findings. Nowhere was this result more prominent than among the Middle Eastern respondents, who, as the large size of the coefficient indicates, placed great weight on world affairs in their evaluations of the United States.

The domestic politics side of the scapegoat hypothesis yields less consistent results. On the one hand, we find that recourse to blaming the United States for an unsatisfactory state of affairs in one's own country appeared in Central and South Asia, East Asia, Eastern Europe, and in the Western democracies. In all of these regions, the negative coefficient on the indicator was significant, which indicates that these respondents were systematically more likely to view the United States in a positive light than respondents who thought well of their own countries' conditions.

The dynamics of blaming the United States, however, were reversed in the Middle East and in Africa. In those two regions, perceptions of the United States were more negative among respondents who felt that things were going fine in their countries. As if they were attuned to a policy discourse coming from their countries' ruling elites, in Africa and the Middle East the image of the United States did not fare well among those who approved of their leaders' governing performance. The internal critics, those dissatisfied with their countries' conditions, on the other hand, viewed the United States more favorably, as if they found in the United States an example and a model to strive to.

Table 5.4.   Estimates for the Scapegoat Hypothesis

	b	Lower bound	Upper bound
Africa			
Satisfied with country conditions	0.102	0.068	0.137
Satisfied with world affairs	−0.437	−0.481	−0.394
East Asia			
Satisfied with country conditions	−0.305	−0.408	−0.203
Satisfied with world affairs	−0.397	−0.538	−0.257
Latin America			
Satisfied with country conditions	−0.016	−0.109	0.078
Satisfied with world affairs	−0.432	−0.623	−0.242
Western democracies			
Satisfied with country conditions	−0.342	−0.419	−0.264
Satisfied with world affairs	−0.448	−0.684	−0.212
Central/South Asia			
Satisfied with country conditions	−0.070	−0.136	−0.004
Satisfied with world affairs	−0.161	−0.220	−0.102
Eastern Europe			
Satisfied with country conditions	−0.231	−0.298	−0.164
Satisfied with world affairs	−0.464	−0.587	−0.340
Middle East			
Satisfied with country conditions	0.317	0.242	0.393
Satisfied with world affairs	−1.033	−1.346	−0.720

Notes: Entries represent the coefficients, and their 95% lower and upper bounds, of ordered logit models. Confidence intervals are based upon Huber/White variance estimates, clustered by country.

In the Middle East, where the dislike of the United States is so widespread, we find that a powerful syndrome frames the mental processes that generate negative opinions of the United States: a sense of deep dissatisfaction with world affairs coupled with the sense that nothing is wrong with one's country.

The Demographic Factors Revisited

What can we learn about the motivations that lead men or women, the young or the old to formulate negative opinions about the United States? In Figure 5.2, we reviewed the *direct* connection between four demographic features—gender, age, education, and religion—and attitudes towards the United States. These four factors affected the patterns of responses differently across regions, which again is indicative of the heterogeneous nature of the phenomenon of anti-Americanism. What we now investigate is whether we can glean from the regression models some additional information about the motivations of survey respondents. To do so, we compare the results presented in Figure 5.2 with the results obtained in the models that include the variables for the causal conjectures. Should any of the causal variables act as the intervening pathway linking demographic factors to the perception of the United States, we would then observe that the associations presented in Figure 5.2 should be substantially reduced. Can we then make claims about the various mechanisms that lead people to form negative opinions of the United States?

As I report in detail in the on-line Appendix, the comparison of all the results across models specifications shows that the coefficients on the demographic factors remain nearly always stable across specifications. Considering the large number of comparisons involved—five models per region—the stability in the coefficients strongly suggests that a large array of reasons animated the popular reactions to the United States, above and beyond the four pathways singled out in this study.

If the regression models do not pinpoint any overriding mechanism, we are then left to conclude that the nature of anti-American sentiments cannot be easily subsumed into any preordained typology that combines basic demographic features with a set of motivations. The large numbers of Muslim respondents who expressed anti-American sentiments, for example, did not simply feel victimized by American foreign policy, or alienated by the modernity of its society, or manipulated by the lack of information. They felt all of that, to different degrees in different regions, but also much else. For any single individual, any of these motivations may have mattered, as the findings on the causal variables clearly indicated, but in the aggregate none gained preeminence.

What do these findings amount to? In the flurry of results and coefficients, two main findings emerge: first, the empirical analyses have shown that the characteristics of the respondents who were more likely to harbor negative feelings towards the United States differed across regions. Thus, the quest for the anti-American version of the "soccer moms" and the "NASCAR dads" that so much intrigue the readers of opinion polls inside the Washington Beltway leaves us with a paltry catch. The anti-American respondent can be either male or female, is more likely to be older in Eastern Europe and Latin America and younger in East Asia, and of Muslim religion, but can have low or high levels of educational attainment. Hence, in the face of what sometimes seems to be a U.S. government belief that there is a single policy problem or a single policy response regarding anti-Americanism, these findings remind us that simple generalizations rarely capture the multifarious responses to the image of the United States and are a poor recipe for any strategy of public diplomacy.

Second, the empirical analyses in this chapter have also shown that the popular perceptions of the United States may be systematically linked to key causal dynamics. However, while all four causal processes investigated here mattered to different degrees in the seven regions, no single causal dynamic could claim the lion's share of the variation in the responses. These two findings again reveal the popular perceptions of the United States as a heterogeneous phenomenon that responds to local context, but they also indicate that popular attitudes towards the United States are not a whimsical reaction impervious to explanation. To different degrees in each region, information, tradition, modernity, and scapegoating affect the psychological and mental processes that give rise to negative attitudes towards the United States.

Of these four processes, dissatisfaction with the state of world affairs appears to be the most prevalent. Blaming the United States for the state of world affairs is as much an acknowledgment of America as arbiter of the current world order as it is a complaint about U.S. foreign policy. At the same time, however, the negative reactions to U.S. foreign policy do not swamp the positive associations that ordinary people establish between the United States and modern life. Beyond the overarching characterization of the United States as the embodiment of modernity, there is the information that ordinary people receive, apart from news media and governmental sources, directly from relatives and friends who have migrated to the United States. That finding speaks to the importance of the communities of immigrants in the American body politic that make the United States seem less alien and less distant to foreigners. But it also speaks to the enduring symbolism of the United States as the land of opportunity.

"Give me your tired, your poor, Your huddled masses yearning to breathe free, The wretched refuse of your teeming shore" are the words that Emma Lazarus penned for the base of the Statue of Liberty.[60] Even in the face of increasing evidence that the American societal model no longer grants superior levels of social mobility (Ferrie, 2005; Solon, 2002), those words, and the opportunity they represent, are a concrete manifestation of the ability to attract that the United States derives from its own unique nature.

Conclusions

The overall pattern of popular anti-Americanism as a multifaceted phenomenon is too loose to be a well-knit ideology and too differentiated to be a cultural syndrome. The general publics surveyed offered overall assessments of the United States that reflected the fundamental experiences of their socialization. At the same time, these publics resorted to systematic elements in their worldviews to express their feelings towards the United States.

Rather than an irrational collection of hatreds, attitudes towards the United States appear to be more predictable and pliable. Modernity, information, and material progress shape the belief systems of ordinary people. All these elements reflect the power of attraction that the United States exerts, but none of these elements may be pronounced enough to allow for straightforward predictions of where any respondent would stand vis-à-vis the United States from knowledge of how he or she would combine specific worldviews, information, and the idiosyncrasies of socialization. The analysis of the sources of anti-American sentiments highlights the fact that the *types* of anti-Americanism identified by Katzenstein and Keohane (2007b) have elusive empirical referents. In the language of Converse's (1964) framework, this finding is another empirical manifestation of a loosely constrained belief system, the belief system that we would expect if we gave credit to the dimensions of America theory which I elaborated in Chapter 2.

CHAPTER SIX

The Sources of the Policy
and Polity Frames

Introduction

Next we shall try to identify some sources of anti-American sentiment by probing the characteristics of the respondents and the political contexts within which they elaborated their opinions in the two samples of data from the 2002 Zogby International Survey and the 2002 Chicago Council on Foreign Relations / German Marshall Fund (CCFR/GMF) survey. From the data analyzed in Chapter 4, we saw that the variation in anti-American sentiment is primarily located at the individual level.[61] What accounts for the patterns of variation in the popular image of the United States is, therefore, the social and political identity of the respondents rather than their country's level of development or its relationship with the United States.

The empirical analyses in this chapter extend the analyses presented in Chapter 4 by including individual- and country-level explanatory variables in the statistical models. The goal is to identify what factors are systematically associated with the propensity to oppose the United States among the mass publics in eight predominantly Islamic countries and in six European countries.[62]

First we will look at how levels of societal and policy-oriented anti-Americanism differed across individuals and across countries. The empirical results presented here illustrate first the individual-level relationships between respondents' identities and patterns of anti-American opinion and, second, the country-level patterns. We will see that attitudes towards the United States systematically varied with respect to levels of information, political attentiveness, and political ideology and that those elements affected the patterns of responses in the two dimensions of the United States that are being investigated: its polity and its policies.

Individual-level Determinants of Anti-Americanism

Starting from the group of Islamic countries in South Asia and the Middle East, the analysis centers on religious affiliation and access to sources of information, beside standard demographic factors such as gender, marital status, and age. While all the countries included in this chapter, with the exception of Lebanon, are predominantly Islamic, it is worth investigating whether the small fractions of individuals who are not Muslim articulated more positive views than those who are. An empirical finding of such nature would replicate, from data measured at the individual level, the aggregate findings on anti-American proneness of Muslims reported in Chapter 1 and, for a different sample of countries, in Chapter 5.

The second set of individual factors is information access: respondents were asked whether they had Internet access, whether they had satellite television, how many newspapers they read, and how many languages they spoke beyond their mother tongue. Each of these indicators captures a different component of respondents' political awareness, under the assumption that the more one reads or watches television, the more likely one is to be exposed to streams of political communication. But the indicators also distinguish between the traditional informational form of the newspaper and the globalized information society exemplified in satellite television and the Internet.

In what seems a direct application of Marshall McLuhan's famous dictum, several scholars have started to argue that the medium through which information is diffused is affecting the dynamics of public opinion formation in the Middle East (Eickelman and Anderson, 2003). Marc Lynch (2003a), for example, traces the transformation of Arab public discourse to the emergence of new media outlets that bypass and undermine state control over information. In an analogous way, Fatema Mernissi (2002, ix–xxi) emphasizes how information technology has the potential to revive the notions of personal opinion and innovation in the Islamic tradition and make them familiar to large portions of the public. Political views previously curtailed receive prime time, often in a style of broadcasting that is American in its inspiration (Ayish, 2001). The political themes that have occupied center stage on the satellite television networks, from the issues of democracy and economic reform to the Palestinian cause and the sanctions and bombing campaigns in Iraq, often carry an intense or outrageous anti-American rhetoric (Lynch, 2003a). Some scholars remain skeptical of the connection between new media diffusion and the emergence of a public sphere; they emphasize that political discourse is shaped more by informal communication in the mosque, the coffeehouses, or the marketplace than by the information flows coming out of satellites and Internet sites (Fandy, 2000). But it behooves us to see whether the balance between form and content of information translates into different patterns of anti-American sentiment on the polity and policy dimensions.

For the group of European countries, four sets of factors are considered: (a) the demographic identifiers of gender and age, (b) levels of education and political ideology, (c) the degree of political knowledge, and (d) a cluster of indicators that specify individual beliefs about the nature of U.S. society and the U.S. political system. These variables not only portray the individuals who are more likely to hold the United States in a negative light but they also distinguish between deeply held factors such as ideological orientation and generational socializing events, on the one hand, and the contingent political considerations that are brought to bear on the process of opinion formation, on the other.

Much interest has been accorded to the diatribe that the conservative commentator Robert Kagan (2003) started about the consequences of power differentials on the collective psyches of the European publics. In Kagan's view, what one thinks of the United States follows from what one thinks of military power in general and U.S. military power in particular, which he elevates to the most sublime feature of the United States from which everything else follows. Other considerations, of course, plausibly shape people's attitudes. Two are evaluated in the empirical analyses that follow: the perception of a commonality of strategic interests beyond the power gaps between the United States and the other members of the transatlantic alliance, and the perception of the role that the United States plays in assisting poor nations through aid.

Political considerations are just one of the possible influences on the popular perception of the United States in Europe. Of these alternative sources, political ideology is the one most often emphasized among European commentators. Sergio Fabbrini (2002, 3), for example, points out that "in (continental) Europe, anti-Americanism seems to be one of the few public philosophies that can unite large sections of the left, the right and the Catholic Church." The domestic ideological bases of the Europeans' perception of the United States would discount, in Fabbrini's assessment, the effects that changes in U.S. foreign policies could have on the image of the United States there. But ideologies can also clarify the extent to which favorable predispositions towards markets and capitalism promote favorable perceptions of the United States, the market and capitalist society *par excellence*.

Country-level Determinants of Anti-Americanism

Differences in individual characteristics can account for part of the variation in anti-American opinion across countries. For example, if younger people are more likely to express positive views of the United States, countries with large cohorts of younger people would be expected to be more pro-American as well. But country differences exist beyond the societal and demographic compositions of their publics, and they reflect distinct processes of opinion formation and the broader political contexts that exist in each country.

This chapter reports the impact of three broad clusters of factors. First, from the venerable tradition of modernization theory comes the conjecture that the more two societies interact and have contacts at the economic and cultural level, the more a sense of "fellow-feeling" between individuals in those societies is likely to emerge (Dore, 1984, 417). Thus, the more the United States trades, invests, and grants visas for a country's students, the more that country's residents will be prone to express positive views of the United States.

The second set of relational variables deals with the diplomatic and military relationships countries have with the United States. While none in the group of Islamic countries being investigated shares a formal alliance with the United States, their levels of military and diplomatic cooperation with America vary sharply. Saudi Arabia and Kuwait host U.S. troops, Egypt receives substantial amounts of U.S. military aid, and Iran is in an antagonistic relationship with the United States. Friendlier relations on the diplomatic or military front might be expected to translate into a closer affinity, primarily at the levels of the political elites, who might see a congruence of interests with the United States. It is more debatable whether these closer connections would necessarily trickle down to the level of the mass publics and be reflected in opinion surveys.

Third, beyond the political, military, and economic conditions that define the position of a country with respect to the United States, publics' attitudes might be shaped by the patterns of elite discourse, how political elites frame the discourse about the United States. To the extent that a public is inattentive to political matters, especially foreign relations, its assessment of the United States is likely to hinge upon the messages from that country's elites. Those messages define what considerations are likely to be salient in people's minds and thus inform their survey responses. This expectation primarily derives from Zaller's (1992) thesis on the "elite domination" of public opinion.

Findings on Respondents' Identities

The discussion of the empirical findings focuses on the regression coefficients, the parameters that summarize how much the variables influence the individual-level propensity to oppose the United States. In the current specification, each of those coefficients represents the expected difference in anti-American opinion between two respondents who differ by one unit in their reaction to the explanatory variable, net of any country effect.[63] The sign of these effects is easily interpreted: a positive coefficient indicates that as a variable's values increase, the levels of anti-Americanism increase, and a negative sign shows that a variable is associated with a decrease in the respondent's hostility towards the United States. As was the case for the results in Chapter 3, I present the results using graphical representations of the coefficients and their confidence intervals.

The Islamic Countries

Starting with the model predicting attitudes towards American culture and society, the upper panel of Figure 6.1, we observe that several variables have a significant impact on the levels of polity anti-Americanism: marital status, age, non-Muslim identity, the Internet, satellite television, and languages.[64] The three remaining explanatory variables—male gender, city dweller, and newspapers read—fail to attain confidence intervals distinct from 0 even with an 80% probability.[65]

Respondents who are not married, young, non-Muslim, have access to the Internet and satellite tv, and who speak foreign languages were more likely to articulate positive views of U.S. culture and society. These results indicate that a generational effect and an information effect underlie the patterns of responses, but in terms of substantive impact, all these factors are overshadowed by the effects of Muslim/non-Muslim identity. With a coefficient as large in absolute terms as -2.3, the non-Muslim minorities in the sample were overwhelmingly more likely to endorse the political and cultural ideals of the United States than were the Muslim respondents. The size of the effect associated with a non-Muslim identity appears in all its prominence if we observe that, for a highly informed respondent with Internet access, satellite tv, and who speaks one foreign language, the latent propensity to oppose American culture and society decreases about half a point, an effect about 80% smaller than the one associated with the non-Muslim variable.[66]

Sociocultural anti-Americanism

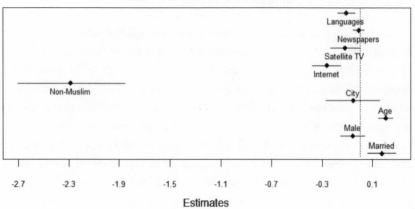

Policy anti-Americanism

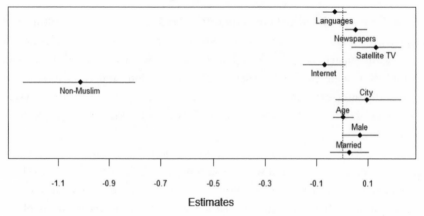

Figure 6.1. Individual-level Sources of Anti-Americanism among Islamic Publics

Notes: The dark dots represent the regression coefficients, and the lines represent the 95% confidence intervals. For the estimation procedure, see the on-line Appendix. Data analysis is based on the Zogby International Ten Nation Impressions of America Poll (2002).

Whether this significance of non-Muslim identity is driven by a reduced sense of cultural distance with the United States or by the fact that the non-Muslim minorities are also different on other counts, such as wealth and education, variables not explicitly included in the models, is not possible to adjudicate on the basis of the individual characteristics that were measured in the Zogby International survey. Indeed, the findings on the country variances, which are reported in the on-line Appendix, show that a considerable part of the individual-level variation remains unaccounted for. Overall, the percentage of the variance at the respondent level explained by the nine explanatory variables is about 21%.[67]

When we shift our attention to the policy dimension, the bottom panel of Figure 6.1, a different pattern emerges. The amount of variation explained in terms of the individual characteristics of the respondents is smaller, about 7%. Three variables turn out to have a significant impact on policy anti-Americanism, namely non-Muslim, satellite tv, and newspapers, while the gender and Internet variables are only significant at the 90% level. Thus, individuals who are Muslim, keep well informed with satellite television and newspapers, and, possibly, are also male are more likely to have negative views of U.S. policies. We still find an informational dynamic underlying attitudes towards the United States, but with a reversal in its effect. While information, from the newer media in particular, helped inspire positive views about the United States as a society and political system, information, through both images and written words, also led to the formation of more negative views about U.S. policies. The combination of the findings on the polity and policy frames in Figure 6.1 indicates that the individuals more likely to experience divergent views about the United States were those who have high levels of information.

These findings also show that the non-Muslim minorities in eight countries in the Middle East and South Asia were more likely than their Muslim countrymen to form consistently positive views of the United States, regardless of whether the frame of reference was American culture and society or American policies. This result apparently corroborates the claims derived from Samuel Huntington's (1996) clash of civilizations thesis: the normative divide between the United States and the West seeps into the perceptions that ordinary people have of the United States and makes those who have a Muslim identity less disposed towards the United States. But this is as much supporting evidence for the clash of civilizations argument as can be squeezed from these findings. For, though non-Muslims are keener on the United States, it does not follow from the empirical data that Muslims are opposed to all dimensions of it.

The empirical record shows that anti-Americanism is not a unified and undifferentiated phenomenon. People exposed to flows of information—and Muslims in particular—formed contradictory views of the United States: more positive with respect to polity and less so with respect to policies. The relationship between opinions towards the United States and the respondents' attentiveness to the political and social conditions of their own societies challenges the view of all those who have depicted anti-Americanism as a syndrome impervious to any form of outside influence (D'Souza, 2002; Krauthammer, 2003; Revel, 2003). It also challenges the view of those who, like Barry Rubin (2002, 83) and Daniel Pipes (2002), have argued that Arab public opinion responds favorably to the United States only when confronted with manifestations of sheer power.

This multifaceted opinion towards the United States is shaped in part by the communication channels of the new media. As Marc Lynch (2003b, 86) has written, speaking of the flourishing market of Arabic satellite television channels, "these new Arab media increasingly construct the dominant narrative frames through which people understand events." These frames are far from unidirectional and predetermined. The results that emerge from this analysis show that these attentive publics yearn for freedom and progress as they are manifested in the U.S. polity while shunning U.S. power as it has been manifested in U.S. foreign policies. It speaks highly of the achievements and symbolism associated with America's society and political system that they remain a source of attraction even amidst some of the sharpest and most obdurate clashes in U.S. history over interests and policies, those existing in the early years of the twenty-first century between the United States and the countries of the Muslim world.

The European Countries

Figure 6.2 reports the findings for the six European countries in the CCFR/ GMF survey—in the top panel the results for the anti-American feeling thermometer, in the bottom panel the results for the policy frame. The statistical models include eleven explanatory variables capturing features of the demographic, societal, and attitudinal profiles of the European respondents.

In the analysis of the anti-American feeling thermometer, we find that the explanatory variables account for about 9.5% of the variation at the individual level of analysis that was found in the baseline model presented in Figure 4.1. Seven variables have 95% confidence intervals that do not include the value of 0; these are gender, ideology, and the five indicators measuring policy orientations. Three variables—age and the two political knowledge indicators—have coefficients that are different from 0 with a 90% probability. Only education fails to achieve statistical significance even at very low probability levels.

Substantively, it appears that older male respondents with a right-wing ideology consistently reported lower scores on the anti-American feeling thermometer than younger women with leftist political orientations. The magnitude of the effect associated with the political beliefs of the respondents is rather large. On

Anti-American feeling thermometer

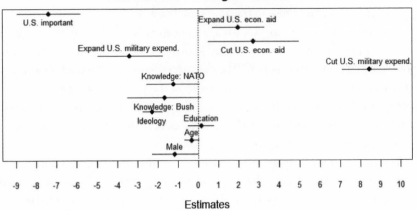

Policy anti-Americanism

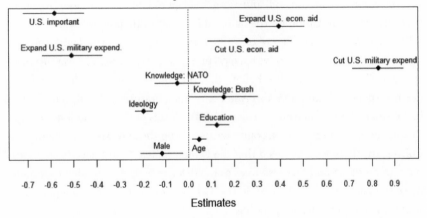

Figure 6.2. Individual-level Sources of Anti-Americanism among European Publics

Notes: The dark dots represent the regression coefficients, and the lines represent the 95% confidence intervals. For the estimation procedure, see the on-line Appendix. Data analysis is based on the the CCFR/GMF Worldviews 2002 survey.

the ideology variable, a 7-point indicator where 1 identifies the extreme left and 7 identifies the extreme right, conservative respondents have anti-American "temperatures" about 10 degrees lower (less opposed) than liberal respondents. The effect of gender and age, on the other hand, is much less pronounced. The models estimate about a 1-point difference between male and female respondents and about a 0.3 decrease in anti-Americanism for any increase on the 6-point age indicator, which amounts to a 1-point difference between respondents in the 55–64 age bracket and those in the 25–34 age bracket.

The findings on the two knowledge indicators show that higher levels of political information—as measured by knowing the identity of the American president and the location of NATO headquarters—are associated with more pro-American views. Thus, while negative views of the United States are as likely to emerge among those with higher levels of education as among the less educated, it appears that the politically attentive were more disposed towards the United States than the politically apathetic.

The last cluster of explanatory variables identifies five foreign policy issues that Europeans might consider when elaborating their views of the United States. These issues capture the publics' attitudes towards three different aspects of U.S. foreign policy and measure the extent to which the United States is seen as a militaristic nation with an oversized defense budget, as a caring nation that distributes economic aid, and as an "indispensable" nation more important than the European Union for the national interests of their countries.

As we can observe in Figure 6.2, all the coefficients associated with these indicators are different from 0 with a 95% probability. Substantively, the survey responses show that those who thought that the United States should cut back its defense spending exhibited anti-American "temperatures" about eight degrees higher than those who were satisfied with the levels of the U.S. defense budget. This is the largest effect in absolute terms among those reported in Figure 6.2. Conversely, those who believed that the United States should have been allocating a greater portion of its resources to the defense budget were about 3.5 points more sympathetic to the United States than the respondents who supported the status quo level of defense spending.

More telling, however, is the fact that when it comes to the support of other nations through economic aid, the United States would be criticized regardless of what course of action it would pursue: both those who believed that the United States should expand its budgetary allocations to foreign aid and those who thought that those allocations should be curtailed had more pronounced anti-American attitudes than the respondents who thought that the level American international aid should be maintained as it was. If we consider that, among the industrialized nations, the United States devotes the smallest percentage of national income to development assistance (Adelman, 2003, 9), we might conjecture that the respondents who would advocate a reduction in U.S. foreign aid are either committed free-marketeers who are skeptical of all types of government intervention in the economy or are committed ideologues who attribute nefarious ulterior motives even to U.S. efforts to alleviate poverty and underdevelopment.

Finally, the respondents who selected the United States over the European Union as the most vital partner for their country's interests held overall views of the United States that are about 7.3 degrees less anti-American than the views of those who declared that the European Union is either more important than the United States, or as important as the United States, for their country's national interests. The perception of a commonality of interests, in other words, fosters a pro-American attitude among the European publics.

Shifting our attention to the results of the IRT model regarding attitudes towards American policies in the bottom panel of Figure 6.2, the 11 explanatory variables contribute to a 24% reduction in the overall individual-level variation. Of the variables, 10 have coefficients that are different from 0 with a 95% probability, and only the knowledge indicator about NATO does not reach statistical significance.

With two exceptions, all of the variables maintain the same sign they had in the models predicting the responses to the anti-American feeling thermometer. The exceptions are age and the knowledge indicator that identified George W. Bush as president of the United States: both of those variables switch their coefficients from negative to positive. Thus, from the estimates in Figure 6.2, it appears that males of younger age with low levels of education and with right-wing ideology were the most supportive of U.S. policies among the European publics. Conversely, highly educated women of older age and leaning towards the left/ liberal side of the political spectrum were the respondents most likely to hold negative views of American foreign policies.

Of the coefficients on the demographic and political characteristics of the respondents, the one associated with political ideology engenders a substantial shift on the propensity to oppose American foreign policy. European conservatives were much less opposed to U.S. policies than European liberals.[68]

The findings on the two indicators measuring levels of political knowledge unveil a revealing pattern: while the respondents who knew where the NATO headquarters were located are no different—in statistical terms—from their less knowledgeable counterparts, those who knew that George W. Bush was the U.S. president tended to dislike U.S. foreign policies more than those who could not name who was at the helm of the American government. These results, therefore, corroborate the widely debated conjecture that animosity towards President Bush, his diplomatic posture and his personal style, underlay the opposition of the European publics in 2002, rather than a sense of aversion to the United States and its power.

Admittedly, the United States was the sole superpower, the arbiter of international affairs, and the unmatched hegemon during the George H. W. Bush and Clinton administrations as much as it was in 2002, the year of the survey, when President George W. Bush was in office. In 1998, Secretary of State Madeleine Albright called the United States "the indispensable nation . . . [that] see[s] further into the future," a statement to which conservative commentators wholeheartedly subscribe (see for example Kagan, 2002–2003, 136).[69] Indeed, Samuel Huntington (1999, 42) had already in 1999 identified an emerging trend of estrangement in which, "in the eyes of many countries [the United States] is becoming the rogue superpower." Similarly, in an overview of the perceptions of the United States in the immediate aftermath of the Kosovo war, François Heisbourg (1999–2000) discussed two referential frames that have gained widespread currency since George W. Bush acceded to power: the "trigger-happy sheriff" and again the "rogue state." At the popular level, however, the inattentive members of a foreign public, who might have believed that they were still in the heyday of the Clinton presidency, appear to have taken a more forgiving stance towards U.S. foreign policies than those who followed international events closely enough to know who had won the U.S. presidential election in the year 2000. In other words, the more informed public detected a change in the foreign policy posture of the United States after George W. Bush's inauguration and expressed its own displeasure with that change.

The coefficient on the survey item identifying the respondents who would have liked the U.S. defense budget to be reduced is positive and, as was the case in the models analyzing the anti-American feeling thermometer, the largest in absolute terms. Respondents who advocated an expansion of the defense budget, on the other hand, came to the opposite conclusion and were more inclined to see the course of U.S. foreign policy in a positive light.

Again, the results in Figure 6.2 indicate that regardless of whether they thought that U.S. foreign aid needed to be expanded or curtailed, the European publics tended to dislike U.S. foreign policy more than the respondents who are satisfied with the current status of U.S. economic assistance.

Finally, the perception of a congruence of interests between the United States and the respondent's own nation is associated with a more favorable attitude towards American foreign policy. The negative coefficient on this survey item indicates that the respondents who considered the United States more important for their country's vital interests than the European Union were more inclined to appreciate U.S. foreign policy than those who thought otherwise.

In sum, these findings show how the perception of the United States in 2002 was shaped by a cluster of factors in which the respondents' political stance about military force, their evaluation of their countries' interests, and their attentiveness to political affairs combined with their fundamental political beliefs and the processes of socialization of their generation. In this cluster, the political ideology of the respondents played a prominent role: liberal left-wing respondents were systematically and consistently more likely to be critical of the United States on issues of both polity and policies.

This finding gives credence to the conjectures of those who have emphasized that European anti-Americanism might be rooted in ideological worldviews rather than in fleeting reactions to the current international role of the United States (Fabbrini, 2002, 3). It also indicates that the left's concerns about the social consequences of markets and capitalism are an essential component of the negative attitudes towards the United States. The arguments of conservative commentators, such as Russell Berman (2004) and Jean-François Revel (2003), who have stressed the inherently anti-market and anti-capitalist mind frame of the "America bashers" among the European elites, might appear vindicated by these results, but they are only partly so. The analysis of the survey data from the CCFR/GMF poll fails to uncover the widespread anti-American animosity that those same commentators have imputed to the European left. Extreme left-wing positions were endorsed by not more than 2.2% of the entire sample of respondents, while the bulk of the European publics located themselves somewhere between moderately conservative and moderately liberal in the political space, which translates into mild positions about the United States as well.

The findings in Figure 6.2 also show the importance of a generational effect: when analyzing *overall* attitudes towards the United States among European respondents, we find that the older generations were more inclined to see the United States in a positive light, whereas when they were evaluating American foreign policy, people from the older generations were more inclined to criticize the policies of the Bush adminstration. If any respondents experienced ambivalent feelings about the United States, it was the World War II generation and the baby boomers born in the 1950s. Socialized to a conception of the United States as the idealistic and internationalist country of the Marshall Plan and the anti-fascist struggle, these respondents still held fond perceptions of the United States despite their growing concerns about the diplomatic postures of the Bush administration. The sign reversal on the coefficients associated with the age variable in the two groups of models, in other words, is indicative of the resilience of the overall image of the United States amidst dissatisfaction about the policy choices of one administration.

Finally, the question of American military power, its desirability and its efficacy, emerges from the empirical patterns as a dividing issue among the European publics. The findings on the indicators measuring the attitudes towards the size of the American defense budget imply that the perception of the United States as a nation that does not eschew military solutions to international issues hurts its overall image in Europe. Different conceptions about the proper conduct of international affairs and the role that military force should play therein underlie the pro- or anti-American attitudes of the European publics.

At first glance, it would appear that the empirical evidence supports the polemical distinction that Robert Kagan (2003) has drawn between "martial" Americans and "effeminate" Europeans, the former conscious of their power and willing to use it and the latter shorn of any power and conspiring to thwart the United States in use of its own. No less than 38% of the European respondents would have approved of a reduction in U.S. defense spending and manifested their displeasure with the United States and what it accomplishes on the international arena.

At the same time, however, 21% of the respondents would have supported an expansion of the U.S. defense budget, and 41% were content with the size of military allocations. Even though the United States was "poised to spend more on defense in 2003 than the next 15–20 biggest spenders combined" (Brooks and Wohlforth, 2002, 21), about 62% in the European publics felt comfortable with the United States and its power and manifested these feelings in their patterns of survey responses. In spite of a sizeable minority in the European publics that hoped to see a less militaristic United States, the majority of the European respondents did not feel alienated or threatened by the overwhelming power of the United States.

The empirical record therefore challenges the idea that power disparities between the United States and Europe translate into a predictable pattern of opinion about the legitimacy and viability of military force. By mechanically inferring psychological stances about military power from the distribution of power itself, Kagan (2003) elevates a political distinction about the centrality of military force in international affairs to the status of an identity defining feature of the American and European political cultures. But in so doing he fails to recognize that ordinary people all over Europe usually feel warmly towards the United States regardless of the size of any countries' military capabilities. By proclaiming, "When the United States was weak, it practiced the strategies of indirection, the strategies of weakness; now that the United States is powerful, it behaves as powerful nations do," Kagan (2003, 10–11) unwittingly denies the notion that the United States and its power might be different, and better, than the power of another nation.

The empirical analysis in this chapter indicates that most Europeans rejected the image of the United States as a one-dimensional nation defined by its military power. Instead, they viewed the United States through intellectual lenses that were primarily shaped by their ideological predispositions, the defining events of their socialization, and their political attentiveness. In the end, there is more to the relationship between the United States and Europe than the psychologies of power and weakness Kagan asserts.

Findings on Country Factors

The models discussed in this chapter investigate a second feature of the process of opinion formation: the effects of the political and economic contexts within which the respondents elaborated their views of the United States. In the discussion of the results in Chapter 4, we saw how the average levels of anti-American sentiment fluctuated across countries. The task of the models in this chapter, then, is to uncover the extent to which such variation can be accounted for by some systematic factors that differentiate countries from each other.[70]

A common element runs through these results: the weakness of the relationships.[71] None of the coefficients has a 95% confidence interval that does not include the value of zero. Underscoring the lack of any strong evidence of country effects, only one of those coefficients is distinct from zero with a 90% probability: the one measuring the effects of the congruence in the voting patterns at the United Nations on the levels of societal and cultural anti-Americanism in the Islamic publics. And only one has an 80% confidence interval distinct from zero: the one measuring the effects of pro-American elite discourse on the policy anti-Americanism in the Islamic publics.

From these findings, then, it would appear that military, economic, and cultural engagement with the United States is not by itself sufficient to create a political context immune to anti-Americanism. Of the two significant relations, the first indicates that in 2002 ordinary people in the Islamic world were more likely to view U.S. culture and society in a negative light if they lived in countries that more often endorsed U.S. positions in the General Assembly of the United Nations over the five-year period from 1997 to 2001 than in countries that systematically voted against U.S. positions. The second statistically significant finding is that popular opposition to U.S. policies was less likely in countries where publics were exposed to a pro-American elite discourse. Interestingly, the insignificant coefficient in the model analyzing societal and cultural anti-Americanism indi-

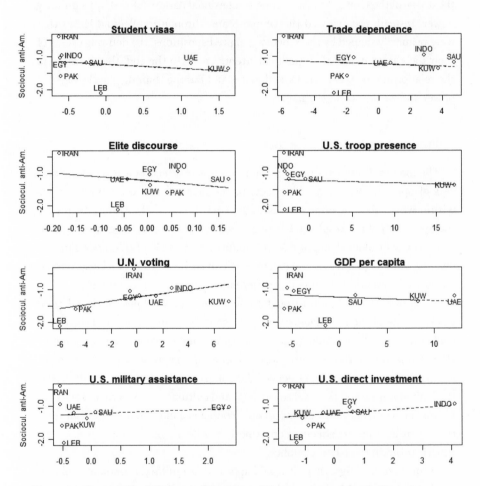

Figure 6.3. Country-level Sources of Anti-Americanism among Islamic Societies

Notes: Each panel represents the mean expected value of a given form of anti-Americanism plotted against a given (mean-centered) country-level variable, with a regression line superimposed. For the estimation procedure and the measurement of the country-level variables, see the on-line Appendix. Data analysis is based on the Zogby International Ten Nation Impressions of America Poll.

cates that more favorable elite discourse translated into more positive attitudes towards U.S. policies, but it is ineffectual with respect to attitudes towards American culture and society.[72]

In order to have a clearer sense of how country-level variables are related to the average level of anti-Americanism, Figure 6.3 shows the country mean levels in anti-American sentiment against the country-level explanatory variables. The broken lines on the plots represent a bivariate regression line.[73]

The flat regression lines in most of the panels corroborate the findings from the statistical models: no single relational measure beyond the two just mentioned

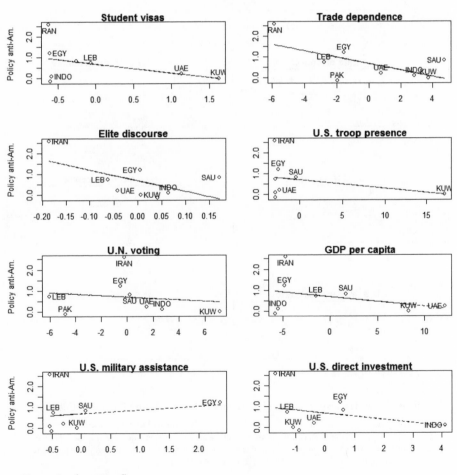

Figure 6.3. (continued)

differentiates the patterns of anti-American opinion across countries. On the one hand, Iran stands out as a country with hardly any U.S. contacts of a military, economic, or cultural nature and with high levels of anti-Americanism. Indeed, the plots offer a portrayal of the antagonistic relationship that exists between Iran and the United States. On the other, Lebanon exhibits relatively low levels

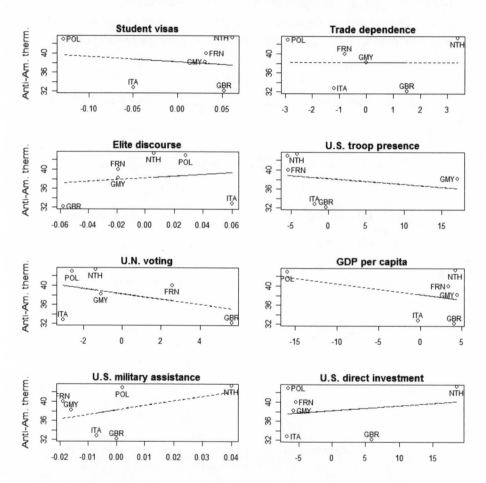

Figure 6.4. Country-level Sources of Anti-Americanism among European Societies

Notes: Each panel represents the mean expected value of a given form of anti-Americanism plotted against a given (mean-centered) country-level variable, with a regression line superimposed. For the estimation procedure and the measurement of the country-level variables, see the on-line Appendix. Data analysis is based on the CCFR/GMF Worldviews 2002 survey.

of anti-Americanism, mostly because of the demographic composition of its population, which confounds effects of other relational variables.

In Figure 6.3 (third row first column), we see that the positive relationship between sociocultural anti-Americanism and voting congruence at the United Nations is generated by the position of Lebanon and Pakistan, two countries that have not toed the U.S. line at the United Nations. Idiosyncratic factors rather than any systematic mechanism enter into this finding. In the upper right corner panel of Figure 6.3, we see that the levels of trade dependence with the United

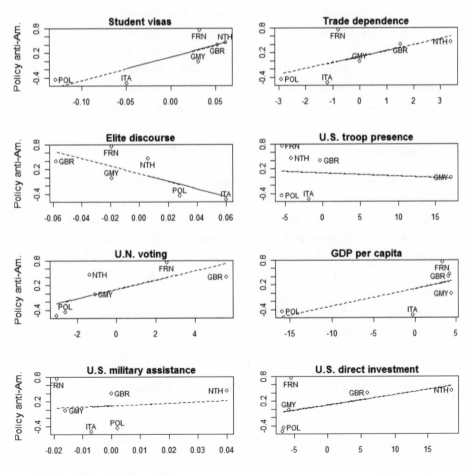

Figure 6.4. (continued)

States are negatively associated with lower levels of popular opposition to American foreign policies.

Figure 6.4 focuses on the group of six European countries. While no systematic relation exists between the country-level variables and the anti-American feeling thermometer, it would seem that some relation may exist with respect to policy anti-Americanism. Cultural contacts as measured by the number of student visas granted, political affinity as measured by the congruence of the voting at the United Nations, and economic interdependence as measured by the levels of bilateral trade are all associated with increased popular opposition to U.S. policies. While such connections should not be overemphasized, given the weak statistical relations, it would seem that the general public voiced open criticism of U.S. policies in countries that interacted closely with the United States. On the other hand, popular approval of American foreign policy seems to have been prevalent in countries such as Italy and Poland where the elites articulated a more predominantly pro-American discourse than is the case in the United Kingdom and France, where elite discourse was less enthusiastic about the United States.

Conclusions

Levels of information, political attentiveness, generational effects, and political ideology constitute some of the basic elements that shape individuals' perceptions of the United States. But, as the analysis has shown, these elements do not necessarily operate consistently across the two dimensions of the United States under investigation: the polity and the policies.

In the group of predominantly Islamic countries, in 2002 non-Muslim minorities held the friendliest opinions of what the United States stood for and what the United States was doing in the international arena, as Huntington's (1996) clash of civilizations thesis would expect. But, the converse empirical statement is not supported by the empirical record: Muslim respondents are not systematically opposed to all aspects of the United States. The survey responses in the Zogby International data instead show that respondents with high levels of information elaborate conflicting views about the United States. The appreciation of the American political and societal ideals coexists in the minds of the highly informed with a rejection of America's foreign policy choices in the Middle Eastern political arena.

The fact that political information mediates the dynamics of opinion formation contradicts the basic explanatory thrust of the clash of civilizations thesis:

the cultural incompatibility of Islam and the West. The results presented in this chapter attribute a key relevance to the political processes of persuasion, diplomacy, and mediation that are channeled through media outlets. The inverse relationship between a pro-American elite discourse and the opposition to American policies offers additional evidence that popular anti-Americanism in the lands of the Prophet Muhammad is not an expression of a longstanding hatred of the United States but a contingent phenomenon that responds to politics more than it does to any forms of civilizational determinism.

The empirical findings for the group of European countries show how the patterns of opinions about the United States are related to fundamental processes of political socialization. We found that political ideology, on the one hand, and common generational experiences, on the other, framed the perspectives through which ordinary citizens viewed the United States. Left-wing respondents, more skeptical of the virtues of capitalism and more concerned about the societal consequences of market competition, saw the United States in a more negative light than did conservative respondents. This finding highlights the importance of domestic ideological sources of anti-American sentiment above and beyond the psychological reactions to the growing unfettered power of the United States.

Moreover, while the perception of the United States as a militaristic power alienated the general publics from the United States, anti-Americanism remained a minority position across Europe. Even when European respondents manifested their displeasure at the diplomatic posture of the George W. Bush administration, as was the case among the more informed public and the older generations, they limited their criticism to the course of American policies while continuing to express warmer feelings towards the United States as a polity and a symbol.

In sum, given the survey items collected in the Zogby International and the CCFR/GMF polls, empirical analysis has revealed a variety of explanatory factors across the two groups of countries under investigation. A common element emerges from this investigation: the United States enters into the ideational worlds of foreign publics as an ideal and an aspiration. Such a perception mediates the popular image of U.S. international political behavior and gives substance to the notion of American exceptionalism in the court of world opinion.

PART IV / Persistence

Part IV / Perception

CHAPTER SEVEN

Anti-Americanism beyond 2002

Introduction

The wide array of empirical evidence presented here mounts a strong challenge to the idea of an anti-American syndrome in the American world order. The perceptions of the United States among ordinary people are multifaceted, not an endemic cultural opposition. When Timothy Garton Ash (2004, 230) writes that we should always challenge claims made in name of *the* Americans or *the* Europeans by asking "*Which* Americans? *Which* Europeans?," he raises a point that has received plenty of empirical support in the analyses presented here.

Still, times might be changing. What was true in 2002 before the Iraq war might not be true in its aftermath. Perhaps the crisis over Iraq and the broader campaign against terrorism have set in motion a chain of consequences that have profoundly altered the popular perceptions of the United States abroad. Joseph Nye chillingly reminds us of how soft power can be lost when policy choices glaringly conflict with the basis of a country's claim to leadership. The comparison Nye (2004, 9) implicitly makes is meant to shock established sensitivities as well as to promote sober reflections: "The Soviet Union once had a good deal of soft power, but it lost much of it after the invasions of Hungary and Czechoslovakia."

Moments of crisis in the popular image of the United States have punctuated U.S. foreign relations. The general publics in Britain, France, Germany, and Italy have expressed serious doubts about the wisdom of U.S. leadership on many occasions since the 1960s. As I show in Figure 7.1, where I plot the percentage of respondents who believed that the United States was dealing responsibly with world affairs, using a long series of data collected by the United States Information Agency over a 42-year period from 1960 to 2002, approval of American international behavior was very erratic at the time of the Vietnam War; it plummeted during the controversy over the deployment of Pershing missiles in Europe

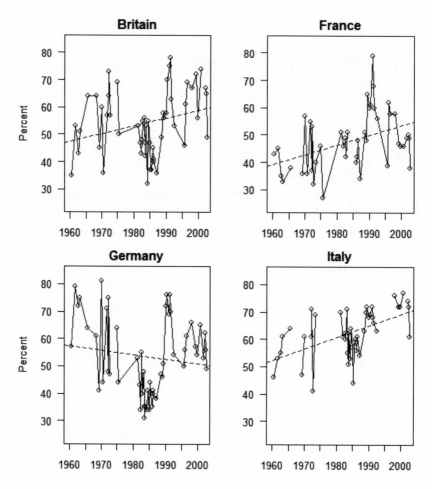

Figure 7.1. Attitudes towards U.S. International Role, 1960–2002

Notes: Solid lines represent the percentage of respondents who believed that the United States was dealing responsibly with world affairs (at the time of the survey). Dotted lines represent bivariate regressions. Data come from U.S. Department of State, Office of Research, "Europeans and Anti-Americanism, Fact vs. Fiction: A Study of Public Attitudes toward the U.S." September 2002.

in the mid-eighties and again during the Bosnia intervention in the mid-1990s. But popular opinion promptly returned to a positive assessment when the crises subsided. Over a long period of time, the perceptions of the U.S. international role showed a remarkable resilience. Waves of anti-Americanism came and went without leaving any major footprint in the survey data, as if anti-Americanism resembled a "bubble," a momentary manifestation of opposition that occasionally emerged and rapidly burst.[74]

For many concerned critics, however, the controversy unleashed by the U.S. anti-terrorist campaigns and the Iraq war is unlike any previous crisis. Michael Cox (2005, 209), for example, refers to it as "the most extended crisis in the history of the transatlantic relationship." He points to the assertiveness on the part of the European countries as a novel development in the transatlantic security relationship. In an attempt to innovate in balance of power theory, Robert Pape (2005) and T. V. Paul (2005) claim that the unilateralist turn in U.S. foreign policy since the election of President George W. Bush has undermined the perception of the United States as a benevolent hegemon with benign intentions, and they view this perceptual change as an unprecedented fracture in a long-standing pattern that will undermine the U.S. ability to assuage fears and defuse power-balancing aspirations. "Soft balancing" is the behavioral consequence of this change and the likely precursor to a traditional hard balancing, unless the United States comes back to its realist senses. But such a dire prognosis is as contested as it is provocative, the discussions in Brooks and Wohlforth (2005) and Lieber and Alexander (2005) attest.

Attributions of novelty to the latest crisis, however, are far from novel and indeed recurrently appear in investigations of the image of the United States, as we saw in Chapter 1 (Free, 1976; Haseler, 1985; Markovits, 1985; Mueller and Risse-Kappen, 1987). Indeed, Lieber and Alexander (2005, 132–133) raise an important objection when they forcefully remind us of how often scholars have identified crises in U.S. relations with the rest of the world, and they sternly declare that as yet they "detect no persuasive evidence that U.S. policy is provoking the seismic shift in other states' strategies toward the United States that theorists of balancing identify."

In the final part of this book, I investigate the persistence of the current wave of anti-American sentiments and assess whether they stem from such sources that they are unlikely to subside even after the termination of the current crisis. The dimensions of America theory presented in Chapter 2 helps us probe whether the factors that shape current popular perceptions of the United States reflect specific contingent circumstances or are indicative of a broader and deeper syndrome that is likely to persist over time and therefore constitutes a novel situation, unlike the crises of the past.

This chapter is divided into an overview of the popular views of the United States since 2002 and a description of an empirical strategy to evaluate the persistence of anti-Americanism. I identify five causal mechanisms that potentially shape popular attitudes towards the United States. These mechanisms specify five alternative hypotheses that will be tested in Chapter 8.

The Image of America in Times of Crisis

As briefly described and documented Chapter 1, attitudes towards the United States in the trying times of the Iraq war and the U.S. campaign against terrorism have been undergoing a period of crisis but have not crashed. In this section, I present additional evidence that corroborates this situation.

The data displayed in Table 7.1 shows that President George W. Bush was clearly not much loved or admired in 2004 outside the United States. Large majorities in the eight countries surveyed by the Pew Research Center Global Attitudes Survey had an unfavorable opinion of him. We should not over emphasize this finding. A mere two years later, even his compatriots were disinclined to see President Bush in a positive light, and even the most appreciative critics of the United States, starting from Alexis de Tocqueville (1947 [1835 and 1840]), have held dim views of its political leaders.[75]

Analogously, support for the U.S. actions in the war on terror has declined since 2002. In Table 7.2, we see that in 2004 about half of the respondents in eight countries disapproved of what the United States was doing to combat terrorism, an increase of about 18 percentage points compared to the 2002 findings reported in Table 3.1. On the other hand, despite all that has occurred in the international arena, foreign publics would not welcome the emergence of a balancing military counterweight to the United States. The percentage of respondents who thought that the world would be safer if there were another country equal in power to the United States was about 32%, which is no different from the percentage found in 2002 in the large sample of 42 countries reported in Table 3.1. In general, large portions of the general publics would not welcome the emergence of a bipolar system where another state would balance the United States. Nonetheless, a shift has occurred in the three European democracies in the sample, particularly in France, where more than 40% of the public thought that the world would be a safer place if another country grew equal in power to the United States.

But even in the finding for the European publics, which clearly indicates stress in the fabric of the transatlantic security community, we can detect that some of the negative opinion may be bluster rather than deep-seated animosity, for at least two reasons. First, these percentages are not as high yet as they were

Table 7.1.   Opinions of President George W. Bush, 2004

Country	Very Favorable (%)	Somewhat Favorable (%)	Somewhat Unfavorable (%)	Very Unfavorable (%)	Don't Know (%)
Britain	8.40	28.20	26.20	32.20	5.00
France	1.59	12.50	33.93	51.19	0.79
Germany	1.00	9.60	45.40	43.00	1.00
Jordan	0.70	2.00	30.80	65.50	1.00
Morocco	1.70	6.10	13.70	76.50	2.00
Pakistan	2.42	5.72	5.15	62.08	24.64
Russia	4.29	24.75	34.43	24.85	11.68
Turkey	4.52	17.01	12.88	53.98	11.60
Total	2.93	12.20	22.38	53.56	8.94

Note: Data are from the 2004 wave of the Pew Global Attitudes Survey.

in the 1960s and 1970s, when the foreign publics repeatedly expressed a preference for power parity between the United States and the Soviet Union, not for American superiority. As Table 7.3 illustrates, in 1974 sizeable majorities in eight countries declared they would prefer to see the U.S. and the U.S.S.R. equal in power.[76] "The reason for this result is simple," commented Russett and Deluca (1983, 192): "parity implies mutual deterrence and caution; superiority implies the possibility of recklessness and adventurism." In direct contrast to the claims that the current crisis is unprecedented, large sections of publics and elites in Europe, the Americas, and Japan were much more concerned about the use of American power at the time of détente than they are now at a time of unipolar power distribution.

Second, when asked in the 2004 Pew Global Attitudes Survey whether they would consider it a positive development if the European Union became as powerful as the U.S., 50% of the public in Britain, 89.5% in France, and 73.4% in Germany, and 67% in Russia and Turkey responded affirmatively. But, when the costs associated with worldwide responsibility for international problems were mentioned in the survey question, those percentages dropped to 41.4% in Britain, to 75.6% in France, to about 52% in Germany and Russia, and to 49% in Turkey. This pattern of "conditional approval" of an expanded international role for the European Union was even more pronounced in the 2004 Transatlantic Trends Survey commissioned by the German Marshall Fund. As we observe in Table 7.4, 64.5% of the respondents in 9 countries in Europe plus Turkey would have ap-

Table 7.2. Opinions about the War on Terror and Balancing U.S. Power, 2004

Country	War on terror			Balancing U.S. power		
	Favor (%)	Oppose (%)	NA (%)	Safer (%)	More dangerous (%)	NA (%)
Britain	62.40	31.40	6.20	43.00	41.80	15.20
France	51.19	46.23	2.58	52.98	40.87	6.15
Germany	50.80	46.80	2.40	42.40	43.20	14.40
Jordan	11.50	78.10	10.40	29.20	53.30	17.50
Morocco	27.50	66.30	6.20	20.80	64.70	14.50
Pakistan	17.95	58.05	23.99	18.20	59.50	22.30
Russia	72.75	20.06	7.19	37.33	44.31	18.36
Turkey	37.27	55.65	7.08	40.61	45.62	13.77
Total	37.62	52.56	9.82	32.62	51.12	16.26

Notes: Data are from the 2004 wave of the Pew Global Attitudes Survey. "NA" stands for "Don't know" or refused to answer.

Table 7.3. Preferred Power Alignments, 1974

	Elites				Publics			
	U.S. more powerful (%)	U.S.S.R. more powerful (%)	About equal (%)	NA (%)	U.S. more powerful (%)	U.S.S.R. more powerful (%)	About equal (%)	NA (%)
Britain	37	1	61	1	49	1	47	3
France	25	5	62	8	21	6	62	11
Germany	35	2	61	2	39	4	51	6
Italy	30	5	60	5	28	6	54	12
Canada	36	2	59	3	30	2	62	6
Mexico	44	3	47	6	37	8	49	6
Brazil	37	2	54	7	42	4	45	9
Japan	29	3	59	9	17	5	59	19
Total	34	3	58	5	33	4	54	9

Notes: Data are taken from the 28th Report of the U.S. Advisory Commission on Information, May 1977, p. 122. "NA" stands for "Don't know."

Table 7.4. Support for the European Union as a Superpower

	Superpower status				If more E.U. military spending		
	U.S. only (%)	E.U. too (%)	No country (%)	NA (%)	Yes (%)	No (%)	NA (%)
Britain	21.00	53.90	16.20	8.90	53.43	41.00	5.57
France	4.97	83.40	10.24	1.39	53.99	43.15	2.86
Germany	9.49	73.23	13.39	3.90	34.92	63.03	2.05
Italy	5.79	73.45	19.56	1.20	56.93	37.23	5.84
Netherlands	8.38	76.35	13.77	1.50	39.08	58.43	2.48
Poland	10.20	68.70	15.80	5.30	46.14	45.27	8.59
Portugal	5.68	65.00	18.25	11.07	59.82	30.21	9.97
Slovakia	3.10	36.20	56.60	4.10	43.65	42.82	13.54
Spain	2.80	74.30	18.70	4.20	47.78	43.88	8.34
Turkey	5.96	40.06	39.56	14.41	48.88	39.70	11.41
Total	7.73	64.46	22.21	5.60	48.49	45.13	6.38

Notes: Data are from the 2004 Transatlantic Trends survey commissioned by the German Marshall Fund. "NA" stands for "Don't know."

proved of the European Union's becoming a superpower "like the United States," about 20% thought that no country should be a superpower, while only 7.7% thought that the United States should be the only superpower. Country variation adds nuance to this finding: the French public was indeed keener on superpower status for the European Union than the other publics, while the Polish were approximately as enthusiastic as the Germans about American preeminence in a unipolar world (10.2% and 9.5%). In Slovakia and Turkey, respectively a freshman member and an aspiring member of the European Union, the general publics were hedging their bets, opting for a position of nonalignment.

What is striking is the substantial number of respondents who promptly revised their opinion when they were asked whether they would continue to approve of a superpower role for the E.U. if it implied increased military spending. For about 45% of the publics a superpower role was deemed acceptable only if obtainable on the cheap. Neoconservative intellectuals would brandish this finding as yet another indication of how Europe is not mature enough to handle threats and risks in the international arena (Kagan, 2003), and they would scornfully hurl back at the Europeans the infamous barb that General de Gaulle directed at the Americans—"They are not serious"—as *Washington Post* commentator George F. Will remarked to Timothy Garton Ash (2004, 206).

But one wonders what image of the United States these respondents had in mind if they had to be reminded that to be a superpower *like the United States* would imply greater allocation of resources to the military. One interpretation of the results in Table 7.4 is that the large but conditional support for a European superpower role reflects superficial dissatisfaction with the United States rather than an entrenched position. If it only takes one calculation of a very prominent aspect of the United States to induce such a large shift in people's attitudes, than those attitudes towards the United States might reflect a momentary anger, definitely shrill and petulant, but also shallow and perhaps short-lived.

Assessing the Persistence of Anti-Americanism

As we would expect in the midst of major political disagreement over the global war on terror, in which harsh words have not been spared, the popular image of the United States shows signs of distress but has not suddenly collapsed. The optimists, who see an opportunity in every danger, say that the U.S. image is slowly returning to the levels of popularity of 2002, and they conclude that this crisis is fostering a moment of clarification that will generate a new consensus on the fundamental rules of the American world order (Pouliot, 2006). The skeptics, who are many and stubborn, would agree with Emily Dickinson that "crumbling is not an instant's act"; rather, the deterioration of U.S. popularity is a consecutive and slow slipping.[77] They point out that the return to "normalcy" is taking longer than was the case for the anti-American mood swings of the Cold War era, and they conclude that we are witnessing the inception of a process of decay and disaffection that will set the United States further apart from the rest of the world (Huntington, 1999; Cox, 2005; Pape, 2005).

No one can conclusively predict the future of America's popularity abroad. Both the pessimistic and the optimistic assessments have a degree of prima facie plausibility and their claims are unlikely to be resolved on the basis of that data alone. Instead of waiting for the future to be the arbiter of this puzzle, however, we can start to build a more comprehensive view of the status of the U.S. image abroad by evaluating what factors shape anti-American views among ordinary people in the heated times of the Iraq crisis. We can assess how the two views of anti-Americanism explored in this book inform the patterns of attitudes towards the United States that have been documented.

On the one hand, we could anticipate that popular opinion will turn into the ideological syndrome that Revel (2003), Rubin and Rubin (2004), Berman (2004), and Joffe (2004) have depicted in vivid language, whereby U.S. culture is seen as oppressive and inauthentic while U.S. power is decried as exploitative and imperial.[78] In that case, the claims of those who see the current wave of anti-Americanism as the harbinger of a long-lasting change in the nature of the transatlantic security community would have stronger empirical grounds. Alternatively, it could be the case that, despite the tensions unfolding on the world stage, ordinary people would still find that the appeal of U.S. culture and values is powerful enough to discount the disagreement and the opposition engendered by the choices, style, and ideology of the George W. Bush administration.

Of the three components of soft power identified by Nye (2004, 11), culture, values, and policies, it is the policies of preemption, unilateralism, and the darker side of the war on terror, exposed by the torture scandals at Abu Ghraib and Guantanamo, that have most prominently changed the American image and that are most strongly denounced as illegitimate and dangerous. As a consequence, we would expect perceptions of the United States to have soured among those who oppose those policies and among those who see in President Bush and his administration the embodiment of a change for the worse in the U.S. international role.

But, as argued in Chapter 2 and illustrated empirically in Chapters 3 and 4, foreign publics form their opinions of the United States on a larger array of factors, not just their immediate policy concerns. Consistent with the dimensions of America theory, the appeal of U.S. popular culture, the respect for the U.S. tradition of liberty and equality, and the sense of opportunity embodied in the American dream are relevant frames in the belief systems of ordinary people. That many ordinary people reveal a positive opinion of the United States *despite* their opposition to the current policies and whoever is president would then count as an indication that the U.S. culture of "can do" and the values of democracy and personal achievement still play a role in the definition of the ideational bases of the U.S. world order.

If we find that negative attitudes towards the United States are no longer mediated by coexisting positive attitudes about other dimensions of the United States, then that finding would count as evidence that the image of the United States has moved closer to the depiction of outright rejection that animates the writings of Revel (2003), Rubin and Rubin (2004), Berman (2004), and Joffe (2004). The current crisis would then be here to stay. On the other hand, if the multiple dimensions of the U.S. continue to figure in the belief systems of ordinary people, then it will show that even in the heat of the current crisis, we can be more confident that the attraction of U.S. norms, popular culture, and institutions can still serve as the pillars upon which U.S. popularity abroad can re-emerge when the current crisis finally subsides.

Five Mechanisms

To assess the empirical underpinnings of these two different conjectures about the future of U.S. popularity abroad, I investigate how five mechanisms hypothetically shape the formation of popular attitudes towards the United States. Each of these mechanisms links specific attitudes, such as dislike of President Bush or the belief that people who migrate to the America lead a better life, with opinions of the United States. More importantly, each of these hypotheses identifies a factor that would clarify how deeply a negative view of the U.S. is engrained. Some factors reflect a reaction to specific contingent circumstances; others point to a broader and deeper pattern of opposition to the United States. By specifying some of the sources of popular anti-Americanism, we can gain empirical insight into the possible persistence of the current opposition to the United States. To an extent, all of these hypothetical mechanisms are likely to be simultaneously at work in many foreign publics, which would make a negative attitude towards the United States overdetermined. But when they are not coincident, we can evaluate the level of psychological relevance that each mechanism exerts in the formation of people's attitudes towards the United States. In detail, I consider the following hypotheses: (a) the Bush hypothesis, (b) the American people hypothesis, (c) the ulterior motives hypothesis, (d) the power hypothesis, and (e) the land of opportunity hypothesis.

The Bush Hypothesis

A popular explanation for the current status of the image of the United States claims that the blame should be placed on the shoulders of President George W. Bush. His style, his political stances, his religiosity are considered insufferable oddities in many quarters and irksome reminders of how the United States is different and proud to be so. In a telling example, Timothy Garton Ash (2004, 10) recalls that his Oxford doctor expressed his irritation about the United States by flippantly remarking, "That Bush is such a cowboy, isn't he?" A sense of elitist snobbery underscores the facile characterizations of President Bush: gun-toting, trigger-happy Texan; unrefined C student bragging about his folksy ways despite his Ivy League degrees. Nevertheless, they appear in cartoons, editorials, and in the responses of ordinary people (Long, 2007; Rubin and Rubin, 2004, 201–202).

This type of response is as often denounced as it is invoked (Ajami, 2003; Kohut and Stokes, 2006; Higley, 2006). On the one hand, the personalization of the criticism of the United States indicates how foreign publics are willing to attribute their displeasure and irritation to a contingent factor, that is a president who came to office in a contested election in a nation split between the political camps of the "blue" Democrats and the "red" Republicans, rather than aiming their disapproval at the country as a whole or at broader causal forces. On the other hand, in the days of tragedy immediately after September 11, 2001, when frightened Americans rallied around the flag and their president, such a distinction was rejected with indignation as the unsympathetic response of heartless critics (Rubin and Rubin, 2004, 201–202).

In the polemical skirmishes that surround the controversy between "anti-Bush-ism" and anti-Americanism, two points are usually overlooked. First, by emphasizing the shortcomings of a specific president, even by impugning his personal character, the critics do not undermine or challenge the justifications for U.S. primacy in the international arena; they are only complaining that in their own view the current president is not living up to what they believe U.S. leadership was in the past and should be in the future. As James Scott (1990, 91) reminds us in his compelling analysis of the forms of opposition to superior power, "it is one thing to claim that *this* king is not as beneficent as his predecessor, another to claim that kings in general don't live up to the beneficence they promise, and still another to repudiate all forms of kingship as inadmissable." Analogously, it is one thing to be scornful of *this* president, another to be critical of American established power, and yet another to reject the material, institutional, and normative bases of the U.S. world order.

Second, the distinction between Bush versus the U.S. obviously implies that a public might like the United States *despite* its contempt for President Bush. The extent to which this pattern occurs, though, is rarely investigated. Given that the personal character of the president, his policies, and his style are likely to feature prominently in the mental references of ordinary people when they are asked to express their attitudes towards the United States as a whole, the numerical relevance of the anti-Bush pro-Americans is a sign of how the image of the U.S. transcends the negative impact of American actions in times of crisis.

Using Friendly's (1999) fourfold plots, introduced in Chapter 3, Figure 7.2 presents a cross-tabulation of the popularity of President Bush and of the United States in the eight countries surveyed in the 2004 wave of the Pew Research Center Global Attitudes Survey.[79] We find that most respondents held both the United States and its president in low esteem (upper left quadrant). For example, those percentages were about 60% in France, Germany, and Turkey, about 36% and 43% in Britain and Russia, and as high as 94% in Jordan. But sizeable numbers of respondents were willing to manifest positive attitudes towards the United States while disapproving of President Bush. The percentage of respondents with an anti-Bush/pro-U.S. position (upper right quadrant) ranges between 25% and 28% in the three Western European democracies and around 22% in Russia and Morocco.

The American People Hypothesis

The second hypothesis shifts the focus from the president to the citizens of the United States. In this perspective, the source of anti-American sentiments is not just *him*, the leader who serves as the agent of the nation, but *them*, the American people. Foreign publics could reach a negative judgment of the United States because they observe that its citizens democratically and constitutionally elected an executive administration that has rejected the tenets of a liberal and multilateral foreign policy, is disinclined to contribute to the provision of international public goods, has endorsed a security doctrine in which the use of force is no longer the *ultima ratio* of statecraft, and many regard as disastrously incompetent.

Anti-American views shaped by negative attitudes towards the American people indicate a more serious problem in the current wave of anti-Americanism, because the people remain as leaders come and go. The distinction between the leader and the people is a principle often invoked in the era of democratic politics. "We have no quarrel with the German people," proclaimed Woodrow Wilson when he addressed Congress to declare war against Germany on 2 April 1917.[80] Since then, many democratic leaders have used this refrain when they were about to launch military attacks against other countries (McGillivray and Smith, 2000). In the case of popular anti-Americanism, the practice of blaming the leader while sparing the people has informed popular judgment, in the past as well as now. Isernia's (2007) analysis of European public opinion in the 1950s and 1960s shows that the distinction between the American people and their government became more pronounced when political relations with the United States were strained. For foreign publics in that analysis, the American people were not part of the problem but an object of sympathy when politics collided.[81]

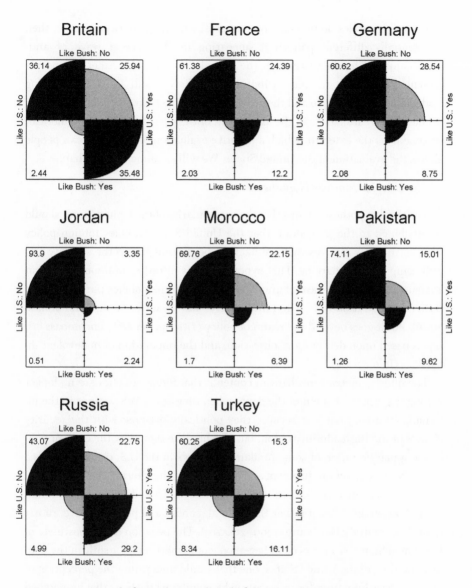

Figure 7.2. Approval of President Bush and of the United States, 2004

Notes: The number in each of the cells represents the percentage of individuals who selected the indicated combination of responses. Data analysis is based on the 2004 Pew Global Attitudes Survey. (See also endnote 29.)

If foreign publics do indeed have a quarrel with the American people, then a potentially different pattern is appearing in the current wave of anti-Americanism. The fluctuations in the attitudes towards the American people presented in Figures 1.2 and 1.3 indicate that there is still a distinction being made between the people and the government by substantial portions of foreign publics. But what matters in the assessment of the persistence of anti-American sentiments is the extent to which a negative evaluation of the American people affects the evaluation of the United States. We will examine this in Chapter 8.

The Ulterior Motives Hypothesis

The third hypothesis claims that the unpopularity of the United States should be attributed to the perception that the United States pursues foreign policy goals for ulterior motives that are likely to be detrimental to the security and well-being of other nations. This hypothesis taps into the common claim that attributes the current wave of anti-Americanism to the policies pursued by the Bush administration in Iraq and in the larger war on terror (Kohut and Stokes, 2006). But it goes beyond the realm of policy criticism per se to encompass critiques based upon denigration, obsession, and the imputation of malevolent intensions (Joffe, 2004).

The ulterior motives mechanism contends that foreign publics are no longer willing to grant the benefit of the doubt when they assess U.S. actions in the international arena, not just because they politically disagree with the security choices of the Bush administration, but also because they view the current policies as a manifestation of some fundamental flaws in the U.S. character or as a pretext for power aggrandizement and domination. The ulterior motives hypothesis, therefore, turns on its head the claim that the United States is a different kind of hegemon, "strong rather than brutal; candid and possibly naive, rather than sly or crafty" (Heisbourg, 1999–2000, 9). The negation of the postulate of the United States as a benevolent hegemon would mark a major shift in the popular standing of the United States, one that would undermine the perception of nonaggressive intentions that allegedly helps counteract the fears that unmatched U.S.power would otherwise generate (Joffe, 2002; Owen, 2002; Risse, 2002; Walt, 2002; Pape, 2005; Mahbubani, 2005).

It follows, then, that if foreign publics form negative views of the United States because they distrust U.S. policy choices to the point of seeing ulterior motives in them, there would be few chances of a return to "normalcy" once the war in Iraq is over. The general foreign public would certainly welcome the end of the Iraq war, but if this hypothesis is true, they would also discount it and soon select other policies as a pretext for articulating preconceived opposition to the United States.

In the 2004 Pew Global Attitudes Survey, two indicators were used to evaluate the extent to which foreign publics attributed ulterior motives to U.S. actions in the international arena. The first indicator distinguishes those respondents who thought that the United States was rightfully concerned about the threat of international terrorism from those who thought that the United States was overreacting to it. The second indicator identifies the respondents who believed that the U.S.-led war on terrorism was a sincere effort to reduce international terrorism rather than a campaign waged for other reasons.[82]

These indicators are closely related but not identical. As an illustration, Figure 7.3 uses Friendly's (1999) fourfold plots to show how the belief that the United States overstates the terrorist threat and instrumentally exploits the war on terror for other goals shapes the views of foreign publics. In all countries but Britain and, by a small margin, Russia, a plurality of the general public views the U.S. anti-terrorist campaigns as a combination of threat exaggeration and hidden agendas (lower right quadrant). In Jordan, Pakistan, and Morocco no less than 70% of the public subscribes to the notion that the United States has ulterior motives in its antiterrorist policies. The Turkish public evaluates the U.S. campaigns against terrorism in a manner that closely resembles that of the French and German publics.

The descriptive analysis of the ulterior motive hypothesis, therefore, addresses the claims of those who, like Josef Joffe (2004), argue that a preconceived bias against the United Sates affects large portions of foreign publics. Widespread though such views are, they might still play only a marginal role in the formation of popular opinion of the United States and so be less relevant than otherwise expected.

The Power Hypothesis

The fourth hypothesis builds upon the effect on foreign opinion of the overwhelming power of the United States. A long tradition of international relations scholarship places power, and the balance of power, at the center of our theoretical understanding of world politics. In a classic statement, Kenneth Waltz (1979, 127), the foremost realist scholar of the past 50 years, wrote. "Secondary states, if

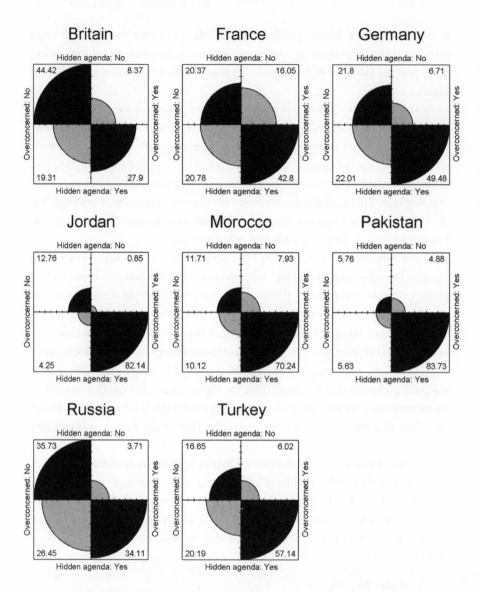

Figure 7.3. Attitudes about U.S. Response to Terrorism, 2004

Notes: The number in each of the cells represents the percentage of individuals who selected the indicated combination of responses. Data analysis is based on the 2004 Pew Global Attitudes Survey. (See also endnote 29.)

they are free to choose, flock to the weaker side; for it is the stronger side that threatens them." When confronted with the increasing power of a nation, wise leaders, according to this theory, would promote the formation of balancing coalitions as well as policies that would increase the military and economic power of their countries. These policies would keep the powerful nation in check and thus help achieve state security. The wise publics, taking the cue from their leaders, would lend support to these balancing efforts because these efforts contribute to the creation of a safer and more stable world.

The conjecture is that unbalanced power generates a sense of threat and insecurity, which then affects popular perceptions of the country with preponderant power. The argument is certainly simple, and it is very common in public discourse. For example, in a perceptive analysis that points to aspects of U.S. power as the driving force of anti-American sentiments, John Ikenberry (2005, 6) writes, "The world worries about American power." Similarly, Fareed Zakaria (1999) argues, "If the past is any guide, America's primacy will provoke growing resistance."

There is no doubt in anyone's mind that the United States is very powerful and has been so since the end of the Second World War. U.S. power, then, would be a constant through the past 60 years and so cannot be invoked to explain the fluctuations and variations in anti-American sentiments during that period. U.S. power, however, has now allegedly reached levels that defy usual categories. At the end of the 1990s, the French foreign minister Hubert Védrine (2000) coined the term *hyperpower* to argue that the United States is no longer *just* a superpower, the old Cold War term, but is now in a category of its own that requires new vocabulary. This kind of power, therefore, might serve as an underlying, and enduring, factor that could shape popular sentiments about the United States.

As shown in Tables 3.1 and 3.2, ordinary people did not feel threatened enough by U.S. power to believe that the emergence of a balancing counterweight to the United States would make the world safer. Tables 7.2 and 7.4 report that popular views about U.S. power continued to be rather qualified even in the midst of the Iraq crisis. While those data cast doubt on the relevance of U.S. power as a source of anti-American attitudes, the hypothesis has an intuitive basis that requires detailed examination. In Chapter 8 I use the indicator measuring whether ordinary people thought that the world would be safer if another power balanced U.S. power, and I assess whether the individuals who held such beliefs also held more negative views of the United States.

The Land-of-Opportunity Hypothesis

The fifth, and final, hypothesis conjectures that belief in the American dream shapes views of the United States. One of the findings reported in Chapter 3 showed that respondents who had friends or relatives in the United States consistently reported more favorable opinions of the United States than those who did not. This systematic difference was taken as an indication that the information provided by friends and family members who had relocated to the United States served as a channel through which a fundamental component of U.S. societal and cultural attractiveness operated. The personal stories of ordinary people who were given a chance by the U.S. and took it are understood to be concrete manifestations of the American dream.

It would thus be a major transformation in the ideational landscape of the American world order if the notion of the American dream were to lose its appeal. A direct comparison with the 2002 survey data is not possible, given that in the 2004 Global Attitudes Survey respondents were not asked whether they were corresponding with friends or relatives living in the United States. Another indicator, though, serves as a reasonable proxy for the perceptions of those aspects of U.S. society and polity that are not directly associated with its government and actions. This indicator measures foreign respondents' perceptions of the quality of life of people who have migrated to the United States. Respondents were asked whether they thought that their compatriots who had migrated to the United States had a better life there, a worse life, or that their life in America was neither better nor worse than the one they would have led in their home country. While not explicitly capturing attitudes towards aspects of U.S. society and values, this measure can illustrate how the perceptions of life in the U.S. are reflected in the overall attitudes towards the United States.

From psychological research, we know that when people try to gauge the happiness of people living in a different region, they predominantly base their evaluations on the ways in which the two regions differ the most, while discounting central aspects of life that would most likely matter in determining life satisfaction (Schkade and Kahneman, 1998). Answers to the question about the quality of life for compatriots who had moved to the United States are therefore likely to reflect the respondent's perceptions of educational and employment opportunities or the broad appeal of America as a welcoming society, rather than any specific knowledge about the life prospects for immigrants in the United States.[83]

As Table 7.5 shows, the belief that life in America was worse was held by only a minority in each of the publics, although between a quarter and a third of the Moroccan and the Pakistani citizens held such a view. The belief that moving to the United States improved the life prospects of migrants from their country was more popular, except for the Germans and the French, who predominantly claimed that life in their countries was as good as life in the United States. Therefore, the respondents who considered life prospects in the United States to be as attractive as those granted by their home country might have implicitly concluded that the United States was becoming an ordinary country with no special claim to an exceptional status.

Survey data offer prima facie evidence that a degree of skepticism colors the popular attitudes towards the quality of life and opportunities that U.S. society and political economy grants to immigrants. It might be expected that, as ordinary people try to imagine the life quality of their compatriots in the United States, their assessments are influenced by how satisfied they are with the state of affairs in their own country. Table 7.5 investigates this option by reporting the distribution of the attitudes towards quality of life in the United States for those who were satisfied with how things were going in their countries and those who were not.

As can be seen, however, satisfaction with their own country only marginally affected respondents' evaluations of life in the United States. The overall distribution of responses on the quality of life measure shows only slight variation across levels of satisfaction with own-country conditions, particularly in Russia and Turkey. Across the board, differences were not large enough to question the ability of this indicator to tap into the popular perceptions of the United States as the land of opportunity.

Summary

Displeasure with President Bush and with the American people, skepticism about the United States as a welcoming society, concerns about the predominance of U.S. power, and the attribution of ulterior motives to U.S. actions are all factors that permeate the psychological calculus underlying popular anti-Americanism. The five mechanisms identified above matter not just because they are likely predictors of anti-American views but because their combination and relative importance offer an important way to assess how deeply anti-American sentiments are ingrained.

How, then, should we assess the persistence of anti-American sentiments in light of the five hypotheses? To answer this question, we should consider whether

Table 7.5. Quality of Life for Migrants to the United States, 2004

	All respondents				Satisfied with their country				Dissatisfied with their country			
	Better	Worse	Same	NA	Better	Worse	Same	NA	Better	Worse	Same	NA
Britain	41.00	6.00	35.20	17.80	34.92	5.29	39.15	20.63	46.85	5.59	32.52	15.03
France	24.40	10.71	56.35	8.53	26.25	5.62	61.25	6.88	23.46	13.20	53.96	9.38
Germany	13.00	15.20	61.60	10.20	6.36	20.91	62.73	10.00	15.26	13.68	60.79	10.26
Jordan	31.20	21.50	28.10	19.20	34.24	21.19	26.27	18.31	28.43	25.75	28.76	17.06
Morocco	46.70	26.70	17.40	9.20	45.04	28.87	16.52	9.57	49.63	24.19	18.45	7.73
Pakistan	30.11	29.47	18.60	21.82	34.17	26.37	17.32	22.15	26.31	35.45	21.27	16.98
Russia	53.09	9.78	17.47	19.66	54.17	10.98	18.56	16.29	53.43	9.64	16.79	20.15
Turkey	50.44	18.98	14.36	16.22	49.51	20.69	10.84	18.97	51.35	17.85	16.67	14.14
Total	38.30	19.20	26.24	16.26	35.12	18.96	21.43	24.48	35.72	16.95	26.01	21.33

Notes: Data are from the 2004 wave of the Pew Global Attitudes Survey. "NA" stands for "Don't know" or refused to answer.

any given factor is a response to some contingent circumstance or reflects a deeper bias of denigration and stereotyping. If the predominant factors shaping attitudes towards the United States are closer to the contingency pole, then we would expect that anti-American views would be shallower and therefore less persistent than would be the case if they reflected denigration and stereotyping. We should also consider whether a factor is likely to be an enduring feature of the current political landscape.

In this logic, we can place four of the five factors on a continuum that has the Bush hypothesis closer to the contingency pole and the ulterior motives hypothesis closer to the denigration pole. The American people hypothesis and the land-of-opportunity hypothesis would then be placed in intermediate positions. Anti-American views that predominantly respond to the dislike of President Bush are qualitatively different from anti-American views that are anchored in the belief that the United States pursues a hidden agenda in its anti-terrorist policies. In the first instance, anti-American sentiments would be a reaction to a president who would soon become a former president, while in the second case they would reflect the belief that there is something inherently "wrong" with the United States. We would then expect that views of the United States predominantly filtered through the Bush hypothesis would be less persistent. If the ulterior motives hypothesis predominated, instead, we would have more reasons to expect that the current anti-American wave would persist well beyond the tenure of the George W. Bush administration.

The American people and the land-of-opportunity hypotheses both identify factors that go beyond a specific political juncture, but they do not develop into an open denigration of the United States. Doubts about the quality of life in the United States would indicate that the United States is no longer seen as the "Empire of the Cool," the land of consumption and opportunities that has so much attracted so many for so long (Wagnleitner, 1999, 506). In Chapter 3, we saw how the attraction of U.S. culture framed popular perceptions and tempered the formation of negative views of the U.S. If the land-of-opportunity mechanism predominates, then, we would expect that anti-American views would lose any virulent edge but would not evaporate once the current crisis is finally resolved.

If a negative view of the United States is a function of a negative view of its inhabitants, we would move closer to the pole of denigration and bias. To dislike a whole people is indeed a mark of prejudicial views, which would be impervious to any change in the international political climate. Nonetheless, the logic associated with the American people hypothesis is less indicative of an anti-American obsession than the logic associated with the ulterior motives hypothesis. The criticism could actually be for specific political and electoral choices, such as those made in the 2004 election. While we should not take lightly any direct criticism of the Americans, we would expect that the anti-American views of those who are disenchanted with the American people might be easily altered, given that the American people have the opportunity to reverse previous political choices at the ballot box.

The power hypothesis, for its part, would predict that anti-American sentiments are here to stay. This is not because a concern about predominant power would be indicative of a syndrome of stereotyping and denigration; concern about unbalanced power is a common feature of world affairs, as Fareed Zakaria (1999) reminded us, while the lack of balancing is a sign that the United States defies history and again asserts itself as exceptional. The persistence of anti-American sentiments would be a consequence of the fact that U.S. power—military, economic, and cultural—is likely to remain vastly superior for a long time. Negative views of the United States that are a reaction to U.S. power probably will be less virulent than those generated under the ulterior motives mechanism, but still enduring.

Conclusions

It certainly cannot be denied that the image of the United States is undergoing a serious crisis (Kohut and Stokes, 2006). If survey data had not registered any deterioration in the overall appreciation of the United States over a period of intense crisis like the one engendered by the Iraq war and the broader U.S. response to the 9/11 terrorist attacks, we would question their reliability as indicators of the status of U.S. popular image abroad. If the past is any guide, however, when periods of crisis have affected relations between the United States and the rest of the world, popular attitudes towards the United States soured, only to recover afterward to earlier overall levels of appreciation. Then, lest we reach the perfect tautological conclusion that in times of crisis, indeed, we find *crisis*, we also need to ask whether the current wave of anti-Americanism, unlike the waves of the past, is likely to persist.

Several scholars and intellectuals have explicitly argued that the current crisis is unlike any other. In their analyses, they depict the end of the West as a political entity and despair about an ineluctable clash of civilizations (Huntington, 1996, 1999; Cox, 2005). While in the end only time will tell, it is possible to have a clearer understanding of the nature of the current crisis in U.S. popular image by looking at factors that shape popular attitudes towards the United States. The five hypotheses developed in this chapter—the Bush hypothesis, the American people hypothesis, the land-of-opportunity hypothesis, the ulterior motives hypothesis, and the power hypothesis—offer ways to explore whether contingent factors, rather than more deep-seated and antagonistic beliefs, contribute to the formation of popular opinion. This approach takes the discussion on anti-Americanism away from the realm of speculation and offers testable hypotheses that ground our conjectures on the persistence of anti-American sentiments in the empirical record.[84] In the next Chapter, I present the empirical findings and analyze their significance.

CHAPTER EIGHT

An Evaluation of the Persistence of Anti-Americanism

Introduction

From the empirical profile of negative public opinions of the United States, we can assess to what extent these opinions are responses to contingent factors, such as the current U.S. president, or to more deeply ingrained and antagonistic beliefs, such as the sense that the United States pursues policies that are purportedly aimed at security but instead have ulterior motives of power aggrandizement and domination.

In this chapter, I analyze how the mass publics in Britain, France, Germany, and Russia, and in Jordan, Morocco, Pakistan, and Turkey viewed the United States in 2004.[85] Very few respondents in the eight countries surveyed ranked the United States negatively on all the indicators I used to measure the five causal mechanisms described in Chapter 7. Overall, there were only 136 individuals in a sample of 6,765 (2.01%) who simultaneously had a low opinion of President Bush, disliked the American people, thought that the United States was excessively concerned about terrorism and had a hidden agenda in the war on terror, believed that the world would be safer if another country balanced U.S. power, *and* were convinced that their compatriots in the United States had a worse life than they would have had in their country. Even if we relax our conditions and count how many individuals stated a negative view on at least five of the six indicators, we find only 893 individuals, or 13.2% of the sample. Still, that means that about 87% of the individuals in the sample expressed a positive view on at least four of the indicators.

These results indicate that the systematic rejection of all aspects of the United States was not common in the spring of 2004, contrary to the theories that view anti-Americanism as a syndrome of total rejection (Revel, 2003; Rubin and Rubin, 2004; Berman, 2004). But, before accepting this finding as evidence that the current wave of anti-Americanism is unlikely to evaporate soon, we need to determine the relative weights of the five factors in shaping popular attitudes towards the United States.

Empirical Findings

What then were the attitudinal profiles of the respondents who expressed negative views of the United States? To answer this question, I rely upon two different modeling approaches: regression analysis and classification tree (CART) models. The regression models evaluate the relative weight that the five causal mechanisms listed above exerted on the overall assessment of the United States, while the classification tree (CART) models offer a visual representation of the combination of factors that most likely lead to the formation of a negative opinion of the United States.[86]

In both sets of models, the dependent variables were coded using a four-level indicator that measured the respondents' overall opinion of the United States on a range from very favorable to very unfavorable. The models were estimated separately for each of the eight countries in the 2004 Pew Research Center Global Attitudes Survey, in order to assess variability in the salience of each causal mechanism in different political and cultural settings.

Regression Analysis

Figures 8.1 and 8.2 present the main results from a series of ordered logit models for the four countries in Europe and for the four countries in the Islamic world, respectively.[87] Each figure reports the coefficients and the 95% confidence intervals around the point estimates. Positive coefficients indicate that a given characteristic was associated with a greater propensity to reveal negative opinions of the United States than was the case in the reference group; negative coefficients indicate a decrease in the propensity to state negative opinions of the United States.[88] Confidence intervals that straddle the zero vertical line indicate that the data did not contain enough information to reject the null hypothesis of no connection between an explanatory variable and the pattern of responses on the dependent variable.

In all eight countries, the most substantial effects on popular opinion towards the United States were associated with the attitudes towards the American people and the attitudes towards President Bush. Positive and significant coefficients are associated with the variables identifying the individuals who strongly disliked President Bush and the individuals who held a very low opinion of the American

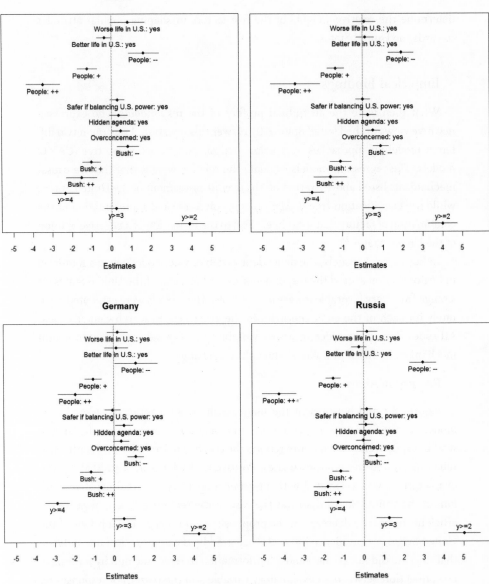

Figure 8.1. Assessment of the Persistence of Anti-Americanism in Four European Societies

Notes: The dark dots represent the regression coefficients, and the lines represent the 95% confidence intervals. Estimates are obtained from a penalized maximum likelihood ordinal logistic model, with Huber/White standard errors. "Bush: ++", "Bush: +", and "Bush: −−" identify the respondents with a very favorable, somewhat favorable, and very unfavorable opinion of President Bush, respectively. "People: ++", "People: +", and "People: −−" identify the respondents with a very favorable, somewhat favorable, and very unfavorable opinion of the American people, respectively. Data analysis is based on the 2004 Pew Global Attitudes Survey.

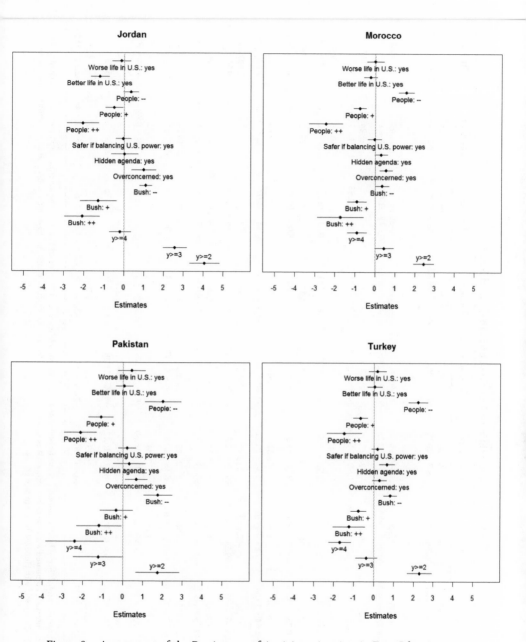

Figure 8.2. Assessment of the Persistence of Anti-Americanism in Four Islamic Societies

Notes: The dark dots represent the regression coefficients, and the lines represent the 95% confidence intervals. Estimates are obtained from a penalized maximum likelihood ordinal logistic model, with Huber/White standard errors. "Bush: ++", "Bush: +", and "Bush: −−" identify the respondents with a very favorable, somewhat favorable, and very unfavorable opinion of President Bush, respectively. "People: ++", "People: +", and "People: −−" identify the respondents with a very favorable, somewhat favorable, and very unfavorable opinion of the American people, respectively. Data analysis is based on the 2004 Pew Global Attitudes Survey.

Table 8.1.   Probabilities of Low Opinion of the United States

	Britain	France	Germany	Russia	Jordan	Morocco	Pakistan	Turkey
Baseline	55.93 41.05 ~ 70.81	63.06 50.86 ~ 75.25	62.36 48.7 ~ 76.01	77.9 67.25 ~ 88.55	92.91 89.01 ~ 96.82	61.19 49.95 ~ 72.42	22.76 2.08 ~ 43.44	40.79 27.67 ~ 53.9
Change from baseline								
Bush: ++	-34.36 -48.92 ~ -19.79	-37.46 -53.39 ~ -21.53	-15.83 -65.44 ~ 33.78	-40.76 -56.88 ~ -24.64	-31.04 -51.47 ~ -10.61	-39.55 -59.64 ~ -19.47	-14.49 -28.98 ~ 0	-24.22 -38.28 ~ -10.17
Bush: +	-24.53 -35.27 ~ -13.79	-26.47 -38.9 ~ -14.04	-28.25 -41.66 ~ -14.84	-25.13 -34.81 ~ -15.45	-14.57 -29.07 ~ -0.07	-22.5 -33.48 ~ -11.53	-5.24 -17.73 ~ 7.25	-16.52 -25.19 ~ -7.84
Bush: --	18.61 6.49 ~ 30.73	17.72 9.71 ~ 25.73	21.14 12.59 ~ 29.69	9.14 3.21 ~ 15.07	4.59 1.85 ~ 7.34	8.2 0.16 ~ 16.23	40.58 27.56 ~ 53.61	20.51 12.58 ~ 28.43
U.S. overconcerned about terrorism	11.1 0.73 ~ 21.46	10.93 3.17 ~ 18.69	8.42 -0.38 ~ 17.21	-0.24 -6.3 ~ 5.82	4.35 1.42 ~ 7.27	12.06 5.03 ~ 19.08	13.76 1.6 ~ 25.91	7.35 -1.54 ~ 16.25
Hidden agenda in war on terror	8.75 -1.64 ~ 19.14	6.05 -2.85 ~ 14.96	11.23 1.36 ~ 21.11	1.88 -4.14 ~ 7.91	0.22 -4.09 ~ 4.53	6.87 -0.34 ~ 14.07	6.09 -8.02 ~ 20.19	16.59 7.52 ~ 25.66
People: ++	-52.16 -66.36 ~ -37.97	-57.33 -69.51 ~ -45.14	-43.39 -59.06 ~ -27.73	-72.96 -82.75 ~ -63.16	-30.48 -50.46 ~ -10.51	-49.37 -60.48 ~ -38.25	-19.36 -36.86 ~ -1.86	-27.26 -39.51 ~ -15.01
People: +	-28.92 -40.73 ~ -17.11	-31.98 -41.46 ~ -22.51	-25.25 -35.13 ~ -15.37	-34 -41.6 ~ -26.4	-4.04 -8.7 ~ 0.62	-19.05 -26.58 ~ -11.52	-13.85 -28.29 ~ 0.59	-14.89 -22.93 ~ -6.86
People: --	30.76 18.57 ~ 42.96	29.08 19.51 ~ 38.66	21.42 5.18 ~ 37.65	20.65 10.64 ~ 30.67	2 -0.14 ~ 4.14	27.01 19.08 ~ 34.93	46.08 30.84 ~ 61.33	45.67 35.91 ~ 55.42
Better life in U.S.	-8.7 -17.99 ~ 0.59	3.12 -6.6 ~ 12.84	3.34 -10.01 ~ 16.69	-4.11 -10.44 ~ 2.23	-13.24 -21.35 ~ -5.12	-5.73 -13.85 ~ 2.39	1.31 -5.99 ~ 8.62	1.1 -8.04 ~ 10.23
Worse life in U.S.	18.7 1.44 ~ 35.97	2.34 -10.09 ~ 14.77	4.73 -6.71 ~ 16.17	2.96 -5.36 ~ 11.28	-0.91 -4.16 ~ 2.35	0.1 -10.07 ~ 10.26	8.73 -2.83 ~ 20.28	4.51 -6.15 ~ 15.17
Safer with power balance	7.26 -1.44 ~ 15.97	0.36 -7.79 ~ 8.52	-1.19 -10.56 ~ 8.19	2.65 -2.26 ~ 7.57	-0.21 -2.7 ~ 2.28	-0.58 -8.72 ~ 7.56	4.02 -3.6 ~ 11.64	4.71 -2.52 ~ 11.94

Notes: The main entries measure the probability of holding a somewhat unfavorable or a very unfavorable opinion of the United States for the baseline respondent and the changes from the baseline. The 95% confidence intervals, computed with the delta method (Wasserman, 2004, 131–134), are shown underneath the main entries. Estimated probabilities are obtained from a penalized ML ordinal logistic model, with Huber/White standard errors.

people. Conversely, approval of President Bush and appreciation of the American people substantially shifted attitudes towards a pro-American stance. On the other hand, the variables capturing the ulterior motives mechanism and those directly measuring the land-of-opportunity mechanism played a more marginal role, as indicated by their smaller and often insignificant coefficients. The power hypothesis received no empirical support in the data. All the coefficients associated with the indicator that identified the respondents who would feel safer if U.S. power was counterbalanced are very close to zero, which indicates that perceptions of U.S. power played no role in determining ordinary people's views of the United States.

For example, as summarized in Table 8.1, respondents who held a somewhat favorable opinion of the American people were substantially less likely to see the United States in a negative light; the drop in the likelihood of a negative opinion of the United States was even more marked among those who strongly liked the American people. Jordan is the only exception. The probability to state a negative opinion of the United States is above 60% among the Jordanians who had very fond perceptions of the American people. In all other countries, those who liked Americans liked the United States.[89]

The "Bush effect" was particularly pronounced in Britain, France, and Germany, where the presence of a somewhat favorable opinion of President Bush instead of somewhat unfavorable resulted in a percentage drop of 25–28 points in attitudinal opposition to the United States. The opinions about specific policies pursued under the aegis of the war on terrorism, on the other hand, had a less marked effect. By themselves, neither the belief that the United States was overstating the terrorist threat nor the belief that it had a hidden agenda in the war on terror changed the baseline probability of low opinion of the United States more than 10 percentage points in general or 16 percentage points in Turkey and Pakistan.

The probability estimates for Pakistan and Turkey show a remarkably low baseline level: on average, respondents in the baseline reference group—that is, respondents who moderately disliked President Bush and the American people, did not believe that the United States pursued ulterior motives in its security policies, viewed power balancing negatively, and did not see a difference in the quality of life for their compatriots living in the United States—had a low propensity to state negative views of the United States: 22.76% in Pakistan and 40.79% in Turkey. Taken individually, the five mechanisms investigated did not much alter the extent of anti-U.S. proclivities of the referent group, with the exception that *strong* dislike for the American people engendered an increase in the baseline probability of more than 45 percentage points. If we consider that 44.3% of the Pakistanis and 53.8% of the Turks had a negative opinion of the American people and that no fewer than 27.5% of the Pakistanis and 23.6% of the Turks strongly disliked President Bush *and* the American people, these low probabilities are not an indication of pro-American sentiments in Pakistan and Turkey. Rather, those probabilities reflect the high concentration of negative attitudes towards the United States on two specific dimensions, while the respondents who did not harbor strong ill feelings towards the president and the American people were more inclined to have milder opinion towards the country as well.

The pattern found in Pakistan and Turkey differs from the one found in Jordan, where anti-American views were so widespread that not even a very favorable opinion of the American people could lower the probability of holding a negative opinion of the United States below the 50 percent threshold. Amidst all this negativity, the only positive indication was the Jordanians' belief that their compatriots living the United States had a better life; such a belief engendered a 13.24% change in the baseline probability, the largest shift in all eight countries.

Finally, the bottom rows of Table 8.1 report that, consistent with the nonsignificant results illustrated in Figures 8.1 and 8.2, the propensity to hold a negative opinion of the United States was unaffected by the belief that a balancing counterweight to the United States would make the world safer.

Classification Tree Models

The results from the regression analyses have shown the importance of two sets of attitudes on the formation of the image of the United States among foreign publics. The largest differences in the perceptions of the United States were associated with attitudes towards the American people and President Bush. Four of the five mechanisms received empirical validation. Concerns over policies and assumptions about life in the United States proved less relevant in the belief systems of ordinary people, and only the power hypothesis found no empirical support.

In reality, however, all of these factors work simultaneously in people's minds. Disapproval of President Bush might be generated from a negative assessment of the decision to employ force in Iraq. Disenchantment with the American people might lead to skepticism about the opportunities offered by life in the United States. Reverse effects are also plausible: for all the populists that view elected officials as the embodiment of the popular will, irritation at President Bush's style and self-assuredness would seep into the perceptions of the American people and, from there, into the evaluations of U.S. foreign policies.[90] While all these factors are plausibly linked, no clear causal priority can be established among them, because none of these attitudinal dimensions is more encompassing than the others.[91] This limitation notwithstanding, the factors' reciprocal relations remain of central importance for the mapping of ordinary people's belief systems about the United States, because they illustrate the clusters of factors that would sustain a negative opinion of the United States.

To explore this effect, I complement the findings from the regression models by using classification and regression tree (CART) models (Therneau and Atkinson, 1997; Hastie, Tibshirani, and Friedman, 2001, 266–279; Venables and Ripley, 2002, 251–269).[92] These models offer a graphical representation of the most likely combinations of factors that would sustain pro- or anti-U.S. views. Each node on the classification tree represents a logical condition that partitions the respondents on the basis of their responses to the explanatory variables. The tree establishes a sequence in which the explanatory factors are ordered according to their level of relevance, that is, their ability to discriminate across response profiles. The labels at the end of the tree ("Anti-US" and "Pro-US") indicate the overall attitudinal result that a given path is likely to generate.

In Figure 8.3, which presents the classification trees for Britain, France, Germany, and Russia, the first key distinction pertains to the attitudes towards the American people. In the simplest case, all we would need to know to predict that someone in these nations harbored a negative opinion of the United States is that the person held a dim view of the American people. On that branch of the classification tree, no other factors played a role; in other words, in the mass publics of Britain, France, Germany, and Russia, none of the other factors had enough psychological force to dislodge an overall negative view induced by a negative opinion of the American people. Indeed, very few individuals stated a pro-U.S. view while disliking the American people: 11 (2.2%) in Britain, 27 (5.36%) in France, 13 (2.6%) in Germany, and 18 (1.8%) in Russia. This form of outright rejection of the American people and their country was particularly pronounced in France. There, we find that 211 individuals in a sample of 504 (41.8%) based their negative opinion of the United States as a country on their negative opinion of its inhabitants.[93]

A positive view of the American people, on the other hand, opened up the attitudinal space. Respondents who liked the American people formed their opinion of the United States by weighing in three additional factors, President Bush

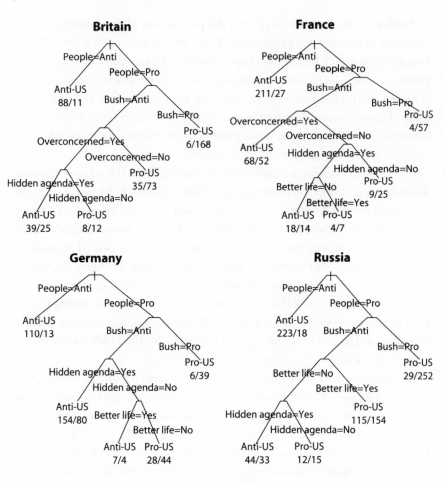

Figure 8.3. CART Models of Anti-American Opinion in European Societies, 2004

Notes: The labels "Pro-US" and "Anti-US" identify respondents who had at least a somewhat favorable and at most a somewhat unfavorable opinion of the United States, respectively. The two numbers listed underneath each terminal node indicate the number of respondents at that node. The number on the left counts the respondents with an "Anti-US" position; the number on the right counts the respondents with a "Pro-US" position. For CART models, see Breiman et al. (1984). Data analysis is based on the 2004 Pew Global Attitudes Survey.

and their more specific views on U.S. foreign policy and of life in the United States. The combination of appreciation of the American people and of President Bush was a sure predictor of appreciation of the United States except for a handful of individuals. More importantly, however, disapproval of the president was not per se sufficient to override all other considerations.

In Britain and Germany, the classification trees show that a negative view of the United States was more likely to be held when the dislike of President Bush combined with misgivings about U.S. foreign policies. If we follow the branches of the classification tree that identify the individuals who liked the American people and disapproved of President Bush, we find that the attribution of ulterior motives to U.S. policies is what weighs in to generate a negative opinion of the United States. Conversely, for the respondents who felt that the United States was rightly concerned about the terrorist threat (in Britain and to a lesser extent in France) and for those who did not attribute U.S. actions to a hidden agenda (in Germany), there was still more to like about the United States than to dislike, despite all the irritation that President Bush might have generated.[94] Interestingly, the classification tree reveals that 44 out of 72 (61.1%) German respondents who liked the American people, disliked the president, did not attribute ulterior motives to U.S. policies, and thought that German immigrants in the U.S. did not have a better life still said that their opinion of the United States was positive overall.[95]

In sum, therefore, members of the publics in Britain and Germany who opposed President Bush and the United States did not do so simply out of divergent visions about values and morality in general; they based their attitudes more specifically on their opposition to the substance and style of the foreign policy course undertaken by that administration. The French public, on the other hand, exhibited a pattern of attitudes that, while still responding to the mediating factors associated with the evaluation of policies and society, was approaching the depiction of a syndrome of rejection in which disliking the American people foreclosed the process of attitude formation for a large portion of the public.

While policy mattered in Western Europe, in Russia the factor that counterbalanced the disapproval of President Bush was the belief that migrating to the United States would improve quality of life. The appeal of the American dream and of American society was still exerting its influence among Russian respondents in 2004, and foreign policy considerations played only a marginal role. The imputation to the United States of ulterior motives in the war on terror affected the formation of the attitudes in respondents who thought that living in the United States would not improve their lot, while those who still had hope in the opportunities granted by U.S. society predominantly downplayed any foreign policy considerations.

Concerns about U.S. power and balancing thereof did not enter into ordinary people's assessment of the United States among the European publics. In none of the four countries described in Figure 8.3 did that indicator emerge as a deciding factor in the CART models. This finding not only confirms the results reported in Table 8.1 about the power hypothesis; it also offers additional support to the conclusion reached in Chapter 6 about the sources of anti-American sentiments in Europe. There, we saw that power considerations were at most a marginal determinant of overall attitudes towards the United States. The simple psychology of power and weakness that Robert Kagan (2003) described under the dichotomy of "Martian Americans" and the "Venusian Europeans" offers a poor guide to the status of U.S. standing in Europe. In Figure 8.3 we observe that, while some parts of same European publics might feel threatened enough by the United States to wish for the emergence of another country to balance the United States, this belief did not affect the formation of popular attitudes towards the United States. Again, as discussed also in Chapter 6, there is more to the relationship between the United States and Europe than a simple psychology of power and weakness.

Figure 8.4 presents the combination of factors sustaining the beliefs about the United States among the publics in four predominantly Islamic societies. On the one hand, it would appear that the basic structure of the attitudes towards the United States in Jordan, Morocco, Pakistan, and Turkey was not so dissimilar to the structure underlying the belief systems in Western Europe and Russia. The classification trees partition the respondents into groupings that resemble the ones depicted in Figure 8.3. This broad similarity, however, should not overlook the fact that in all four countries the overwhelmingly predominant cluster of attitudes combined a dislike of the American people, a dislike of the president, and a dislike of the United States.

This pattern pertains in its most extreme form to the Jordanian public: in a sample of 1,000 respondents, 775 ranked the president, the people, and the country in a negative way. Of those who expressed positive feelings towards the American people (only 187 individuals), 153 (81.8%) let their opposition to U.S. policies drive their overall perceptions of the United States. In Morocco, Pakistan, and Turkey in 2004, there was not yet found the outright rejection of all that the United States does and stands for which the widespread dislike of President Bush and the American people led to among the Jordanians. But even in those three countries, few positive results emerged. As was the case among the European publics, the attribution of ulterior motives combined with a dislike for President Bush to overturn positive feelings engendered by the appreciation of the American people. In Morocco, in particular, we find only 101 individuals

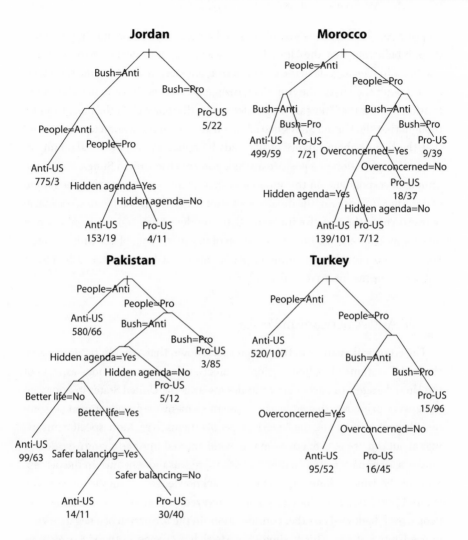

Figure 8.4. CART Models of Anti-American Opinion in Islamic Societies, 2004

Notes: The labels "Pro-US" and "Anti-US" identify respondents who had at least a somewhat favorable and at most a somewhat unfavorable opinion of the United States, respectively. The two numbers listed underneath each terminal node indicate the number of respondents at that node. The number on the left counts the respondents with an "Anti-US" position; the number on the right counts the respondents with a "Pro-US" position. For CART models, see Breiman et al. (1984). Data analysis is based on the 2004 Pew Global Attitudes Survey.

(out of 240, about 42%) who still reported a positive view of the United States despite believing that the United States was exaggerating the terrorist threat and had a hidden agenda in the war on terror, and despite disliking the president, even though they liked the American people. Moreover, if we follow the classification tree for the Pakistani respondents who disapproved of the president and thought that the United States had a hidden agenda in the war on terror, we find that the beliefs about quality of life and the belief about power balancing affected the formation of a positive attitude towards the United States. While the sample of respondents in this group was small, still, we observe that the notion of the American dream, the dream of a better life in the United States, is capable of overturning the negative influence that President Bush and the imputation of ulterior motives exerted on the formation of negative views of the United States. For that to occur, though, ordinary people must not feel threatened by power imbalance in the international arena.

Will Anti-Americanism Persist?

The empirical analysis in this chapter has shown that, even in times of crisis, the belief systems of ordinary people reflect evaluations of various aspects of the United States. In particular, attitudes towards the United States in 2002 and 2004 were primarily shaped by the "human element": a president who personifies a hegemonic era and the American people themselves. More specific misgivings about the use of U.S. power in the world entered into the cognitive calculus only as a secondary factor. In other words, there was more nuance in the perceptions of the United States than is usually acknowledged. Nonetheless, for substantial portions of the foreign publics surveyed, a dim view of the American people overshadowed all other considerations in the formation of a negative view of the United States. This finding suggests that a change in the U.S. executive administration would not be sufficient by itself to alter popular attitudes towards the United States. For that to occur, views of the American people will have to improve as well.

In light of these findings, will anti-Americanism persist or will it melt into air as soon as the current political juncture is past? While one should always take heed of movie tycoon Samuel Goldwyn's aphorism "Never prophesy, especially about the future" the analyses presented in this chapter help place the question of the persistence of anti-American sentiments into a fuller context. As the dimensions of America theory posits, the recurrence of moments of intense opposition to the United States and moments of attitudinal truce reflects a shifting balance between positive and negative opinions. In that balance, we find an empirical barometer of the status of U.S. popularity. The five mechanisms introduced in Chapter 7 and tested in this chapter indicate that a variety of conjunctural factors contribute to the formation of the popular belief systems of foreign publics, while the structural factor of U.S. power does not exert a determining influence on popular opinion.

Reassuring though this finding might be for Americans, its continuation is neither inevitable nor ineluctable. Still, the recent wave of anti-American sentiments has exacted a toll on U.S. popular standing. It has not, however, as yet metastasized into an enduring popular opposition to the United States.

Conclusions

In 2004, when the international tensions generated by the Iraq war were reverberating in the political arena, the image of the United States was less bright than it was before the war. As several commentators have pointed out, the perceptions of the United States had definitely soured on many dimensions (Kohut and Stokes, 2006). But even among many signs of distress, evaluations of the United States were still influenced by the diverse aspects of the United States that elicit distinct responses in people's hearts and minds. Dislike of the president could not be equated with dislike of the United States. This result gives empirical validation to the conceptual discussion underlying the Bush hypothesis, that blaming a powerful political leader was not yet tantamount to blaming the country over which that leader was presiding. The aspirations associated with the American dream were definitely less effective among the publics of three Western European democracies but still salient enough among the Russian public to overcome their disapproval of President Bush.

A sense of disillusionment with the United States has started to take hold of the collective imagination in many quarters of the world. But if there is disillusionment, there is not yet hatred or revolt. Amidst so many indicators pointing to a negative outlook of the United States, very few people have expressed a desire for the termination of the American world order. Many foreign publics seem to have adopted a notion of the United States that parallels Churchill's comment about democracy; they see it as the worst hegemon except for all the others. It is truly remarkable that in a period of time when war, torture, sexual abuse, extraordinary rendition, and human rights violations have clouded U.S.

actions in the international arena we can still find favorable nuances and qualifications in the popular perceptions of the United States.

Three decades ago, an unpopular war severely taxed America's international standing. But, as Joseph Nye (2004, 14) points out, "When the policy changed and the memories of the war receded, the United States recovered much of its lost soft power." In times of crisis that generated no less anguish and no less condemnation than has the current one, the United States was able to reassert itself as a symbol and an aspiration. The road back from the abyss might be strenuous, but it has been traveled before.

CHAPTER NINE

Conclusions

E lusive or ubiquitous, pernicious or irrelevant, anti-Americanism has been a staple feature of the discourse on international politics in the dawning years of the American world order. It informs everyday conversations, journalistic commentaries, and academic reflections in a variety of guises, from the virulent to the bewildered. But despite its being fiercely debated or sternly stigmatized, anti-Americanism remains a poorly understood phenomenon. What is anti-Americanism? Where does it emerge? What forms does it take?

In this intensive investigation of the nature and features of anti-American sentiment among the general publics in a large number of countries in 2002 and 2004, we have seen that popular perceptions of the United States cannot be subsumed under a single encompassing element. As ordinary people reflect on the multiple aspects of the United States, they form opinions that are at times positive, at times contradictory, but rarely systematically negative.

All of the scholars who have depicted anti-Americanism as an encompassing syndrome of rejection and opposition would expect attitudes towards the U.S. polity and attitudes towards U.S. policies to be tightly tied, with few respondents supporting the United States on both counts and large portions of the publics revealing a consistent dislike of what the United States is and does (Berman, 2004; D'Souza, 2002; Krauthammer, 2003; Revel, 2003). Instead, the empirical map emerging from this book reveals that anti-Americanism amounts to a loosely constrained belief system. Ambivalence—one of the most enduring features of the American people's own political and social attitudes (Alvarez and Brehm, 2002; Zaller, 1992)—is also a defining feature of how the United States is perceived worldwide.

The conjecture of a consistent belief system in which the United States is either loved or hated is supplanted by a less structured but more complex belief system in which the United States is both loved and hated. This book, however, also identified important regional variation in the perceptions of the United States. In the Middle East, in particular, there was not only a greater propensity to hold a negative opinion of the United States but also a stronger tendency to discount the multifaceted nature of U.S. polity and society in people's evaluations of the United States.

These findings show how Joseph Nye's (2004) mechanism of soft power defines an ideational environment within which positive views of U.S. policy choices can emerge. However, admiration for U.S. political and societal ideals is not per se sufficient to foster a positive outlook on U.S. diplomacy. At best, it creates the conditions under which a positive assessment can be elaborated. As a tool of public diplomacy, soft power is hardly the panacea that would make U.S. diplomacy and international behavior accepted in many quarters of the world. The multifacetedness of world opinion is, therefore, a mixed blessing. On the one hand, it tempers the emergence of a syndrome of opposition to the ideational basis of the American world order; on the other hand, it dampens the efficacy of soft power as a strategy of public diplomacy.

The relevance of these results finds corroboration in the empirical evidence presented in Chapters 5 and 6. There, we saw that regardless of whether the countries analyzed in this book entertained economic, military, or cultural connections to the United States, they were not more or less prone to anti-American sentiment. Although country-level connections and contacts had scant leverage on the patterns of popular opinion about the United States, I found that a large set of individual characteristics was consistently associated with popular anti-Americanism. The processes through which attitudes towards the United States are formed take place through political attentiveness, generational experiences, and political ideology. In other words, far from being an unpredictable attitudinal stance, linked to the imponderable emotional reactions of envy or resentment, as some writers contend, popular anti-Americanism appears to be a societal phenomenon in which political socialization and levels of information play a major role.

These results, however, do not indicate that the popular foreign sentiment regarding the United States responds uniformly to the same informational and generational stimuli or to the same attitudinal stances. Levels of information, attentiveness, and generational experiences, as well as the dynamics associated with traditional worldviews, pro-market orientation, and scapegoating give rise to systematic but not necessarily consistent patterns of views of the United States. For those who fear an onslaught of anti-American opinion that will take hold of the imagination of the mass publics worldwide or the formation of an embryonic balancing opposition, this finding should be reassuring. Anti-Americanism is too variegated a phenomenon to be the ideational epitome of a transnational move-ment aimed at counterbalancing the United States.

These findings, however, have a flip side that is less reassuring for all those who would want an easy recipe for combatting anti-American sentiments world-wide. The disaggregated, multidimensional, nature of popular attitudes towards the United States implies that anti-Americanism is not a single policy problem that calls for a single policy response. Rather, it requires sophisticated policies of public diplomacy that pay attention to the multifarious details that region by region characterize the popular view of the United States.

In sum, the image of the United States is not as tarnished as is often dreaded nor is it as shiny as is occasionally dreamed. The unfolding of the diplomatic crisis over the war in Iraq and the torture scandals at Abu Ghraib and Guantan-amo have definitely exacted a heavy toll on the image of the United States. None-theless, the United States still exerts considerable attraction among ordinary people. Of the five hypotheses I tested to evaluate the potential for persistence of anti-American sentiments, the ones that received the most empirical support were those that linked the popular opinions about the American people and Pres-ident Bush to the overall attitudes towards the United States. Factors that would indicate a broader syndrome of denigration, such as the imputation of ulterior motives to U.S. foreign policy, and factors that would indicate a structural basis for anti-Americanism, such as a reaction to the overwhelming power of the United States, played at most a marginal role in the formation of popular opinion. This finding indicates that current anti-Americanism might be less enduring and less deep-seated than is often declared.

For friends and supporters of the United States, true believers, and true admir-ers, the empirical findings presented in this book lend credence to a belief that they have had all along: that the United States is a different kind of nation, benign and benevolent, that promotes a vision of a better world. Henry Luce (1999, 169) said it best, while extolling the "American Century," at a time when the world had plunged into war and needed hope: "Unlike the prestige of ancient Rome or Genghis Khan or 19th Century England, American prestige throughout the world is faith in the good intentions as well as in the ultimate intelligence and ultimate strength of the whole American people."

But the contrast between the appreciation of U.S. political values—"a love of freedom, a feeling for the equality of opportunity, a tradition of self-reliance and in-dependence and also of co-operation" as Luce (1999, 170) summarized them—and the disaffection with U.S. policies creates a tension that has repeatedly tested the strength of the popular appeal of the United States. The country has risen to the occasion of those challenges throughout the twentieth century. Now that it is more powerful than ever, it should be mindful of the words of George Kennan, writing as "Mr. X," in 1947 in *Foreign Affairs* magazine, cautioning that U.S. conduct in the foreign arena should have "nothing to do with outward histrionics: with threats or blustering or superfluous gestures of outward 'toughness.'" While the United States charts its course in the treacherous waters of world politics in the unipolar era, the American flag remains an endearing symbol the world over, as Jean Baudrillard (1988, 86) depicted it, "the trademark of a good brand."

Notes

1. The conventional wisdom about anti-Americanism is articulated in its most elaborate form in Hollander (1995), Revel (2003), and Rubin and Rubin (2004).

2. The main referents are Converse (1964), Zaller (1992) and Alvarez and Brehm (2002).

3. I rely upon the work of Converse (1964), Zaller (1992), and Alvarez and Brehm (2002) in particular.

4. The text of the House hearings on the image of America in the Arab world is available at http://purl.access.gpo.gov/GPO/LPS39591. Information on the conference on anti-Americanism sponsored by the State Department's Bureau of Intelligence and Research is available at http://usinfo.state.gov/regional/nea/sasia/afghan/text/0828state.htm. Three contenders for the U.S. presidency, Senator McCain on the Republican side and Senators Clinton and Obama on the Democratic side, stated that the restoration of U.S. standing and trust abroad would be a high priority of their administrations (Clinton, 2007; McCain, 2007; Obama, 2007).

5. The text of the *Arbella Covenant* is available at http://history.hanover.edu/texts/winthmod.html.

6. These words, equally immortal as Winthrop's, are those of President Abraham Lincoln from the Annual Message to Congress of 1862, available at http://showcase.netins.net/web/creative/lincoln/speeches/congress.htm.

7. The search finds the articles that included the word anti-Americanism in their text.

8. This allusion to the opening lines of the *Communist Manifesto* was also used by Stephen Haseler (1985, 1) in a pamphlet published in 1985, which revealingly underscores how the contemporary debate on anti-Americanism shares themes and metaphors with previous debates.

9. With one exception, as Hobsbawn (1994) quickly added, and Markovits and Hellerman (2001) elegantly documented: sports.

10. Henry Luce's celebrated essay was published in the 17 February 1941 issue of *Life*. It is reprinted in Luce (1999), from which the quoted passages are taken.

11. The 2002 Pew Global Attitudes Project survey included 44 countries. The two countries excluded from this count are the United States itself and China where questions about the United States were not asked. The surveys were conducted through face-to-face or telephone interviews conducted mostly in July and

August of 2002. The interviews were conducted in September and October of 2002 in Egypt, Ghana, India, Ivory Coast, Jordan, Lebanon, Mali, Nigeria, Senegal, and Uganda.

12. The index of anti-Americanism, which reflects both the presence and the intensity of anti-American opinion, is formally defined in the on-line Appendix (see note 14 below). The variables plotted in Figure 1.1 include levels of development, regime type, U.S. investments, trade dependence, U.S. economic aid, U.S. troop presence, voting similarity at the United Nations, pro–U.S. elite discourse, cultural connections through presence of foreign students in the United States, the presence of Peace Corps programs in a country, the extent of U.S. military assistance, and the percentage of Muslim population. In the on-line Appendix, I report the results of a regression model that includes all these variables.

13. The 2005 wave of the Pew Global Attitudes Survey was conducted in May of 2005 as allegations about the desecration of the Quran at Guantanamo Bay were reported worldwide. The Pew researchers analyzed the responses given before and after May 11, 2005—the day the allegations became public knowledge—and found that the percentage of favorable responses dropped from 30% to 16% in Pakistan and increased from 9% to 26% in Jordan; they were unable to make comparisons in the remaining countries. See Pew Global Attitudes Project 2005, 13.

14. The on-line Appendix is available on my faculty webpage at Vanderbilt University (currently at http://sitemason.vanderbilt.edu/site/d4M7ja) and on the book webpage at Johns Hopkins University Press (at http://www.press.jhu.edu/).

15. In an address before a joint session of the Congress on the termination of the Gulf War in March 1991, President George H. W. Bush proclaimed, "Now, we can see a new world coming into view. A world in which there is the very real prospect of a new world order. In the words of Winston Churchill, a world order in which 'the principles of justice and fair play protect the weak against the strong.' A world where the United Nations, freed from cold war stalemate, is poised to fulfill the historic vision of its founders. A world in which freedom and respect for human rights find a home among all nations." The speech can be retrieved from http://www.presidency .ucsb.edu/ws/index.php?pid=19364&st=&st1=.

16. The text of Whitman's poem, "Song of Myself," can be found at http://rpo .library.utoronto.ca/poem/2288.html.

17. These words are an adaptation of Freud's classic statement, which can be found in an essay entitled "The Taboo of Virginity," and are inspired by Michael Ignatieff's (1997) insightful application of Freud's logic to the dynamics of identity formation during ethnic conflict.

18. Buruma and Margalit's (2004) approach is reminiscent of one of Sartori's (1970) strategies of conceptual innovation: a movement up the ladder of conceptual generality which specifies fewer defining attributes to a concept and extends its realm of empirical referents. This approach, while allowing for a synthesis of different perspectives, comes at the cost of a loss of conceptual differentiation.

19. For well-informed definitional distinctions between these two alternative forms of authoritarian rule see Linz (1964) and Arendt (1966).

20. Halper and Clarke (2004, 233) attribute this sentence to the influential policy consultant Richard Perle.

21. The obligatory reference for the analysis of concept formation and comparison is Sartori (1970).

22. Of the three, Adorno was the most skeptical, particularly during his exile in California. But, as Offe (2005, 89) points out, in his later years in Frankfurt, "Adorno developed a diametrically opposite picture of the United States as a beacon of civil freedom that Europe, and specially defeated Germany in its state of moral catastrophe, had to take and study as its model."

23. This is the sense that underlies Neil Smelser's (1998) theoretical analysis of ambivalent sentiments. Katzenstein and Keohane (2007b, 15–19) also draw a distinction between multidimensionality and ambivalence.

24. Cohen's statement is representative of what William Riker (1982) calls the populist interpretation of voting whereby elected officials embody the will of the people.

25. Examples of citations of these data include Lambert (2003), Berman (2004), Nye (2004), *Economist* (2005), and Mahbubani (2005).

26. The sample of countries and the timing of the survey are described in footnote 11.

27. The percentage of respondents who declared they had at least a somewhat favorable opinion of the United States was 62.2% in India, 77.2% in Nigeria, 64.7% in Senegal, and 81.7% in Venezuela. The percentage was lower in Bangladesh, but still above half the sample: 51.96%.

28. Katzenstein and Keohane (2007a, 311), for example, assess how three broad macro perspectives—power imbalances, the globalization backlash, and conflicting identities—would help account for patterns in anti-Americanism worldwide. They conclude that "focusing closely on only one of the three explanatory conjectures . . . is unlikely to advance our understanding much when confronting the complex array of anti-American views in contemporary world politics."

29. Fourfold display plots present in both graphical and numerical format the information of a 2×2 table wherein two (dichotomous) categories are presented on the vertical and horizontal axes, respectively. The pie shapes depict the percentage of respondents in each cell using a quarter-circle whose radius is proportional to the cell count. The frequencies, conventionally reported in a 2×2 table, are shown in the corners of each cell. Friendly (1999) offers an introduction to this technique for representing categorical data organized in $2\times2\times k$ tables.

30. The sample of countries does not include Egypt and Vietnam because the survey question measuring people's attitudes towards American ideas about democracy was not asked in those countries. I compute Huber/White robust standard errors; the standard errors are also computed by clustering by country in the regression

model including all the countries and in the models by region. Missing values due to survey non-response on any items were imputed by generating ten simulated data sets with a semiparametric imputation model that relies upon the approximate Bayesian bootstrap to approximate the process of drawing predicted values from a full Bayesian predictive distribution (Rubin and Schenker, 1991, 588). The imputation model draws a bootstrap sample with replacement, which provides between-imputation variability; it then fits a flexible additive model to predict all of the original missing and nonmissing values for the target variable; finally, it uses predictive mean matching to impute the missing values. This procedure was implemented using Frank Harrell's *aregImpute* function in R. Regression coefficients and estimate uncertainty were then summarized using Rubin's rules (Schafer, 1997). The on-line Appendix to Chapter 3 offers a more detailed presentation of the model for the missing data. In the Appendix, I also present a data analysis conducted on each sample of countries separately.

31. At first glance, this finding is consistent with the conclusions reached by Katzenstein and Keohane (2007a) about the difficulty in explaining anti-Americanism on the basis of standard international relations arguments. But, in interpreting this result, we should also take into account the greater complexity that the power balancing survey item had compared to the complexity of items inquiring about popular culture or the spreading of American customs and ideas.

32. More precisely, in Tables 3.2 and 3.3 I report the probability that an individual will hold a somewhat unfavorable or a very unfavorable opinion of the United States. I also report the 95% confidence intervals computed around the estimated probabilities. Thus, Tables 3.2 and 3.3 convey information both about the magnitude of the effect associated with any attitudinal scenario and about the degree of uncertainty that surrounds those estimates. Overlapping confidence intervals indicate that respondents' evaluations were not systematically different across attitudinal scenarios but were affected by random uncertainty in the data. The confidence intervals are computed on the basis of standard errors that are calculated using the Delta Method, an analytic approximation for nonlinear transformations of the data and the parameters (see, for example, Fox and Andersen, 2006; Wasserman, 2004, 131–134).

33. Percentages are computed by combining the response categories of "somewhat favorable" and "very favorable" into a common category of "positive" opinion and by combining the response categories of "somewhat unfavorable" and "very unfavorable" into a common category of "negative" opinion.

34. For an overview of the transatlantic tensions during the diplomatic crisis leading to the Iraq war, see Pond (2004). The most vivid intellectual catalyst of the debate over the European perceptions of the United States is Kagan (2003).

35. Holsti and Roetter (2005) offer a more systematic analysis and distinguish between what the United States *does* and what the United States *is*.

36. In Chapter 6, the focus will turn to how individual and country factors account for popular perceptions of America. In sum, the analyses in these two Chapters identify the underlying dimensions structuring popular attitudes towards the United

States, specify the sources of variability in those attitudes, and offer a characterization of the nature and content of anti-American opinion in a group of predominantly Islamic countries and a group of European countries.

37. Two surveyed countries have been excluded from the analysis in this chapter, France and Venezuela, because they are not predominantly Muslim.

38. More specifically, I estimated a Bayesian multilevel ordinal item response theory (IRT) model. The Appendix presents a more extensive discussion of this model.

39. While innovative for a political science audience, the Bayesian multilevel ordinal item response theory (IRT) models bear a family resemblance to factor analysis and Lisrel-type models insofar as they assess how survey items "load" onto the latent propensity, but they go beyond those more traditional approaches by respecting the ordinal measurement of the survey items and by incorporating a hierarchical structural model that measures how respondents' and countries' characteristics explain the latent traits. Applications of Bayesian IRT models can be found in the literature on roll call votes in the U.S. legislature (Clinton, Jackman, and Rivers, 2004) and in the General Assembly of the United Nations (Voeten, 2004).

40. The propensities are called latent because they are not directly measurable but are retrieved through statistical modeling. The latent propensities are given an arbitrary zero point. Specifically, in the sociocultural dimension, zero is the level of anti-Americanism that leads a respondent to be at most "somewhat favorable" to U.S. education with a probability equal to 50%; in the policy dimension, zero is the level of anti-Americanism that leads a respondent to be at most "somewhat favorable" to the U.S. policy to fight terrorism with a probability equal to 50%; finally, in the model of the attitudes towards U.S. policies among European publics, zero is the level of anti-Americanism that leads a respondent to have at most a "good opinion" of the U.S. handling of relations with Europe with a probability equal to 50%.

41. The on-line Appendix presents a more extensive discussion of the results summarized in Figure 4.1.

42. The overall mean value is -1.329. In the on-line Appendix, I present detailed information about the probability estimates associated with different values of the latent propensity to oppose U.S. culture and society.

43. The estimate for Iran is -0.485.

44. This parameter is the intraclass correlation coefficient, ρ.

45. The overall average latent propensity to oppose American policy is 0.716. The on-line Appendix presents an extensive discussion of how the latent propensity scores translate into probabilities to oppose U.S. policies.

46. In the on-line Appendix, I also report the findings about the variance in the anti-American propensity scores propensity. The data show that there is greater variability in the sociocultural dimension than in the policy dimension of anti-Americanism. Moreover, most of the variance is located between countries rather than within countries. About 59% of the variance occurs between countries.

47. The relevant parameter is the variance across countries (τ^2) which has a posterior mean equal to 101.7. These findings are reported in the on-line Appendix.

48. An alternative specification of the model, which is discussed at length in the on-line Appendix, finds that the proportion of the variance occurring across countries is even less prominent (about 6%).

49. In the on-line Appendix, I present color versions of Figures 4.2 and 4.4.

50. A variance ratio that is probabilistically different from the value 1 gives a statistical validation to the conjecture of non-equal variances. Using a noninformative reference prior, the posterior distribution for the ratio of the variances of two normally distributed random variables, $\eta = \frac{\phi_1}{\phi_2}$, follows a Snedecor's F distribution with degrees of freedom equal to the number of observations in each sample minus 1. That is, $\eta \sim S_1 / S_2 \, F_{n_1-1, \, n_2-1}$, where S_1, and S_2 are the variances in the two samples, and n_1 and n_2 are the sample sizes (Lee, 1997, 149–151).

51. I coded the demographic variables as follows: (a) Gender—a dichotomous indicator coded 1 for males and 0 for females. (b) Age—coded using six age groups: 25 years old or younger, 26–35 years old, 36–45 years old, 46–55 years old, 56–65 years old, and 66 years old or older. The youngest cohort serves as the reference category in the regression models. (c) Education—coded using four dichotomous indicators that denote completion of elementary school, middle school, high school, or college. Respondents with no education serve as the baseline category of comparison in the regression models. (d) Religious affiliation—a series of dichotomous indicators distinguishing seven types of religious affiliation: Christian, Orthodox, atheist/no religion, Muslim, Hindu, Buddhist, and a residual category that incorporates other religious groups. Christian serves as the reference category in the regression models.

52. These conjectures were first elaborated in Chiozza (2007).

53. For a discussion of this issue, see also Gentzkow and Shapiro (2004).

54. This argument is analogous to the one Katzenstein and Keohane (2007b, 31) subsume under the label of social anti-Americanism.

55. See, for example, Berman (2004), Joffe (2004), Revel (2003), Rubin and Rubin (2004). For a sophisticated analysis of French *anti*-anti-Americanism see Gopnik (2003).

56. The findings about the individual profiles of anti-American attitudes were obtained by running a series of ordered logit regression models. I computed Huber/White robust standard errors clustered by country. Missing values were imputed using the approach described in footnote 30 and in the on-line Appendix. The three threshold parameters associated with the ordered logit model are not reported in the graphs in this volume. Tables with the regression coefficients, standard errors, and significance tests of the coefficients are presented in full in the on-line Appendix.

57. We can follow the logic in Figure 5.1. If the Z factors are the exclusive intervening variable between the demographic factors and the popular attitudes towards the United States, the direct link between X and Y, which is labeled A, will be *insignificant*. If there are other mechanisms that connect X and Z beyond those subsumed under Z, the direct link A will be significant. Blalock (1979), King (1991), and Ray (2003) offer clear expositions of the logic underlying the modeling of variables that

intervene in a causal pathway. Gelpi and Grieco (2001) present an application of this modeling logic.

58. Given that there were only eight respondents of Muslim religion in the East Asian sample, they were included in the residual category "other religion."

59. As Moisés Naím (2005) aptly reminds us, the 2000 U.S. Census shows that Arab Americans fare much better than the average American in terms of wealth and education.

60. The text of Emma Lazarus's poem, *The New Colossus* can be retrieved from http://xroads.virginia.edu/~CAP/LIBERTY/lazaruspoem.html.

61. The parameter that summarizes how variation is partitioned across the individual and the country levels of analysis is rather small in three of the four models estimated in Chapter 4, thus indicating that differences across countries are not as conspicuous as those within countries.

62. The models estimated in this chapter take the form of two variants of the Ancova model (Raudenbush and Bryk, 2002, 25–26): the ordinal IRT Ancova model was applied to the two batteries of six indicators from the Zogby International survey and the battery of seven indicators from the Chicago Council on Foreign Relations/German Marshall Fund survey; and the conventional random-effects Ancova model was used with the anti-American feeling thermometer. These two flavors of the Ancova model differ in that the ordinal IRT model assesses the impact of the explanatory variables on the latent propensity to respond in a consistently anti-American manner to a cluster of related survey questions, whereas the conventional random-effects Ancova model directly measures the effect of the explanatory variables on the mean of the anti-American feeling thermometer itself. Otherwise, the two models convey the same empirical information about effects and variances of the explanatory variables. For each cluster of anti-American attitudinal indicators, I consider four alternative model specifications. These specifications differ in terms of the country-level variables accounting for the variation in the mean levels of anti-American sentiment across countries. For all the models, the Gibbs sampler was run for 16,000 iterations, discarding the first 2,000 iterations as a burn-in phase. Every tenth iteration was retained for inference, which provides 1,400 samples from the posterior distribution of the model parameters. The visual inspection of the trace plots and of the within-chain autocorrelation plots indicates that the chains had good mixing and low autocorrelations. Convergence to the stationary posterior distribution was also assessed, using the formal tests of Geweke's and Heidelbeger and Welch's diagnostics (Gill, 2002, 398–399, 405–408), which also corroborate that the chains have reached the stationary distribution.

63. This interpretation follows because I use a country mean centering of the explanatory variables (see Raudenbush and Bryk, 2002, 135–139, 141).

64. These coefficients have posterior distributions whose 95% confidence interval do not cross the 0 threshold.

65. These are Bayesian confidence intervals.

66. This estimate is obtained by computing the sum of the coefficients associated with the Internet, satellite tv, and languages variables.

67. The proportion of the variance explained at the unit level—ψ—is defined as $\dfrac{\sigma^2_{\text{Anova}} - \sigma^2_{\text{Ancova}}}{\sigma^2_{\text{Anova}}}$, where σ^2_{Anova} and σ^2_{Ancova} are approximated by the mean of the country variances σ^2_j which are reported in greater detail in the on-line Appendix (Raudenbush and Bryk, 2002, 79).

68. If we compare conservative and liberal individuals, we obtain a .78 shift on the latent propensity to oppose U.S. policies. A shift of such magnitude noticeably increases the anti-American edge to the survey responses.

69. Secretary Albright's full statement comes from an interview on NBC's *Today* show where she was discussing the prospects of a bombing campaign against Iraq. In her own words, "If we have to use force, it is because we are America. We are the indispensable nation. We stand tall. We see further into the future" (quoted in Herbert, 1998).

70. The on-line Appendix specifies the terms of the relationship estimated in the models: country means are modeled as a function of an overall population intercept and as a linear function of two explanatory variables per model. Given the choice to employ country mean centering for the individual-level explanatory variables, the intercept parameters β_{0j} represent the unadjusted mean levels of anti-Americanism (Raudenbush and Bryk, 2002).

71. These findings are presented in greater detail in the on-line Appendix.

72. Two factors might underlie these weak statistical patterns: the small number of units—eight countries in the Zogby International survey and six countries in the CCFR/GMF survey—and the specification of vague priors on the variance components of the models, as specified in the on-line Appendix.

73. The explanatory variables are centered at their mean, as they were in the Ancova models.

74. If anything, the linear trend of the data indicates *increasing* confidence in the U.S. role over time in Britain, France, and Italy, rather than an ineluctable slipping to the worst.

75. Tocqueville (1947 [1835 and 1840], 184) was not very kind towards President Andrew Jackson: "General Jackson, whom the Americans have twice elected to be the head of their Government, is a man of a violent temper and mediocre talents; no one circumstance in the whole course of his career ever proved that he is qualified to govern a free people, and indeed the majority of the enlightened classes in the Union has always been opposed to him." For an overview of the collapse of President Bush's approval ratings in his second term, see Nagourney and Thee (2006).

76. This data comes from the 28th Report of the United States Advisory Commission on Information (1977, 122).

77. The full text of this Emily Dickinson poem can be found at http://www .repeatafterus.com/title.php?i=2849.

78. For a description of these forms of anti-Americanism as manifested in France, see Bowen (2007) and Meunier (2007).

79. In these graphs the percentage of respondents in each cell of a 2×2 cross-tabulation is represented by a quarter circle whose radius is proportional to the cell count, along with 95% confidence bounds. For example, in Figure 7.2, 36.14% of the British public disliked both the United States and President Bush; 25.94% disliked President Bush but liked the United States; 35.48% liked both the United States and President Bush; and 2.44% liked President Bush and disliked the United States. Data analysis is based on the 2004 wave of the Pew Research Center Global Attitudes Survey.

80. The text of President Wilson's speech can be retrieved at http://net.lib.byu .edu/~rdh7/wwi/1917/wilswarm.html.

81. In a game-theoretic analysis of cooperation in the international arena, McGillivray and Smith (2000) show that punishment strategies specifically aimed at the political leaders, rather than at the country as a whole, foster greater cooperation in countries with accountable political systems. In their model, punishment for defection continues until the leader is replaced. Agent-specific punishment strategies give the public an incentive to remove the leaders who transgress from a cooperative arrangement, given that the removal of the leader restores cooperative relations. Leaders who value their office tenure would then be less inclined to grab the short-term gains of unilateral defection. McGillivray and Smith offer a functionalist argument that explains the origins of the leader-people distinction in the foreign policy of democratic countries.

82. In the tables and figures, the first indicator is identified with the label "Over-concerned"; the second is labeled "Hidden agenda."

83. As a matter of fact, historical data show that the prospect for upward social mobility in the United States no longer matches the dazzling extent that impressed Alexis de Tocqueville or Werner Sombart (Ferrie, 2005), while other societies have achieved patterns of social mobility that are either no different or even more fluid than those found in the United States (Solon, 2002). Current circumstances in the United States therefore can, indeed, be less bright than they were in the past.

84. Robert Singh's (2006, 37) perceptive analysis of the different layers of anti-Americanism is an excellent example of the speculative character of most current predictions about the persistence of anti-Americanism. Singh argues that antipathy to the Bush administration's foreign policy is insufficient to explain the current spread of anti-American sentiments, and from that he concludes, "Change in that foreign policy, equally, may mute but is unlikely to silence anti-Americanisms." The extensions of the dimensions of America theory elaborated in this chapter instead offer an indication of which contributing factors would make anti-American sentiments last beyond the current phase in U.S. foreign policy.

85. Data cited in this paragraph come from the Pew Research Center's 2004 Global Attitudes Survey.

86. For an introduction to classification tree (CART) models, see Breiman et al. (1984) and Venables and Ripley (2002, 251–269). For an application in the political science literature, see Gleditsch and Ward (1997).

87. The models were estimated by penalized maximum likelihood (with a penalty factor equal to 1) to minimize the problems associated with empty or sparse cells in the design matrix for the Jordan sample (Harrell, 2001, 207–210). I computed Huber/White robust standard errors. Missing values due to survey non-response on items were imputed using the same approach employed in Chapters 3 and 5, that is, by generating 10 simulated data sets with a semiparametric imputation model based upon the approximate Bayesian bootstrap to approximate the process of drawing predicted values from a full Bayesian predictive distribution. Regression coefficients, standard errors, and p-values are reported in the on-line Appendix, along with the estimates obtained with ML estimation.

88. All the variables in the models are dichotomous indicators. The baseline, or reference, category, which corresponds to respondents who were coded "zero" on all the indicators, identifies respondents who (a) had a somewhat negative opinion of President Bush, (b) thought that the U.S. did not have a hidden agenda and was not over reacting in the war on terrorism, (c) had a somewhat negative opinion of the American people, (d) thought that the world would be safer if the United States remained the only superpower, and (e) believed that their quality of life in the U.S. would be the same as it was in their own country.

89. The probabilities reported in Table 8.1 were computed using the estimates of the penalized ML ordered logit models presented in Figures 8.1 and 8.2. The confidence intervals around the probability estimates were computed using the Delta method (Wasserman, 2004, 131–134).

90. The distinction between populist and liberal/madisonian theory of voting is most clearly developed in Riker (1982).

91. This is the criterion that Hurwitz and Peffley (1987) identify to establish causal relations among attitudinal dimensions, as was discussed in Chapter 2.

92. The estimates are computed using a 10-fold cross-validation and a complexity parameter α equal to .01. The complexity parameter α was chosen to be approximately within 1 standard deviation from the minimum cross-validation error rate. The complexity parameter α was set to .005 in the Russian sample to increase the descriptiveness of the tree. A more detailed description of the CART models is presented in the on-line Appendix.

93. The proportion is similar in Russia, although the number is about double (223 individuals disliked both the American people and the United States, but the Russian sample was twice as large—1,002 respondents were surveyed in Russia).

94. In both France and Germany, the classification trees further split the responses according to the belief expressed about the quality of life in the United States. Those groupings, however, are too small—comprising 20–30 respondents in samples of about 500—to be given any substantive interpretation.

95. The belief that life in the United States would be worse did not contribute to the overall opinion of the United States in any of the countries. This implies that the branches labeled "Better life=No" identify both respondents who thought that quality of life in the United States would be worse and those who thought it would be the same.

References

Acheson, Dean. 1965. "The American Image Will Take Care of Itself." *New York Times.* 28 February 1965:SM24.

Adelman, Carol C. 2003. "The Privatization of Foreign Aid: Reassessing National Largesse." *Foreign Affairs* 82(6):9–14.

Ajami, Fouad. 2003. "The Falseness of Anti-Americanism." *Foreign Policy* (138): 52–61.

Alesina, Alberto, Rafael Di Tella, and Robert MacCulloch. 2004. "Inequality and Happiness: Are Europeans and Americans Different?" *Journal of Public Economics* 88(5–6):2009–2042.

Almond, Gabriel A. 1960. *The American People and Foreign Policy.* New York: Praeger.

Alvarez, R. Michael, and John Brehm. 2002. *Hard Choices, Easy Answers: Values, Information, and American Public Opinion.* Princeton, NJ: Princeton University Press.

Amis, Martin. 1986. *The Moronic Inferno and Other Visits to America.* New York: Viking.

Arendt, Hannah. 1966. *The Origins of Totalitarianism.* New York: Harcourt, Brace & World.

Ayish, Muhammed I. 2001. "American-Style Journalism and Arab World Television: An Explanatory Study of News Selection at Six Arab World Satellite Television Channels." *Transnational Broadcasting Journal* (6):www.tbsjournal.com/Archives/ Spring01/Ayish.html.

Bacevich, Andrew J. 2002. *American Empire: The Realities and Consequences of U.S. Diplomacy.* Cambridge, MA: Harvard University Press.

Bachrach, Peter, and Morton S. Baratz. 1963. "Decisions and Nondecisions: An Analytic Framework." *American Political Science Review* 57(3):632–642.

Bartels, Larry M. 2003. "Democracy with Attitudes." In *Electoral Democracy*, ed. Michael B. MacKuen and George Rabinowitz. Ann Arbor: University of Michigan Press, pp. 48–82.

Baudrillard, Jean. 1988. *America.* New York: Verso.

Berinsky, Adam J. 2004. *Silent Voices: Public Opinion and Political Participation in America.* Princeton, NJ: Princeton University Press.

Berman, Russell A. 2004. *Anti-Americanism in Europe: A Cultural Problem.* Stanford, CA: Hoover Institution Press.

Blalock, Hubert M., Jr. 1979. *Social Statistics*. New York: McGraw-Hill.

Bow, Brian, Peter J. Katzenstein, and Arturo Santa-Cruz. 2007. "Anti-Americanism in Canada and Mexico." Paper presented at the Annual Meeting of the American Political Science Association, Chicago, 30 August–2 September 2007.

Bowen, John R. 2007. "Anti-Americanism as Schemas and Diacritics in France and Indonesia." In *Anti-Americanisms in World Politics*, ed. Peter J. Katzenstein and Robert O. Keohane. Ithaca, NY: Cornell University Press, pp. 227–250.

Breiman, Leo, Jerome Friedman, Charles J. Stone, and R. A. Olshen. 1984. *Classification and Regression Trees*. Boca Raton, FL: Chapman & Hall/CRC.

Brooks, Stephen G., and William C. Wohlforth. 2002. "American Primacy in Perspective." *Foreign Affairs* 81(4):20–33.

Brooks, Stephen G., and William C. Wohlforth. 2005. "Hard Times for Soft Balancing." *International Security* 30(1):72–108.

Bueno de Mesquita, Ethan. 2005. "The Quality of Terror." *American Journal of Political Science* 49(3):515–530.

Buruma, Ian, and Avishai Margalit. 2004. *Occidentalism: The West in the Eyes of Its Enemies*. New York: Penguin Press.

Carr, Edward Hallett. 1946. *The Twenty Years' Crisis, 1919–1939*. New York: Harper & Row.

Chiozza, Giacomo. 2002. "Is There a Clash of Civilizations? Evidence from Patterns of International Conflict Involvement, 1946–97." *Journal of Peace Research* 39(6):711–734.

Chiozza, Giacomo. 2007. "Disaggregating Anti-Americanism: An Analysis of Individual Attitudes towards the United States." In *Anti-Americanisms in World Politics*, ed. Peter J. Katzenstein and Robert O. Keohane. Ithaca, NY: Cornell University Press, pp. 93–126.

Chua, Amy. 2003. *World on Fire: How Exporting Free Market Democracy Breeds Ethnic Hatred and Global Instability*. New York: Doubleday.

Clinton, Hillary Rodham. 2007. "Security and Opportunity for the Twenty-first Century." *Foreign Affairs* 86(6):2–18.

Clinton, Joshua, Simon Jackman, and Douglas Rivers. 2004. "The Statistical Analysis of Roll Call Data." *American Political Science Review* 98(2):355–370.

Cohen, Roger. 2004. "France Says, Love the U.S., Hate Its Chief." *New York Times*. 6 June:D14.

Converse, Philip E. 1964. "The Nature of Belief Systems in Mass Publics." In *Ideology and Discontent*, ed. David E. Apter. New York: Free Press, pp. 206–261.

Converse, Philip E. 1970. "Attitudes and Non-Attitudes: Continuation of a Dialogue." In *The Quantitative Analysis of Social Problems*, ed. Edward R. Tufte. Reading, MA: Addison-Wesley, pp. 168–189.

Cox, Michael. 2005. "Beyond the West: Terrors in Transatlantia." *European Journal of International Relations* 11(2):203–233.

Crenshaw, Martha. 2008. "Why the United States Is Targeted by Terrorism: An Approach and a Case Study." Paper presented at Responses to Political Violence and the Growth of Anti-Americanism Conference, Center for the Advanced Study in the Behavioral Sciences, Palo Alto, CA, 22–23 May 2008.

Crockatt, Richard. 2003. *America Embattled: September 11, Anti-Americanism, and the Global Order*. London: Routledge.

Cunliffe, Marcus. 1986. "The Anatomy of Anti-Americanism." In *Anti-Americanism in Europe*, ed. Rob Kroes and Maarten van Rossem. Amsterdam: Free University Press, pp. 20–36.

Dahl, Robert A. 1957. "The Concept of Power." *Behavioral Science* 2(3):201–215.

Deudney, Daniel, and G. John Ikenberry. 1999. "The Nature and Sources of Liberal International Order." *Review of International Studies* 25(2):179–196.

Dore, Ronald. 1984. "Unity and Diversity in Contemporary World Culture." In *The Expansion of International Society*, ed. Hedley Bull and Adam Watson. Oxford: Clarendon Press, pp. 406–424.

D'Souza, Dinesh. 2002. *What's So Great about America*. New York: Penguin Books.

Economist. 2005. "Anti-Americanism: The View from Abroad." *Economist*. 19–25 February 2005:24–26.

Eickelman, Dale F., and Jon W. Anderson, eds. 2003. *New Media in the Muslim World: The Emerging Public Sphere*. 2nd ed. Bloomington: Indiana University Press.

Fabbrini, Sergio. 2002. "The Domestic Sources of European Anti-Americanism." *Government and Opposition* 37(1):3–14.

Fandy, Mamoun. 2000. "Information Technology, Trust, and Social Change in the Arab World." *Middle East Journal* 54(3):378–394.

Ferguson, Niall. 2003. "An Empire in Denial: The Limits of US Imperialism." *Harvard International Review* 25(3):64–69.

Ferrie, Joseph P. 2005. "The End of American Exceptionalism? Mobility in the United States since 1850." *Journal of Economic Perspectives* 19(3):199–215.

Fish, M. Steven. 2002. "Islam and Authoritarianism." *World Politics* 55(1):4–37.

Fox, Jean-Paul. 2003. "Multilevel IRT Using Dichotomous and Polythomous Response Data." Unpublished typescript, University of Twente, Netherlands.

Fox, Jean-Paul, and Cees A. W. Glas. 2001. "Bayesian Estimation of a Multilevel IRT Model Using Gibbs Sampling." *Psychometrika* 66(2):271–288.

Fox, Jean-Paul, and Cees A. W. Glas. 2003. "Bayesian Modeling of Measurement Error in Predictor Variables Using Item Response Theory." *Psychometrika* 68(2): 169–191.

Fox, John, and Robert Andersen. 2006. "Effect Displays for Multinomial and Proportional-Odds Logit Models." *Sociological Methodology* 36(1):225–255.

Free, Lloyd A. 1976. *How Others See Us: Critical Choices for Americans*. Vol. 3 Lexington, MA: D. C. Heath.

Friedman, Thomas L. 2003. "A Theory of Everything." *New York Times*. 1 June:D13.

Friendly, Michael. 1999. "Visualizing Categorical Data." In *Cognition and Survey Research*, ed. Monroe G. Sirken, Douglas J. Herrmann, Susan Schechter, Norbert Schwarz, Judith M. Tanur, and Roger Tourangeau. New York: John Wiley & Sons, pp. 319–348.

Garton Ash, Timothy. 2003. "Anti-Europeanism in America." *New York Review of Books* 50(2):32–34.

Garton Ash, Timothy. 2004. *Free World: America, Europe, and the Surprising Future of the West.* New York: Vintage.

Geddes, Barbara, and John Zaller. 1989. "Sources of Popular Support for Authoritarian Regimes." *American Journal of Political Science* 33(2):319–347.

Gelpi, Christopher, and Joseph M. Grieco. 2001. "Attracting Trouble: Democracy, Leadership Tenure, and the Targeting of Militarized Challenges." *Journal of Conflict Resolution* 45(6):794–817.

Gentzkow, Matthew A., and Jesse M. Shapiro. 2004. "Media, Education, and Anti-Americanism in the Muslim World." *Journal of Economic Perspectives* 18(3): 117–133.

Gill, Jeff. 2002. *Bayesian Methods: A Social and Behavioral Science Approach.* Boca Raton, FL: Chapman & Hall/CRC.

Gilpin, Robert. 1981. *War and Change in World Politics.* New York: Cambridge University Press.

Glaeser, Edward L. 2005. "The Political Economy of Hatred." *Quarterly Journal of Economics* 120(1):45–86.

Gleditsch, Kristian S., and Michael D. Ward. 1997. "Double Take: A Reexamination of Democracy and Autocracy in Modern Polities." *Journal of Conflict Resolution* 41(3):361–383.

Gopnik, Adam. 2003. "The Anti-Anti-Americans." *The New Yorker* 79(24):30.

Greene, Graham. 2002. *The Quiet American.* New York: Penguin Books. First published in 1955.

Halper, Stefan, and Jonathan Clarke. 2004. *America Alone: The Neo-Conservatives and the Global Order.* New York: Cambridge University Press.

Harrell, Frank E., Jr. 2001. *Regression Modeling Strategies: With Applications to Linear Models, Logistic Regression, and Survival Analysis.* New York: Springer.

Haseler, Stephen. 1985. *The Varieties of Anti-Americanism: Reflex and Response.* Washington, DC: Ethics and Public Policy Center.

Hastie, Trevor, Robert Tibshirani, and Jerome Friedman. 2001. *The Elements of Statistical Learning: Data Mining, Inference, and Prediction.* New York: Springer.

Heisbourg, François. 1999–2000. "American Hegemony? Perceptions of the US Abroad." *Survival* 41(4):5–19.

Henderson, Errol A., and Richard Tucker. 2001. "Clear and Present Strangers: The Clash of Civilizations and International Conflict." *International Studies Quarterly* 45(2):317–338.

Herbert, Bob. 1998. "War Games." *New York Times* 22 February:D17.

Higley, John. 2006. "The Bush Elite: Aberration or Harbinger?" In *The Rise of Anti-Americanism,* ed. Brendon O'Connor and Martin Griffiths. London: Routledge.

Hobsbawm, Eric. 1994. *The Age of Extremes: A History of the World, 1914–1991.* New York: Vintage.

Hoge, Warren. 2003. "Bush and Blair Say Bombings Fortify Resolve." *New York Times.* 21 November:A1.

Hollander, Paul. 1995. *Anti-Americanism: Irrational and Rational.* New Brunswick, NJ: Transaction Publishers.

Holsti, Ole R., and Natasha C. Roetter. 2005. "How Publics Abroad View the United States." Paper presented at the Annual Meeting of the American Political Science Association, Washington, DC, 1–4 September 2005.

Huntington, Samuel P. 1982. "American Ideals versus American Institutions." *Political Science Quarterly* 97(1):1–37.

Huntington, Samuel P. 1996. *The Clash of Civilizations and the Remaking of World Order.* New York: Simon & Schuster.

Huntington, Samuel P. 1999. "The Lonely Superpower." *Foreign Affairs* 78(2):35–49.

Hurwitz, Jon, and Mark Peffley. 1987. "How Are Foreign Policy Attitudes Structured? A Hierarchical Model." *American Political Science Review* 81(4):1099–1120.

Ignatieff, Michael. 1997. *The Warrior's Honor: Ethnic War and the Modern Conscience.* New York: Holt.

Ignatieff, Michael, ed. 2005. *American Exceptionalism and Human Rights.* Princeton, NJ: Princeton University Press.

Ikenberry, G. John. 2005. "Anti-Americanism in the Age of American Unipolarity." In *Korean Attitudes toward the United States: Changing Dynamics*, ed. David I. Steinberg. Armonk, NY: M. E. Sharpe, pp. 3–20.

Ikenberry, G. John, ed. 2002. *America Unrivaled: The Future of the Balance of Power.* Ithaca, NY: Cornell University Press.

Isernia, Pierangelo. 2007. "Anti-Americanism in Europe during the Cold War." In *Anti-Americanisms in World Politics*, ed. Peter J. Katzenstein and Robert O. Keohane. Ithaca, NY: Cornell University Press, pp. 57–92.

Joffe, Josef. 2001. "Who's Afraid of Mr. Big?" *National Interest* (64):43–52.

Joffe, Josef. 2002. "Defining History and Theory: The United States as the 'Last Remaining Superpower.'" In *America Unrivaled: The Future of the Balance of Power*, ed. G. John Ikenberry. Ithaca, NY: Cornell University Press, pp. 155–180.

Joffe, Josef. 2004. "The Demons of Europe." *Commentary* 17(1):29–34.

Johnson, Chalmers. 2004. *The Sorrows of Empire: Militarism, Secrecy, and the End of the Republic.* New York: Metropolitan Books.

Kagan, Robert. 2002–2003. "One Year After: A Grand Strategy for the West?" *Survival* 44(4):135–139.

Kagan, Robert. 2003. *Of Paradise and Power: America and Europe in the New World Order.* New York: Alfred A. Knopf.

Kagan, Robert. 2004. "America's Crisis of Legitimacy." *Foreign Affairs* 83(2):65–87.

Kaplan, Lawrence F., and William Kristol. 2003. *The War over Iraq: Saddam's Tyranny and America's Mission.* San Francisco, CA: Encounter.

Katzenstein, Peter J., and Robert O. Keohane. 2007a. "Conclusion: Anti-Americanisms and the Polyvalence of America." In *Anti-Americanisms in World Politics*, ed. Peter

J. Katzenstein and Robert O. Keohane. Ithaca, NY: Cornell University Press, pp. 306–316.

Katzenstein, Peter J., and Robert O. Keohane. 2007b. Varieties of Anti-Americanism: A Framework for Analysis. In *Anti-Americanisms in World Politics*, ed. Peter J. Katzenstein and Robert O. Keohane. Ithaca, NY: Cornell University Press, pp. 9–38.

Kennedy, David M. 2007. "Imagining America: The Promise and Peril of Boundlessness." In *Anti-Americanisms in World Politics*, ed. Peter J. Katzenstein and Robert O. Keohane. Ithaca, NY: Cornell University Press, pp. 39–54.

Keohane, Robert O., and Peter J. Katzenstein. 2007. "Introduction: The Politics of Anti-Americanisms." In *Anti-Americanisms in World Politics*, ed. Peter J. Katzenstein and Robert O. Keohane. Ithaca, NY: Cornell University Press, pp. 1–6.

King, Gary. 1991. "'Truth' Is Stranger than Prediction, More Questionable than Causal Inference." *American Journal of Political Science* 35(4):1047–1053.

Kohut, Andrew. 2003. "Anti-Americanism: Causes and Characteristics." Available at people-press.org/commentary/display.php3?AnalysisID=77.

Kohut, Andrew, and Bruce Stokes. 2006. *America against the World: How We Are Different and Why We Are Disliked*. New York: Times Books.

Krastev, Ivan. 2004. "The Anti-American Century?" *Journal of Democracy* 15(2):5–16.

Krauthammer, Charles. 1990–1991. "The Unipolar Moment." *Foreign Affairs* 70(1): 23–33.

Krauthammer, Charles. 2003. "To Hell with Sympathy." *Time* 162(20)(17 November): 156.

Kupchan, Charles A. 2002. *The End of the American Era: U.S. Foreign Policy and the Geopolitics of the Twenty-First Century*. New York: Knopf.

Kuran, Timur. 1995. *Private Truths, Public Lies: The Social Consequences of Preference Falsification*. Cambridge, MA: Harvard University Press.

Lacorne, Dennis, and Jacques Rupnik. 1990. "Introduction: France Bewitched by America." In *The Rise and Fall of Anti-Americanism: A Century of French Perception*, ed. Dennis Lacorne, Jacques Rupnik, and Marie-France Toinet. New York: St. Martin's Press, pp. 1–31.

Lambert, Richard. 2003. "Misunderstanding Each Other." *Foreign Affairs* 82(2):62–74.

Lapham, Lewis. 2002. *Theater of War*. New York: New Press.

Laski, Harold J. 1947. "America—1947." *The Nation*. 13 December:641–644.

Lee, Peter M. 1997. *Bayesian Statistics: An Introduction*. 2nd ed. London: Arnold.

Lieber, Kier A., and Gerard Alexander. 2005. "Waiting for Balancing: Why the World Is Not Pushing Back." *International Security* 30(1):109–139.

Linz, Juan J. 1964. "An Authoritarian Regime: Spain." In *Cleavages, Ideologies, and Party Systems: Contributions to Comparative Political Sociology*, ed. Erik Allardt and Yrjo Littunen. Helsinki: Academic Bookstore, pp. 291–341.

Lipset, Seymour Martin. 1997. *American Exceptionalism: A Double-Edged Sword*. New York: Norton.

Locke, John. 1988 [1690]. *Two Treatises of Government*. New York: Cambridge University Press.

Long, J. Scott. 1997. *Regression Models for Categorical and Limited Dependent Variables.* Thousand Oaks, CA: Sage.

Long, Mark. 2007. "Exploring Anti-Americanism in Post-9/11 Editorial Cartoons in the U.S. and Spain." *PS: Political Science and Politics* 40(2):279–286.

Luce, Henry R. 1999. "The American Century." *Diplomatic History* 23(2):159–171.

Lynch, Marc. 2003a. "Beyond the Arab Street: Iraq and the Arab Public Sphere." *Politics and Society* 31(1):55–91.

Lynch, Marc. 2003b. "Taking Arabs Seriously." *Foreign Affairs* 82(5):81–94.

Mahbubani, Kishore. 2005. *Beyond the Age of Innocence: Rebuilding Trust between America and the World.* New York: Public Affairs.

Mann, Michael. 2003. *Incoherent Empire.* New York: Verso.

Markovits, Andrei S. 1985. "On Anti-Americanism in West Germany." *New German Critique* 34:3–27.

Markovits, Andrei S., and Steven L. Hellerman. 2001. *Offside: Soccer and American Exceptionalism.* Princeton, NJ: Princeton University Press.

McAdam, Doug. 2007. "Legacies of Anti-Americanism: A Sociological Perspective." In *Anti-Americanisms in World Politics*, ed. Peter J. Katzenstein and Robert O. Keohane. Ithaca, NY: Cornell University Press, pp. 251–269.

McCain, John. 2007. "An Enduring Peace Built on Freedom." *Foreign Affairs* 86(6):19–34.

McGillivray, Fiona, and Alastair Smith. 2000. "Trust and Cooperation through Agent-specific Punishments." *International Organization* 54(4):809–824.

McNeill, William H. 1993. "Fundamentalism and the World of the 1990s." In *Fundamentalisms and Society*, ed. Martin E. Marty and R. Scott Appleby. Chicago, IL: University of Chicago Press, vol. 2 pp. 558–573.

McPherson, Alan. 2002. "Latin American Anti-Americanism and U.S. Responses: Venezuela 1958." Unpublished typescript, Howard University.

McPherson, Alan. 2003. *Yankee No! Anti-Americanism in U.S.–Latin American Relations.* Cambridge, MA: Harvard University Press.

Mead, Walter Russell. 2004. *Power, Terror, Peace, and War: America's Grand Strategy in a World at Risk.* New York: Alfred A. Knopf.

Mernissi, Fatema. 2002. *Islam and Democracy: Fear of the Modern World.* 2nd ed. Cambridge, MA: Perseus Publishing.

Meunier, Sophie. 2007. "The Distinctiveness of French Anti-Americanism." In *Anti-Americanisms in World Politics*, ed. Peter J. Katzenstein and Robert O. Keohane. Ithaca, NY: Cornell University Press, pp. 129–156.

Midlarsky, Manus, and Raymond Tanter. 1967. "Toward a Theory of Political Instability in Latin America." *Journal of Peace Research* 4(3):209–227.

Mueller, Harald, and Thomas Risse-Kappen. 1987. "Origins of Estrangement: The Peace Movement and the Changed Image of America in West Germany." *International Security* 12(1):52–88.

Naghmi, Shafqat Hussain. 1982. "Pakistan's Public Attitude toward the United States." *Journal of Conflict Resolution* 26(3):507–523.

Nagourney, Adam, and Megan Thee. 2006. "Poll Gives Bush Worst Marks Yet on Major Issues." *New York Times.* 10 May:A1, A18.

Naím, Moisés. 2005. "Arabs in Foreign Lands." *Foreign Policy* (148):95–96.

Norris, Pippa, and Ronald Inglehart. 2004. *Sacred and Secular: Religion and Politics Worldwide.* Cambridge: Cambridge University Press.

Nye, Joseph S., Jr. 1990. *Bound to Lead: The Changing Nature of American Power.* New York: Basic Books.

Nye, Joseph S., Jr. 2002. *The Paradox of American Power: Why the World's Only Superpower Can't Go It Alone.* Oxford: Oxford University Press.

Nye, Joseph S., Jr. 2004. *Soft Power: The Means to Success in World Politics.* New York: Public Affairs.

Obama, Barack. 2007. "Renewing American Leadership." *Foreign Affairs* 86(4):2–16.

Odom, William E., and Robert Dujarric. 2004. *America's Inadvertent Empire.* New Haven, CT: Yale University Press.

Offe, Claus. 2005. *Reflections on America: Tocqueville, Weber, and Adorno in the United States.* Malden, MA: Polity Press.

Owen, John M., IV. 2002. "Transnational Liberalism and American Primacy; or, Benignity Is in the Eye of the Beholder." In *America Unrivaled: The Future of the Balance of Power,* ed. G. John Ikenberry. Ithaca, NY: Cornell University Press, pp. 239–259.

Pape, Robert A. 2005. "Soft Balancing against the United States." *International Security* 30(1):7–45.

Paul, T. V. 2005. "Soft Balancing in the Age of U.S. Primacy." *International Security* 30(1):46–71.

Pew Global Attitudes Project. 2004. "A Year after Iraq: Mistrust of America Even Higher, Muslim Anger Persists." Technical report by the Pew Research Center for the People and the Press. Available at people-press.org/reports/pdf/206.pdf.

Pew Global Attitudes Project. 2005. "American Character Gets Mixed Reviews: U.S. Image up Slightly, but Still Negative." Technical report by the Pew Research Center for the People and the Press. Available at pewglobal.org/reports/pdf/247.pdf.

Pew Global Attitudes Project. 2006. "America's Image Slips, but Allies Share U.S. Concerns over Iran, Hamas." Technical report by the Pew Research Center for the People and the Press. Available at pewglobal.org/reports/pdf/252.pdf.

Pew Global Attitudes Project. 2007. "Global Unease With Major World Powers; Rising Environmental Concern in 47 Nation Survey." Technical report by the Pew Research Center for the People and the Press. Available at http://pewglobal.org/reports/display.php?ReportID=256.

Pipes, Daniel. 2002. "A New Round of Anger and Humiliation: Islam after 9/11." In *Our Brave New World: Essays on the Impact of September 11,* ed. Wladyslaw Pleszczynski. Stanford, CA: Hoover Institution Press, pp. 41–61.

Pond, Elizabeth. 2004. *Friendly Fire: The Near-Death of the Transatlantic Alliance.* Washington, DC: European Union Studies Association / Brookings Institution Press.

Pouliot, Vincent. 2006. "The Alive and Well Transatlantic Security Community: A Theoretical Reply to Michael Cox." *European Journal of International Relations* 12(1):119–127.

Raudenbush, Stephen W., and Anthony S. Bryk. 2002. *Hierarchical Linear Models: Applications and Data Analysis Methods*. 2nd ed. Thousand Oaks, CA: Sage.

Ray, James Lee. 2003. "Explaining Interstate Conflict and War: What Should Be Controlled For?" *Conflict Management and Peace Science* 20(2):1–31.

Revel, Jean-François. 1974. *Without Marx or Jesus: The New American Revolution Has Begun*. New York: Laurel Editions.

Revel, Jean-François. 2003. *Anti-Americanism*. San Francisco, CA: Encounter Books.

Riker, William H. 1982. *Liberalism against Populism: A Confrontation between the Theory of Democracy and the Theory of Social Choice*. Prospect Heights, IL: Waveland Press.

Risse, Thomas. 2002. U.S. Power in a Liberal Security Community. In *America Unrivaled: The Future of the Balance of Power*, ed. G. John Ikenberry. Ithaca, NY: Cornell University Press, pp. 260–283.

Rosecrance, Richard. 1976. "Introduction." In *America as an Ordinary Country: U.S. Foreign Policy and the Future*, ed. Richard Rosecrance. Ithaca, NY: Cornell University Press, pp. 11–19.

Rubin, Barry. 2002. "The Real Roots of Arab Anti-Americanism." *Foreign Affairs* 81(6):73–85.

Rubin, Barry, and Judith Colp Rubin. 2004. *Hating America: A History*. New York: Oxford University Press.

Rubin, Donald B., and Nathaniel Schenker. 1991. "Multiple Imputation in Health-Care Databases: An Overview and Some Applications." *Statistics in Medicine* 10(4):585–598.

Russett, Bruce, and Donald R. Deluca. 1983. "Theater Nuclear Forces: Public Opinion in Western Europe." *Political Science Quarterly* 98(2):179–196.

Russett, Bruce, John R. Oneal, and Michaelene Cox. 2000. "Clash of Civilizations, or Realism and Liberalism Déjà Vu? Some Evidence." *Journal of Peace Research* 37(5):583–608.

Russett, Bruce M. 1963. *Community and Contention: Britain and America in the Twentieth Century*. Cambridge, MA: MIT Press.

Safire, William. 2003. "Nixon on Bush." *New York Times*. 7 July:A13.

Sardar, Ziauddin, and Merryl Wyn Davies. 2002. *Why Do People Hate America?* New York: Disinformation.

Sartori, Giovanni. 1970. "Concept Misformation in Comparative Politics." *American Political Science Review* 64(4):1033–1053.

Schafer, Joseph L. 1997. *Analysis of Incomplete Multivariate Data*. New York: Chapman & Hall.

Schkade, David A., and Daniel Kahneman. 1998. "Does Living in California Make People Happy? A Focusing Illusion in Judgements of Life Satisfaction." *Psychological Science* 9(5):340–346.

Scott, James C. 1990. *Domination and the Arts of Resistance: Hidden Transcripts.* New Haven, CT: Yale University Press.

Shafer, Byron E. 1999. "American Exceptionalism." *Annual Review of Political Science* 2:445–463.

Shepherd, Robin. 2004. "A Bigger EU, and Not So Anti-American." *Washington Post.* 9 May:B03.

Singh, Robert. 2006. "Are We All Americans Now? Explaining Anti-Americanisms." In *The Rise of Anti-Americanism,* ed. Brendon O'Connor and Martin Griffiths. London: Routledge.

Smelser, Neil J. 1998. "The Rational and the Ambivalent in the Social Sciences." *American Sociological Review* 63(1):1–16.

Smith, Steven K., and Douglas A. Wertman. 1992. *US-West European Relations during the Reagan Years: The Perspective of West European Publics.* New York: St. Martin's Press.

Solon, Gary. 2002. "Cross-Country Differences in Intergenerational Earnings Mobility." *Journal of Economic Perspectives* 16(3):59–66.

Strauss, David. 1978. *Menace in the West: The Rise of French Anti-Americanism in Modern Times.* Westport, CT: Greenwood.

Tai, Chong-Soo, Erick J. Peterson, and Ted Robert Gurr. 1973. "Internal versus External Sources of Anti-Americanism." *Journal of Conflict Resolution* 17(3):455–488.

Tajfel, Henry. 1982. "Social Psychology of Intergroup Relations." *Annual Review of Psychology* 33:1–39.

Tessler, Mark. 2002. "Islam and Democracy in the Middle East: The Impact of Religious Orientations on Attitudes toward Democracy in Four Arab Countries." *Comparative Politics* 34(3):337–354.

Therneau, Terry M., and Elizabeth J. Atkinson. 1997. "An Introduction to Recursive Partitioning Using RPART Routines." Technical Report 61, Department of Health Science Research, Mayo Clinic, Rochester, MN.

Tocqueville, Alexis de. 1947 [1835 and 1840]. *Democracy in America.* Translated by Henry Reeve. New York: Oxford University Press.

Todd, Emmanuel. 2003. *After the Empire: The Breakdown of the American Order.* New York: Columbia University Press.

United States Advisory Commission on Information. 1977. "The 28th Report." Washington, DC.

Védrine, Hubert. 2000. "L'Hyperpuissance Américanine." *Les Notes de la Fondation Jean-Jaurès* 17:13–34.

Venables, W. N., and B. D. Ripley. 2002. *Modern Applied Statistics with S.* 4th ed. New York: Springer.

Verba, Sidney. 1996. "The Citizen as Respondent: Sample Surveys and American Democracy. Presidential Address, American Political Science Association, 1995." *American Political Science Review* 90(1):1–7.

Voeten, Erik. 2004. "Resisting the Lonely Superpower: Responses of States in the United Nations to U.S. Dominance." *Journal of Politics* 66(3):729–754.

Wagnleitner, Reinhold. 1999. "The Empire of the Fun, or Talkin' Soviet Union Blues: The Sound of Freedom and U.S. Cultural Hegemony in Europe." *Diplomatic History* 23(3):499–524.

Wallerstein, Immanuel. 2003. *The Decline of American Power: The U.S. in a Chaotic World*. New York: New Press.

Walt, Stephen M. 1998–1999. "The Ties That Fray: Why Europe and America Are Drifting Apart." *National Interest* (54):3–11.

Walt, Stephen M. 2002. "Keeping the World 'Off Balance': Self-Restraint and U.S. Foreign Policy." In *America Unrivaled: The Future of the Balance of Power*, ed. G. John Ikenberry. Ithaca, NY: Cornell University Press, pp. 121–154.

Walt, Stephen M. 2005. "Taming American Power." *Foreign Affairs* 84(5):105–120.

Waltz, Kenneth N. 1979. *Theory of International Politics*. New York: McGraw-Hill.

Waltz, Kenneth N. 1991. "America as a Model for the World? A Foreign Policy Perspective." *PS: Political Science and Politics* 24(4):667–670.

Wasserman, Larry. 2004. *All of Statistics: A Concise Course in Statistical Inference*. New York: Springer.

Waterbury, John. 2003. "Hate Your Policies, Love Your Institutions." *Foreign Affairs* 82(1):58–68.

Watts, William, and Lloyd A. Free. 1974. *State of the Nation 1974*. Washington, DC: Potomac Associates.

X. 1947. "The Sources of Soviet Conduct." *Foreign Affairs* 25(4):566–582.

Yan, Yunxiang. 2002. "Managed Globalization: State Power and Cultural Transition in China." In *Many Globalizations: Cultural Diversity in the Contemporary World*, ed. Peter L. Berger and Samuel P. Huntington. New York: Oxford University Press, pp. 19–47.

Zakaria, Fareed. 1999. "Best Treaty: The Empire Strikes Out." *New York Times Magazine* April 18:99.

Zakaria, Fareed. 2003. *The Future of Freedom: Illiberal Democracy at Home and Abroad*. New York: Norton.

Zaller, John R. 1992. *The Nature and Origins of Mass Opinion*. Cambridge: Cambridge University Press.

Index